# TOLSTOY'S 'WAR AND PEACE'

## A STUDY

# TOLSTOY'S
# 'WAR AND PEACE'
## *A Study*

BY

R. F. CHRISTIAN

CLARENDON PRESS · OXFORD

*Oxford University Press, Ely House, London W. 1*

GLASGOW  NEW YORK  TORONTO  MELBOURNE  WELLINGTON
CAPE TOWN  SALISBURY  IBADAN  NAIROBI  LUSAKA  ADDIS ABABA
BOMBAY  CALCUTTA  MADRAS  KARACHI  LAHORE  DACCA
KUALA LUMPUR  HONG KONG  TOKYO

FIRST PUBLISHED 1962
PRINTED IN GREAT BRITAIN AT
THE UNIVERSITY PRESS, ABERDEEN
REPRINTED LITHOGRAPHICALLY IN GREAT BRITAIN
AT THE UNIVERSITY PRESS, OXFORD
BY VIVIAN RIDLER
PRINTER TO THE UNIVERSITY
1968

# PREFACE

THIS is a book about a book, and as such it is doubtful whether it would meet with Tolstoy's approval if he were alive today. Tolstoy rightly believed that books are better than books about books. 'Critics', he wrote, forestalling the sentiments of Shaw, 'are always people who have tried to be artists and failed'. On another occasion he expressed the opinion that 'of all the boring things in the world, criticism is the most boring'.

And yet people will continue to write about Tolstoy, as they continue to write about Shakespeare. The purpose of this book is in the first place to acquaint the English reader with material which will facilitate an understanding of the process of writing *War and Peace*—material which for the most part has not been translated into English, and which is not always easily obtainable in Russian: draft versions of the novel, Tolstoy's diaries, notebooks and letters, the historical and biographical sources he used, and the secondary critical literature about the novel. In the second place I have attempted to consider certain aspects of the finished work—structural, linguistic, and ideological—and to offer very briefly some possible lines of approach to Tolstoy's art as a novelist. As a general rule I have resisted the temptation to expand, and I have often been content with one example when I should like to have given many more. If as a result the book appears to be too condensed, and to broach topics without proper amplification, this is to some extent due to my wish to raise as many problems as possible and to illustrate them very briefly, but not to give an exhaustive, or even remotely exhaustive treatment of any one of them. My object is to stimulate further enquiry, and I hope that my work will be of some use and interest both to university students of Russian and to the far wider public who read Russian literature in translation. I should add that it will be of no use to those who have not already read *War and Peace* in Russian or in English.

The reader will notice that some proper names and place names are not spelt in the generally accepted manner. I have in all cases transliterated Russian names and not given English translations (Prince Andrei and Nikolai, not Prince Andrew and Nicholas), on the principle that we always talk about Ivan, and not John Karamazov. Where the name is French or German in the first place (Pierre, Schöngraben) I have tried to give the correct spelling in the original language, and not to reproduce commonly accepted but sometimes inaccurate forms. All translations from the Russian are my own.

The book was read in typescript by Professor Roy Pascal and Dr. Inna Arian-Baykov of Birmingham University, Professor D. P. Costello of Manchester University and my wife Rosalind Christian. I am very grateful to them for their comments and criticisms, many of which I have gladly availed myself of in the course of revision. Finally I would like to acknowledge the help I have received from the magnificent 90-volume edition of Tolstoy's works, the Jubilee Edition (Polnoe Sobranie Sochinenii, Moscow, 1928–58), which must surely rank as one of the great achievements of Soviet scholarship. This edition is referred to by the abbreviation J.E. My references to volumes I–IV of *War and Peace* are to volumes 9–12 in the Jubilee Edition, and correspond to books 1–3, 4–8, 9–11 and 12–15 in the translation by Louise and Aylmer Maude.

R. F. C.

# CONTENTS

# I: THE EVOLUTION OF THE NOVEL

## THE FIRST STEPS

How does a novel begin? Certainly not with the first words of the first draft plan. The further one delves down into the youth and even the childhood of the novelist, the more one extracts which is in some way relevant to the writing of his novel—childhood experiences and emotions, youthful thoughts, interests, prejudices and ideas. Ideally speaking, the reader of this book should also read a good biography of the young Tolstoy, should be familiar with the numerous autobiographical features of his *Childhood, Boyhood,* and *Youth,* should have some knowledge of his way of life at Yasnaya Polyana as a proud member of the landowning aristocracy, his military service in the Caucasus, his participation in the Crimean War and the stories he wrote on the basis of it, his educational experiments at his Yasnaya Polyana school and the close contacts he maintained with the peasantry, his attitude to love and the family as revealed in *Family Happiness,* and the first happy years of his married life which were the background to the writing of *War and Peace.* Ideally he should know a little about the ferment of ideas in Russia in the late 50's and early 60's, the events leading up to the Emancipation of the Serfs in 1861, the beginning of the so-called 'great reforms'. the emergence of radical revolutionary thought and activity and the growing faith among certain sections of the Russian Intelligentsia in science, progress and the possibility of man-made solutions to all human problems. This book cannot provide him with this material, but there are other books in English which can.

The English reader, however, it at a disadvantage in that he is denied access to much of the material about Tolstoy and about *War and Peace* which can be found in the now complete 90-volume Soviet edition of his works. *War and Peace* is the longest nineteenth-century Russian novel. It occupied Tolstoy more or less exclusively for the better part of seven years. The standard English translation runs to some 1,650 pages. And yet if we compare the size of the definitive version with the quantity of draft versions and amended proofs which have already been published in the Soviet Union and with the manuscripts which have not been published, we might be pardoned for referring to it, in reviewers' jargon, as 'this slim volume'. To understand *War and Peace* better and to appreciate the magnitude of Tolstoy's achievement, it is necessary to take into account these volumes of trial and error which have not yet been absorbed by English writers in their studies of Tolstoy's novels.

But the foundations of *War and Peace* were laid long before Tolstoy began to plan his great novel. They rest in that deep and lasting interest in history which he acquired as a young man. In his early twenties he read the long standard histories of his own country and major works by European historians. In particular he was fascinated by the theme of the Napoleonic wars, and he read through the detailed works on 1812 and 1813 by the official Russian historian Mikhailovsky-Danilevsky and the volumes on the same period by the French historian Thiers. His comments in his diaries reveal the unfavourable impression they made on him. 'To compile a true, accurate History of Europe in this century'; he wrote as a young man of 24, 'There is a task for a life-time.'[1] As his reading continued he became more convinced of the inadequacy or inaccuracy of what he read, and of the enormity of the gulf between the truth of history and the truth of the historian. With his interest centring particularly on the recent history of his own country and with his ability as a writer already acknowledged by the success of his early stories, he slowly evolved the idea of writing a novel on a Russian nineteenth-century historical theme. Some years later he was to say that 'the first germ of interest in history arises out of contemporary events';[2] and in the case of his first novel, his intention was to write about one of his own contemporaries returning to Russia in 1856 after thirty years of exile in Siberia for his part in the abortive Decembrist uprising which coincided with the accession of Nicholas I to the throne in 1825. This is how he spoke of his work in a letter of March 26th, 1861 to A. I. Herzen whom he had very recently met in London:

[1] J.E. XLVI. 141.
[2] Quoted by Aylmer Maude, *Life of Tolstoy*, I, Oxford, 1930, 265.

About four months ago I began a novel, the hero of which is to be a Decembrist returning from exile—I wanted to have a talk with you about it, but I didn't manage to. My Decembrist is to be an enthusiast, a mystic, a Christian, returning to Russia in 1856 with his wife and his son and daughter, and applying his stern and somewhat idealised views to the new Russia. Please tell me what you think about the propriety and the opportuneness of such a subject. Turgenev, to whom I read the beginning, liked the first chapters.[3]

In fact only three chapters of this novel *The Decembrists* were ever written before Tolstoy discarded it (although he returned to it for a while in the 1870's). The first chapter begins with a vehement attack on contemporary Russia, written with heavy sarcasm and in a spirit of angry declamation. Here are some extracts from it:

It was a short while ago, in the reign of Alexander II, in our time—the time of civilization, progress, *questions,* the renaissance of Russia etc. etc.; the time when the victorious Russian army was returning from Sevastopol which it had surrendered to the enemy, when the whole of Russia was celebrating the destruction of the Black Sea fleet and white-stoned Moscow was welcoming and congratulating on this happy event what was left of the crews, treating them to a good old Russian glass of vodka and to bread and salt as the good old Russian custom has it, and prostrating itself before them . . . ; the time when journals appeared under diverse colours—journals developing European principles on a European ground but with a Russian philosophical outlook, and journals standing exclusively on Russian ground developing Russian principles but with a European philosophical outlook; the time when all of a sudden there appeared so many journals that it seemed as if all titles had been exhausted: *The Messenger* and *The Word* and *Talk* and *The Observer* and *The Star* and *The Eagle* and many others, and despite this more and more titles kept appearing; the time when pleiads of writers and thinkers appeared, contending that science is popular and that science is not popular and that science is non-popular and so on, and pleiads of writers and artists describing a grove and a sunrise and a storm and the love of a Russian girl and the idleness of one official and the bad behaviour of many officials; the time when *questions* arose on all sides, questions of cadet corps, universities, the censorship, public court proceedings, finance, the banks, the police, emancipation and many others; everyone was trying to find still more questions and everyone was trying to solve them; people read, wrote and talked projects, wanted to improve, to destroy, to change everything, and all Russians to a man were in an indescribable state of excitement—a state which occurred twice in 19th century Russia: first when we gave Napoleon I a beating in 1812, and secondly when Napoleon III gave us a beating in 1856. What a great, unforgettable time, the renaissance of the Russian people!!!![4]

[3] J.E. LX. 374.       [4] J.E. XVII. 7.

Against this ironical background of Russia in 1856 the reader is introduced to the Labazov family—Pierre and Natasha and their two children Sergei and Sonya. Pierre emerges as a kindly good-natured, venerable old man, an aristocrat, proud to be a Russian, delighted at the great changes for the better which he had witnessed on his journey back to Moscow, and in sympathy with the liberal measures of the new government. The word *people* (*narod*) is on his lips, and he even goes so far as to say 'I am of the opinion that Russia's strength is not in us but in the people'.[5] It seems that Pierre's character was modelled on that of S. G. Volkonsky, an exiled Decembrist who returned to Moscow in 1856 and whom Tolstoy met in Italy a few years later. The name may owe something to that of another Decembrist acquaintance of Tolstoy, Zavalishin, as there is a noticeable similarity between Labaz- and Zaval- in reverse, especially when one remembers Tolstoy's fondness for interchanging the letters b and v (e.g. Volkonsky and Bolkonsky). There is hardly time for any action to develop in the three short chapters which were written, and the scenes are confined to the family homecoming and reunions in Moscow, a church service in the Kremlin and brief glimpses of the young generation with its representatives of the new Moscovite *jeunesse dorée*. On the basis of this rather slender evidence a distinguished Soviet Tolstoyan scholar has written: 'One can say with confidence that the old Decembrist—an aristocrat grown wise through past experience—was conceived as a contrast to "the new people", who knew no other religion but the religion of progress and no other laws but the laws of history.'[6]

It must remain a matter of speculation whether *The Decembrists* was intended to be a polemic against new radical ideas, but there is no doubt that it left some traces on Tolstoy's first completed novel. In an unpublished draft foreword to *War and Peace* the author gave his reasons for shifting the focus of his attentions from 1856 to 1812. These reasons will be quoted shortly when we come to consider the opening chapters of that book. But before we turn to our main subject—the examination of the various draft versions and the part they played in the evolution of *War and Peace*—it will be convenient to record

[5] J.E. XVII.
[6] B. M. Eykhenbaum, *Lev. Tolstoy, kniga vtoraya*, Leningrad-Moscow, 1931, p. 199.

briefly the main stages in the history of the writing of the novel.

## THE CHRONOLOGY OF *WAR AND PEACE*

The earliest plans and drafts of Tolstoy's first novel date back to 1863. At that time it was referred to by Tolstoy as 'a novel of the 1810's and 1820's',[7] and by his wife as 'a history of 1812'.[8] The first chronological landmark was the publication in the January and February issues of *The Russian Messenger* for 1865 of thirty-eight chapters of a work entitled *1805* (Tolstoy expressly forbade the editor to call it a novel), the chapters roughly corresponding in extended form to the twenty-five chapters of Volume I, Part 1 of the definitive text of *War and Peace*. The vast scope of the future novel could not be imagined from these few, essentially domestic chapters about the life of the Rostovs, the Bolkonskys and the St. Petersburg nobility, and the impression was later gained by some influential critics that Tolstoy originally intended to write a sort of family chronicle with a military background, but that he changed his purpose and consciously elevated his work into a historical novel which duly became a national epic. This impression was strengthened by the following entry in Tolstoy's diary in March 1865:

I have become engrossed in the history of Napoleon and Alexander. The idea of writing a psychological history of the romance of Alexander and Napoleon has swept over me like a cloud of joy and awareness of the opportunity to do a great thing. All the baseness, all the empty words, all the folly, all the contradictions of them themselves and of the people round them . . . [9]

and here follows a précis of the characters and actions of the two men, in Napoleon's case wholly unfavourable, in Alexander's largely sympathetic. But the evidence, I think, is against any elaborate change of plan. Historical figures, including Napoleon and Alexander, had been introduced into draft versions long before this entry in Tolstoy's diary. The first drafts of some of the battle scenes were already being written in 1863. The theme of war, the campaign of 1812, the historical role of the leaders of

[7] J.E. LXI. 23.
[8] *Dnevniki S. A. Tolstoi 1860–1891*, Moscow, 1928, p. 80.
[9] J.E. XLVIII. 60.

nations and armies all occupied Tolstoy's thoughts from the very first.

During 1865 Tolstoy continued writing the second part of *1805*, revising the battle scenes he had already written and rejected as one of many possible openings to his book, and adding new scenes (Schöngraben) which do not appear in the earlier drafts. This next instalment, entitled *War,* came out in the February, March and April numbers of *The Russian Messenger* for 1866; it corresponds closely to Volume I, Part 2 of *War and Peace.* By this time Tolstoy had made a rough plan of the division of the rest of his material into parts, which would take his story as far as the retreat from Moscow in 1812. So confident was he of the course his book would take that he was able to write in April 1866 that he hoped to publish the finished work the following year under the title *All's Well That Ends Well.* It is interesting to see how he envisaged the ending at this stage. As the title suggests, it is to be a happy one. A draft version of 1866 spares Prince Andrei's life.[10] He recovers from his wounds. But when he comes to a full realization of Natasha's love for Pierre, he sacrifices his own feelings for her so as not to stand in his friend's way. Likewise Sonya is moved by Prince Andrei's sacrifice to surrender her claim to Nikolai so that he may be free to marry Princess Marya. Petya is not killed in battle. There is no hint of Karataev. Pierre's regeneration is achieved without him. Finally the two couples marry on the same day before Nikolai and Prince Andrei rejoin their units and go with the Russian army to Paris. This is the happy ending which Tolstoy had promised some years earlier that he would not provide to the work which he had refused to call a novel.

In June 1866 the parts already published in *The Russian Messenger* came out in book form, still with the title *1805.* Meanwhile Tolstoy had left this stage a long way behind. In 1867 he was negotiating for the printing of the work as a whole. In the text of a draft agreement dated March 1867 and referring to the author's book, the title *1805* is crossed out by Tolstoy and the words *War and Peace* inserted—as far as we know the first time this title was ever used. In the summer of the same year Tolstoy revised the already published *1805* and made fairly substantial reductions in it. By the end of the year the forth-

10 J.E. XIV. 127 ff.

coming publication of *War and Peace* in four volumes was announced, the first three to be available at once and the fourth to follow. In March 1868 another notice appeared. The work would now be in five volumes and those who bought their copies before the fourth volume appeared would get the fifth volume free. At the same time Tolstoy's famous article 'A Few Words About *War and Peace*', in which he sought to 'express his own views' about his work 'and thus counteract misunderstandings which might arise in the reader's mind', was printed in the March number of *The Russian Archives*, when in fact only three volumes of the 'novel' had been published. The fourth volume duly appeared in 1868, and not only the fifth, but also a sixth and final volume were published the following year, the ending being considerably different from that foreshadowed in the later parts of the manuscript referred to above.

In 1873 Tolstoy drastically revised his book. Some of the reflective or philosophical passages were cut out altogether. Others, including the second epilogue, were removed piecemeal and reassembled for publication as a separate volume. All the French was translated into Russian. The number of volumes was reduced from six to four. Finally in 1886 Tolstoy's wife (presumably with his tacit acquiescence though certainly not with his active approval) undid her husband's work and produced a version which is virtually the same as that of the 1868–69 edition, the only important difference being that the later division into four volumes was retained. This has become the definitive text and it is the one with which all English readers will be familiar.

So much then for the bare chronological background to the history of the writing of the novel. In this chapter we shall concentrate on certain aspects of Tolstoy's work of revision (and we must remember that of the alterations made by him some involved the rewriting of his manuscripts, others were emendations made after the type had been set up, others again were corrections to proofs and still others were revisions of material already published) which seem to us to illustrate best his technique as a novelist. We are interested in the rough material for what it can tell us about the finished product.

### THE OPENING CHAPTERS

One of the most difficult and laborious tasks which Tolstoy ever undertook was the writing of the opening chapters of *War and Peace*. It is only necessary to compare the definitive version of these chapters with the dozen or more false starts to be assured of this. The first question which we shall try and answer, therefore, is why Tolstoy eventually began his book in the way he did and not in one of the various other ways which he might have done and had tried to do. The novel, in its final version, opens with a scene in Anna Scherer's salon in St. Petersburg in the year 1805. The celebrated hostess is talking to Prince Vasily. The reception which follows is the occasion for introducing the Prince's son and daughter, Hippolyte and Hélène; Prince Andrei Bolkonsky and his young wife Lisa; and Andrei's friend Pierre. As the scene shifts from St. Petersburg to Moscow and from Moscow to the country estate of Bald Hills, the author introduces in turn the Rostov circle and the other members of the Bolkonsky family. All the characters of any importance who are not historical characters make their appearances quite early on in the first part of volume one. But only one scene can actually be first—and it is the soirée in the Scherer salon. This is the opening which finally satisfied Tolstoy more than any other:

'Eh bien, mon prince, Gênes et Lucques ne sont plus que des apanages, landed estates, de la famille Buonaparte. Non, je vous previens, que si vous ne me dites pas, que nous avons la guerre, si vous vous permettez encore de pallier toutes les infamies, toutes les atrocités de cet Antichrist (ma parole, j'y crois)—je ne vous connais plus, vous n'êtes plus mon faithful slave, comme vous dites. Well, hello, hello. Je vois que je vous fais peur, sit down and talk to us.'

These words were spoken in July 1805 by the well-known Anna Pavlovna Scherer, maid of honour and confidante of the Empress Marya Fedorovna, as she greeted Prince Vasily, a man of high rank and importance, who was the first to arrive at her reception.[11]

Several facts emerge from these few introductory sentences. First Tolstoy begins with the spoken word before announcing who is speaking. Secondly the speaker uses French almost entirely. Thirdly, the words spoken are followed by a sentence defining the time and place of the scene, and the social position of the speaker and the man she is addressing. Fourthly, as we

[11] *War and Peace*, I. 1. 1.

see later, the speakers themselves are peripheral figures who first talk about, then serve to introduce some of the major characters. Finally a reference is made in the very first sentence—a disparaging reference as the spelling Buonaparte indicates—to Napoleon and to the subject of the impending war with France. We must keep these facts in mind as we examine the early plans and draft versions of the beginning of Tolstoy's novel.

There is no exact chronology of the existing drafts which Tolstoy wrote between the spring of 1863 and the spring of 1864 as he laboured on the opening scenes of the novel which was later to be called *War and Peace*. Any attempt to establish the order in which they were written is bound to be hypothetical, and here we follow the plausible reconstruction postulated by the Soviet scholar E. E. Zaidenshnur.[12] The earliest fragment of Tolstoy's monumental work would seem, from internal evidence, to be a brief plan in note form with the curt beginning:

In 1811 the young Zubtsov visits old Prince Volkonsky.[13]

These words are deleted and in their place follows a brief sketch of the main characters of the embryonic novel. Recognizable from the novel as it now stands are Prince Bolkonsky (he is here called Volkonsky) and his daughter Marya; the family of Count Rostov (here called Tolstoy); the future Pierre (here Ilya, 'married to a beautiful b . . .', as Tolstoy puts it); Berg, and the Kuragin family (again under different names). An allusion is made at the end of the plan to the marriage of four couples, but the partnerships do not correspond to the associations actually formed in *War and Peace*.

In this brief sketch there is no reference to war or to any historical figures. It is essentially a family affair. But significantly enough, there is no Prince Andrei as yet. This fact alone suggests that it is probably the earliest 'version' we have.

When Tolstoy began what was probably his first attempt at writing the first chapter of his work he gave it the title *Three Eras*.[14] This title suggests that he was thinking in terms of a prelude to his discarded, fragmentary novel *The Decembrists*.

[12] J.E. XVI. 19 ff.
[13] J.E. XIII. 13.
[14] ibid. 77. ff.

The three eras were to be 1812, 1825 and 1856 and Part 1 is entitled *1812*. The first chapter is called *Général en chef*. It begins in a conventional way with a factual narrative introduction of a secondary character, the old Prince Volkonsky, including his age, position and the year in which the action begins. The two most interesting things about it are the hesitations Tolstoy had, as shown in his deletions in the manuscript, first over the choice of date (1811 is altered to 1805), and secondly over the question whether to introduce a new character not envisaged in the original plan—Volkonsky's son Prince Andrei. At first Volkonsky is described as having only a daughter. Then 'one daughter' is crossed out and 'a son and daughter' substituted. The son appears originally in an unfavourable light. His young wife has been left pregnant and resourceless in Moscow, and it is the general's daughter, Princess Marya, who rescues her and brings her to Bald Hills. The son has been disowned by his father and his name is not allowed to be mentioned in the house. This original situation is toned down somewhat in the amended manuscript. Prince Andrei's marriage is still disapproved of, but his father allows him to return to Bald Hills with his bride before he leaves for his regiment. At first sight the date 1805 would suggest that Tolstoy intended, even in the earliest stages, to advance the beginning of his story to Napoleon's first war with Russia, despite the title 1812. It is probable, however, that the emendations in the manuscript were made at a later date, and that the events culminating in Austerlitz did not fit in to Tolstoy's original conception of the novel.

The character of the old prince and his relations with his daughter Marya are substantially the same as in the definitive version—though there they are introduced at a much later stage—with the notable exception of the reference to the prince's mistress who bears him five children, all dispatched à la Rousseau to the foundlings home. The draft version states in abbreviated form that two guests (both fools) and an abbé arrived at the Volkonskys; that the elder of the two began to flirt with Princess Marya much to her disgust; and that the Prince began to talk about Napoleon ('he saw his strength but despised him'). These few bare sentences make it clear that Tolstoy wished at the very beginning of his book to introduce the subject of Napoleon, and to do so in an unflattering way. Why did he abandon this opening? Because, it has been suggested, the company present were not the right people to broach a serious conversation on a serious subject. Two fools, an abbé (who 'despised the revolution') and a retired general in disfavour were hardly representative of conflicting public opinion. Probably too because the main characters were not yet clearly conceived in Tolstoy's mind. A draft plan[15] of about the same period provides the earliest detailed notes of nearly all the main fictional characters in the novel. Among the nineteen people whose principal characteristics are listed and in several cases grouped under headings such as property, social status, love relationships, mental faculties, family, and the curious one 'poetry' are Pyotr (who at this stage has some features of Pierre, some of Anatole Kuragin), Nikolai, Boris, Natasha and Sonya. There is no entry for Prince Andrei. Boris, however, is very different from the Boris Drubetskoy of *War and Peace* and has much in common with the later Andrei Bolkonsky, in particular in so far as his relations with Natasha and his experiences in the army are concerned. In several cases the ages of the characters are given, and more important, what they were doing in the years 1811–13. The focal point of the work, even at this early stage in its production, is clearly intended to coincide with the title of its first part, *1812*, although the plan itself contains no details of any historical characters, rulers, generals or statesmen. There is, however, unmistakable evidence of Tolstoy's intention from the start to include battle scenes, and allusions are made in the thumb-nail sketches of some of the characters to their conduct at the battle of Borodino or their participation in the guerilla warfare during the retreat from Moscow. Finally, the attitude of the male characters to Napoleon is briefly defined. The old Count Tolstoy (i.e. Rostov) does not know whether to praise or blame him. Pyotr is jealous of him, although he hates him as a man. Boris adores him.

   It is worth translating two of these entries—those for Natasha and Pyotr. They will show, I think, that in the case of his heroine Tolstoy had all the essential features clear in his mind when he began writing and that he adhered to them faithfully throughout many years of work. The same is largely true of

[15] J.E. XIII. 13 ff.

all the other women characters—whose attributes are similarly listed in this draft plan—of Countess Tolstaya (i.e. Rostova), Lisa (i.e. Vera) and Sonya. It is true too of such male characters as Berg and Nikolai who, like the women, had little or nothing of Tolstoy in them. On the other hand the draft sketch of Pyotr who has most of Tolstoy in him and for that reason is more mobile and elusive, corresponds much less closely to the finished portrait, and is very much a cross between Anatole Kuragin and Pierre.

Of the future Natasha it is said (the entry is short and is not divided up by headings):

Natalya. 15 years old.
Terribly generous.
Believes in herself. Naughty, and always gets away with it, a nuisance to everybody and loved by everybody.
Ambitious.
Has a command of music, understands and feels it acutely.
Suddenly sad, suddenly terribly happy. Dolls.
*Love*: crying out for a husband, two even, needs children, love, bed.
Foolish but nice, uneducated, knows nothing and always knows how to hide it.
In love with teacher, Boris, doll Bibi, friendship with Sonya. First ball, in love with tsar. Country, Mikhail, ['Anatole' has been crossed out by Tolstoy], love, fall. Horror and cheerfulness. Concert. Relations of half friendship with Arkady. With Pyotr. Wants to kill herself. He is wounded. She runs away from him. Explanation. Wedding—clothes.[16]

These are the first rough notes about Pyotr:

*Property* Father wealthy. Son squandered everything given him, debts paid twice, refused. Generous, a gambler, knows poverty, keeps his wits about him.
*Society* Knows people, can easily deceive, and laughs. Can play any part—nobleman, beggar. Despises contacts, everything himself. More than usually ambitious. Doesn't know duty and always does the opposite. Doesn't acknowledge order of things. Cruel and kind *ad infinitum*.
*Love* Loves quickly, passionately, and at once hates the person loved. Despises women. Can't bear company of women—all fools.
*Poetry* Passionately fond of music, voice not good. Sings ['dances *à la russe*' has been crossed out by Tolstoy]. In love, remembers nothing before success, passionately fond of Russia, loyal in friendship.
*Intellect* Quick at understanding everything. Eloquent in all ways. Far-sighted. So much a philosopher that he's afraid of himself. Often

[16] J.E. XIII. 18.

speaks of immortality, and tormented by the question. Jealous of Napoleon.

*Family* Father—minister, Frenchman. Brother—diplomat whom he hates, cousin a Volkonskaya on mother's side. Mother née Ofrosimova.[17]

There follows a fairly lengthy account in note form of his activities for the years 1811 to 1813 which, while making reference to gambling and to escapades with a bear and a policeman, is substantially different from the story of Pierre in *War and Peace* and closer to that of Anatole. These early plans put the emphasis entirely on the fictional characters in the book and their relationships in time of peace and war. But it does not follow, as some people have assumed, that, because there is no preliminary sketch of historical figures or of battle scenes, the 'war' side of *War and Peace* was something of an afterthought, a later development at a time when the original concept of a family novel had become inflated into a national epic. As a novelist Tolstoy always thought first about people. Once the characters were clear in his own mind they could safely be taken through the events of 1812.

What is believed to be the next stage chronologically in the task of launching the novel involves two new methods of approach. The first is to begin with an important social occasion, a society ball, at which the conversation hinted at in the earlier version at the Volkonskys (Napoleon, the military campaigns) could perhaps be developed in a wider and more appropriate setting and among a more intelligent and illustrious company. The second is to experiment with a historical introduction which would serve as a prelude to the events of 1811–13.

One of two similar versions (probably written at the end of 1863 or the beginning of 1864) starts with a ball at a nobleman's house in St. Petersburg in the year 1811. The Emperor Alexander is to be present. There is the conventional narrative opening paragraph defining time and place, and reference is made at the very beginning to well-known historical figures: 'In 1811, just at the time when Napoleon I's letter to Alexander I had been received in St. Petersburg and Caulaincourt had been replaced by Lauriston, a ball was held in the city at the house of Prince N., a nobleman of Catherine's day. . . .'[18] There is a similar but longer version extant which, unlike the

other, is prefaced by a lengthy historical paragraph on the
situation in Europe between Tilsit and the fire of Moscow.[19] It is
polemical in tone and patently ironical at the expense of
Napoleon ('He never thought, but did the first thing that came
into his head'). It has the advantage of preparing the way for
the letter referred to in the opening paragraph above. But it
did not satisfy Tolstoy, perhaps because it too prejudges the
issue of Napoleon—a topic which Tolstoy seemed determined
to have ventilated by different people with different points of
view, for all his own firm views about it.

Among the company assembled for the ball are Boris Zubtsov,
just back from the wars in Turkey (an embryonic Prince
Andrei); a certain Kushnev, strikingly similar to the Pierre of
War and Peace; and the young roué Pyotr Kurakin, who has
many features of the later Anatole Kuragin. A complete break
has been made between Pyotr on the one hand, and the 'Pierre-
type' character, Kushnev, who is given no Christian name. Two
interesting facts emerge from a reading of the ball scenes. First
there is virtually no dialogue in French. This is in striking
contrast to the opening of War and Peace. Tolstoy absolves
himself from the necessity of using French by inserting the
author's comment: 'there is no need to mention that everything
was said only in French.' Why he subsequently changed his policy
is something we shall have to consider at a later stage. Secondly
it is interesting to see that once the topic of Napoleon has been
raised at the ball in conversation between Kushnev and Zubtsov,
it is dropped almost at once, and the amorous activities of
Kurakin occupy Tolstoy's attention. It would seem that the
author has still not found the right setting for broadly representative, though not necessarily very intelligent, discussion.
The occasion is less appropriate than the company.

The Napoleon theme occurs at the very beginning of what is
assumed to be the next variant of the opening of the novel—the
name-day party at Count Prostoy's house in Moscow, 1808. Like
the final version, it opens with a few spoken words followed by
the name of the speaker, and here again Napoleon is the subject
of the conversation:

'But nobody said that I consider Bonaparte [without the u] a good
Christian. I didn't say so, I didn't say so at all, I say he's a great man,'

[19] J.E. XIII. 58.

said a tall stout youth breathlessly and almost foaming at the mouth . . . It was the young Bezukhoy arguing with Prince V[asily] about Napoleon.[20]

The occasion is a dinner party and the host is Count Prostoy (literally Count Simple). The level of 'discussion' is painfully low:

'What do you think, count,' said Prince V[asily] to him in Russian (the count spoke French badly). 'Will Napoleon get to Moscow or not?' 'Oui, pas de doute,' cried the count. 'Très bien, très bien.' Everybody laughed.[21]

Count Prostoy's table is evidently not the place for coherent conversation about important matters. Besides, who is Count Prostoy?

A new beginning extending to nine chapters and incorporating this variant was written towards the end of 1863 or the beginning of 1864 and entitled *A Day in Moscow*[22] (another title —*Name-day in Moscow, 1808*—is deleted). The first four chapters answer the question who are the Prostoys (the name is sometimes Plokhov—'Bad'—sometimes Rostov). The next two are devoted to the death of old Count Bezukhoy. The last three deal with the name-day, and the chapter just referred to is introduced at the appropriate stage. The names are still in a state of flux. Pierre is sometimes Arkady, sometimes Leon. There are many signs of inconsistency and clumsiness. As the old Bezukhoy lies dying he talks to the future Princess Drubetskaya (here Shchetinina) about the present régime and about Speransky—an improbable enough subject of conversation between such people at any time, still more so on the count's deathbed. But although this introduction is by no means a polished one, nearly all the substance of it is used in one place or another in the finished novel. Tolstoy hated to waste material. He would revise again and again. He would condense, amplify, transfer from one place to another. But he would very seldom (except for reasons of propriety) discard altogether a scene he had once got down on paper. The manuscript of this variant breaks off in the middle of chapter nine, which had opened with the ponderous statement that the discussion about Napoleon, the peace of Tilsit, the meeting at Erfurt and the merits of Napoleon continued throughout dinner, and which had been

[20] ibid. 169.    [21] ibid. 171    [22] ibid. 150 ff.

abruptly and vividly transformed into a fragment of Yasnaya Polyana domesticity as Natasha rushes in and asks what the sweet will be. The writing of such scenes was an easy matter for Tolstoy. But in rejecting this draft he seems to be acknowledging his intuitive feeling that the simple, domestic concerns of the Prostoy family—perhaps because there is nothing about them to suggest Moscow 1812, while they might well have undertones of Yasnaya Polyana 1863—are not a sufficiently weighty subject with which to begin a 'story of 1812'. And it is undoubtedly 1812 and its wider implications which are uppermost in his thoughts. That this is so can be seen from the short preface to be found in the same manuscript as *A Day in Moscow*, and beginning: 'Countless are the times I have begun and given up writing the story of 1812 which has been growing clearer and clearer in my mind and which has been crying out more and more urgently to be written down in clear concise forms.' Explaining the reasons for his numerous false starts he says:

Above all I was hampered by traditions both of form and content. I was afraid to write in a language which would not be the same as everybody else's; I was afraid that what I wrote would not fit into any category, whether novel, short story, poem or history; I was afraid that the need to describe important people of 1812 would compel me to be guided by historical documents and not the truth . . .

But he goes on to add: 'I have decided to put all these fears aside and to write only what I need to express, without worrying what the result of it all will be and without giving any title to my work.' [23]

This preface is important because it proves convincingly that Tolstoy is already thinking at this early stage of something bigger than a family novel in the English style, which is what some critics have considered the starting point of *War and Peace* to have been. It is 1812, the historical characters of 1812, the truth about 1812 which Tolstoy is concerned with, and was concerned with from the very beginning.

What was probably the next version of the opening chapters of Tolstoy's novel departs from all previous versions in two respects. It begins with 'authentic' historical events, with a narrative description of episodes of recorded military history, and not with a fabricated conversation piece in dining-room or salon.

[23] J.E. XIII. 53.

It also takes the time of the action yet another stage further back—not 1812, not 1811, not 1808, but 1805. Clearly Tolstoy already felt, as he later explicitly stated, that the events of 1812 could not be understood without reference to their causes, and that these causes must be traced back to the time of Russia's first encounter with Napoleon, many years before the invasion of Russia was ever contemplated. The text now begins with a factual narrative statement: 'On the 12 November 1805 the Russian armies under the command of Kutuzov, having retreated to Brunn under the pressure of Murat's entire army, were getting ready for the review by the Russian and Austrian emperors at Olmütz.'[24]

It is the night before the review. The future Nikolai Rostov (here called Prostoy, and rather more like Dolokhov at this stage than Nikolai) is with the army. The following pages describe the Olmütz review, the events leading up to Austerlitz (but not as yet the action at Schöngraben), and the battle of Austerlitz itself. It is evident that it was Tolstoy's intention even at this early date (the manuscript was probably written early in 1864) not only to include battle scenes in his book but also to devote a good deal of space to them. Historical characters—Alexander, Napoleon, Kutuzov, Bagration—are introduced into the action for the first time. There are short author's digressions on history and military science. The phrase 'the spirit of the army', so important to Tolstoy's later thesis, occurs here. And Tolstoy's own negative attitude to Napoleon is bluntly and unequivocally stated:

. . . he kept on winning his battles, not because he was a genius (I am convinced he was very far from that), but on the contrary because he was more stupid than his enemies, could not be carried away by logical deductions and only bothered about seeing that his soldiers were well-fed, embittered, obedient and as numerous as possible.[25]

Perhaps the most interesting feature of this lengthy opening is the much clearer definition of Prince Andrei's character. At first, it will be remembered, there was no Andrei, although the original Boris was endowed with many of his features. Then Tolstoy decided that he 'needed a brilliant young man to die at Austerlitz'[26] and so he gave old Bolkonsky a son. But now the

[24] ibid. 95.
[25] ibid. 137.
[26] Letter to L. I. Volkonskaya, 3 May 1865, J.E. LXI. 80.

plan is changing. Prince Andrei is to be reprieved. He is only
to be wounded. He is to be needed later on, although it is not
yet decided for what purpose. Possibly this version breaks off
when it does because of the need to think out Andrei's future
more clearly. It has been suggested also that Tolstoy was worried
about the way he was actually handling his material, especially
the extent to which he was interfering in the story with his
author's comments. When he said later in life[27] that description
of a thing coming from the author is bad and that you need to
describe how this or that thing is reflected in your characters,
he had in mind, I think, primarily that sort of situation where
the author takes the reader into his confidence about his characters—a thing which Tolstoy rarely or never does. The 'bar-
parlour chattiness' of Fielding and Thackeray, as E. M. Forster
calls it,[28] when the author gossips to his reader about his
characters is something very different from the digressions in
which Tolstoy indulges, and which are a more conspicuous
feature of the definitive version than of these early drafts. As
Forster says: 'It is not dangerous for a novelist to draw back
from his characters . . . and to generalize about the conditions
under which he thinks life is carried on. It is confidences about
the individual people that do harm. . . .'[29] To suggest that
Tolstoy abandoned the military opening because he found himself making pronouncements *ex cathedra* as it were is not convincing. It is much more likely that he preferred to introduce
his characters in situations and environments which were typical
of their normal daily life. The life of Prince Andrei or Nikolai
is not bounded or determined by the army. They are men first
and soldiers incidentally, and for a time. Similarly Anna
Karenina is not an habitual adulteress. She is a woman who
incidentally becomes involved in an adulterous situation.
Whether or not this is the correct explanation of Tolstoy's
dissatisfaction with this beginning, it is certainly a fact that
the experiment of an opening military scene is not repeated.
Significantly enough, however, the material is not wasted. Suitably
revised it will reappear in Parts 2 and 3 of Volume I.

About the same time as Tolstoy broke off the version just

[27] To V. G. Chertkov, 1909. Quoted in *Literaturnoe Nasledstvo, 37/38,*
Moscow, 1939, p. 533.
[28] E. M. Forster, *Aspects of the Novel,* London, 1927, p. 111.
[29] ibid. p. 112.

referred to, he probably returned to his *Three Eras*, revised it and altered the date from 1811 to 1805, as mentioned above. He did not, however, continue it. The next development of import-ance is to shift the opening scene to St. Petersburg and to make the early story centre on two characters, Prince Andrei and Pierre, who at this stage are sometimes called Andrei Volkonsky and Pyotr Medynsky. There are several similar openings in this vein. The action takes place still earlier, in the summer of 1805, and the scene is set at a dinner party in St. Petersburg given by the newly wed Volkonskys. One text[30] contrives to tell us in the very first sentence that at the time everybody in St. Petersburg was talking about Buonaparte. Another[31] pays more attention to the married couple, while nevertheless paving the way for a discussion of Napoleon at the dinner party which Prince Andrei and his wife are giving (the well-known emigré abbé Piatoli is present and M. Pierre is expected at any moment)—when the text ends. Clearly by now 1805 is to be the starting date. Clearly too Napoleon has to be worked in as early as possible. But now the talking is to be done, not by the simple Prostoy or the old Volkonsky, but by Prince Andrei and Pierre. And there is to be a foreigner present too.

All these features are incorporated in a new draft which has its own title and which for the first time calls the projected work a novel:

*From 1805 to 1814*

*Novel by* COUNT L. N. TOLSTOY

1805. Part I

Chapter I

The opening paragraph is interesting is so far as it shows that the Decembrist idea—the germ of *War and Peace*—is still present in Tolstoy's mind. He begins:

It would be difficult for those who knew Prince Pyotr Kirilovich B. at the beginning of Alexander II's reign in the 1850's, when Pyotr Kirilovich had come back from Siberia a hoary old man, to imagine him the care-free, muddle-headed, wild young man he was at the beginning of Alexander I's reign, soon after his return from abroad where he had been finishing his education at his father's wish.[32]

[30] J.E. XIII. 174.          [31] ibid. 174–7.          [32] ibid. 184.

Although the action has been pushed back to 1805, the three-fold division inherent in the title *Three Eras* (namely, 1812, 1825, and 1856) has not been lost sight of altogether.

This version is artistically speaking a very good one. There is a nice balance between early description and later discussion. First Pierre (Pyotr Kirilovich) and his closest friends Prince Andrei and Anatole Kuragin are described. Pierre arrives late to dinner at Prince Andrei's. He and Andrei are afterwards to go on to Anna Pavlovna Scherer's. At the dinner table are seated a foreigner and 'un homme de beaucoup de mérite'. Prince Andrei's wife, Lisa, is in the background. The conversation turns to the projected reforms in Russia, the constitution, Speransky. It works round to France and Napoleon, and Prince Andrei and Pierre voice their admiration of Napoleon as the greatest man in history. This version clearly has much in common with the definitive text. Towards the end even the use of French is apparent to a greater extent than in any previous variant—although it is still extremely discreet compared with its use or abuse in the opening pages of *War and Peace*. It is such a good beginning in fact that it is hard to say if much is gained by transferring the scene to Anna Scherer's salon. Perhaps Tolstoy thought it was unwise to play his two trump cards too soon—to give the two friends the floor from the very beginning and to do so in the comparative intimacy of one of their private homes. Perhaps he felt the need for neutral ground, a social milieu into which Prince Andrei and Pierre could enter gradually and as a matter of course, without attracting all the attention to themselves—a soirée large enough not only for two but for many characters to make their entrance, where a Kuragin could breathe side by side with a Volkonsky, where there was room for the widest possible range of people and opinions, clever men and fools, liberals and royalists; and where, one might add, a mildly satirical note could better be sounded. At all events, the transition to the Scherer salon is now an easy one, once the decision to abandon the private and exclusive dinner party has been taken.

What is not so easy is for Tolstoy to decide whether or not to preface his opening by a short historical introduction as he had attempted to do before. There are in fact at least two further versions, one with and one without such an introduction. The text of the introduction itself is of considerable interest—being, it is thought, written early in 1864 at a time when the work as a whole was still very much in the formative stages—for Tolstoy, having dated the period and the events of which he is to write, namely, the early years of Alexander's reign in Russia and of Napoleon's power in France, continues as follows:

But neither Napoleon nor Alexander, Kutuzov nor Talleyrand will be my heroes: I shall write a history of people freer than statesmen, a history of people living in the most favourable conditions, free from poverty, free from ignorance, independent people not having those shortcomings necessary for traces of them to be left on the pages of historical chronicles. . . .

And he goes on to criticize: 'the historians—les chroniqueurs des fastes de l'histoire—who see only the conspicuous monstrosities of human life and think that they are life itself'.[33] Tolstoy's bias against 'great men' and against the professional historians' methods of writing history is already much in evidence.

Once the historical introduction has been concluded the stage is set for the story to begin: 'In the old winter palace all the ladies-in-waiting were discussing the war.' We are now very close, if we subtract the introduction, to the opening of the final version, the salon of Anna Scherer, lady-in-waiting to the empress.

It now remains for us to mention the foreword, planned in 1864 but never used, to the first version of *1805*, which was due to appear in serial form. This discarded fragment is a most interesting document, and we quote one version of it in full:

In publishing the beginning of my projected work, I do not promise a continuation or a conclusion. We Russians generally speaking do not know how to write novels in the sense in which this genre is understood in Europe, nor is the projected work a long short story; no single idea runs through it, no contention is made, no single event is described; still less can it be called a novel with a plot, with a constantly deepening interest, and with a happy or unhappy dénouement destroying the interest of the narrative. In order to explain to the reader what the projected work is I find it most convenient to describe how I began to write it.

In 1856 [1860 according to Tolstoy's letter to Herzen quoted above] I began to write a story with a definite tendency, the hero of which was to have been a Decembrist returning with his family to Russia. From the present I involuntarily moved to 1825, the period of the delusions

[33] J.E. XIII. 73.

and misfortunes of my hero, and I abandoned what I had begun. But even in 1825 my hero was already a grown-up man with a family. In order to understand him, I had to carry myself back to his youth, and his youth coincided with Russia's glorious period of 1812. Once again I discarded what I had begun, and took as my starting point the year 1812, the smell and sound of which can be apprehended by us and are dear to us, but which is now so far removed from us that we can think about it calmly. But for a third time I abandoned what I had begun, not now because I needed to describe my hero's early youth: on the contrary, in the midst of the semi-historical, semi-public, semi-imaginary great typical faces of a great period, the personality of my hero receded into the background, and the young and the old, the men and the women of that time interested me equally and came to the fore. I turned back a third time, from a feeling which might seem strange to the majority of readers, but which, I hope, will be understood by those whose opinion I value: I did so from a feeling not unlike shamefacedness and which I cannot define in one word. I felt ashamed to write about our triumph in the struggle against Bonapartist France without having described our failures and our shame. Who has not experienced that secret but unpleasant feeling of shamefacedness and mistrust when reading patriotic works about 1812? If the cause of our triumph was not accidental, but lay in the essence of the character of the Russian people and army, this character ought to have been expressed still more clearly in the period of failures and defeats.

And so having gone back from 1856 to 1805, I now intend to lead not one, but many heroes and heroines of mine through the historical events of 1805, 1807, 1812, 1825, and 1856. I do not foresee in any one of these periods a dénouement in the relationships between these people. However much I tried at first to think up a novel-like plot and dénouement, I was convinced that it was not within my means, and I decided in describing these people to bow to my own practices and my own powers.

A few more words of justification against the reproach that many people will make. In my work (they will say) the only people who act are princes speaking and writing French, counts and so on—as though the whole of Russian life of the time centred on these people. I agree that this is untrue and illiberal, and I can give only one answer, an irrefutable one. The lives of officials, merchants, theological students and peasants do not interest me and are only half comprehensible to me; the lives of the aristocrats of that time, thanks to the documents of that time and other reasons, are comprehensible, interesting and dear to me.[34]

This tentative preface, rejected as it was, raises some interesting questions of the genre, the historical compass and even the polemical nature of Tolstoy's work, to which we shall have to return later. Meanwhile, now that the stages through which Tolstoy passed to reach a satisfying beginning to his book have

[34] J.E. XIII. 54.

been traced, the question arises whether the final version is an improvement over the many discarded ones. The answer, I think, is undoubtedly yes. Once the decision had been taken to dispense with a historical introduction—and there is nothing in the draft introductions which cannot be as well or better incorporated into the main body of the work—one can understand Tolstoy's reluctance to begin with a camp or battle scene in which the heroes of the novel would have to make their first appearance outside their normal milieu, and in which there would be no place for the civilian Pierre or the equally important womenfolk. Given the fundamental importance in the context of the work of Napoleon's invasion of Russia it seems logical to begin with an expression of differing opinions about the man and his achievements, ill-informed and ludicrous as some of these opinions are. And given the desirability of this divergence of views and a superficially serious level of discussion, coupled with the wish to introduce as many important men and women characters as possible in the early pages of the book, the choice of a distinguished salon providing the semblance of up-to-date serious discussion in the midst of tittle-tattle, and a mobility created by the constant arrivals and departures, is an improvement over the more static and archaic setting of the Rostovs' house or Bald Hills, and also the restricted intimacy of Prince Andrei's flat. But perhaps the decisive reason for Tolstoy's choice of this particular opening and not any other was the opportunity it gave him to start off in a gently satirical vein and to poke fun at the pretentiousness of the *haut monde* and the intellectual poverty of the 'important' people who imagined themselves to be in the vanguard of public opinion. The contrast between the natural and the conventional is an important theme of *War and Peace*. In the scene in Anna Scherer's salon we have the first hint of the antithesis of the 'natural' Pierre and the 'unnatural' Francophile society in which, reluctantly and against his better judgment, he moves and has his being.

### THE CHARACTERS AND THEIR RELATIONSHIPS

We have devoted much space to the opening chapters of *War and Peace* because they caused Tolstoy more difficulty than any other comparable section of his book. But a study of the draft versions of the novel reveals many other significant changes, some of which can now be briefly illustrated. Broadly speaking we can distinguish between two sorts of textual alterations: those which concern the handling of characters, their introduction, the impression they make on one another, their mutual relationships, the handling of their emotional crises, the dramatization of the events in which they are involved; and secondly the more narrowly stylistic emendations, improvements in syntax and vocabulary, balance and rhythm, verbal changes of one sort or another. Each of these two broad divisions covers much ground and has many ramifications. We shall begin with the first, and can note in passing that the tendency of the definitive text as compared with the early drafts is nearly always in the direction of greater individualization of character and less concern with holding an impartial balance between the good and bad features of any given person. Thus some positive heroes such as Kutuzov and Natasha—simple, 'natural', Russian men and women—have some 'unnatural' features attributed to them in some of the early drafts and plans: Natasha, for example, is said to ape the court circle in everything; Kutuzov to be a great general but 'not a Russian'. Conversely those characters such as Boris and Anna Scherer who are more the butt of Tolstoy's satire in *War and Peace,* appear at first in a much more favourable light. The urge to differentiate more sharply between the true and the false elements in Russian society was something which became more pronounced as the writing of the book got under way.

Of all the principal characters in *War and Peace* it was Prince Andrei who proved to be the most troublesome to handle and the conception of him was considerably modified once the decision had been taken to include him at all, and then to allow him, contrary to the original intention, to survive the battlefield of Austerlitz. In the early drafts several interesting modifications were made in the portrait of Prince Andrei which was taking shape under Tolstoy's pen. To give one or two examples. In a manuscript of 1864,[35] Prince Andrei's treatment of his young wife Lisa in the company of Pierre is not merely ungallant but pointedly and deliberately rude. When the two are later alone, Andrei loses his temper again over a *billet doux*

[35] J.E. XIII. 268-71.

which Hippolyte had sent to his wife. White with rage he sends
Hippolyte a letter, threatening him with a duel. These scenes
create an unfavourable impression of Andrei's bad manners and
unjustified outbursts of jealousy. They lower him in the reader's
eyes, quite apart from the fact that his behaviour towards
Hippolyte is internally inconsistent. A man of his breeding
would hardly involve himself with people he despised. To bully
and threaten Hippolyte would be to demean himself in his own
esteem. We can safely assume that these scenes were discarded
as being unworthy of the cold, correct, vain, self-possessed and
brilliant young man whom Tolstoy was in the process of
creating.

In another early draft, Prince Andrei is seen engaging in
literary exchanges with Pierre, and expressing his opinions about
different writers and thinkers. He is severe on the 'boring',
'untrue', 'overdone' ballads of Goethe. He likes Racine, Voltaire,
Rousseau (*Le Contrat Social*, that is, *not La Nouvelle Héloïse*)—
'but the rest—these Iliads and Shakespeares and Mm. Suza—all
that is for women's albums'.[36] These and similar recognizably
Tolstoyan eccentricities of taste foisted on to Prince Andrei are
later deleted, not necessarily because they are out of keeping
with his character, but rather, one suggests, because they were
felt to be *longueurs*—and Tolstoy was sensitive about his tendency towards prolixity. As he said to Fet a couple of years later:
'Turgenev's opinion that one can't spend ten pages describing
what N.N. did with his hand helped me very much.'[37] When
the first part of *1805* was published, Prince Andrei came in for
criticism, especially from Fet, for being a tedious and static
figure. Tolstoy acknowledged the justice of Fet's criticism, tried
to explain the reason for it and expressed the hope that he had
profited by it. Referring to Fet's negative remarks about Prince
Andrei, Tolstoy says in agreement:

It is true, he is tedious, monotonous, merely *un homme comme il faut*
throughout the first part. But it is not his fault, it is mine. Apart from
my conception of the characters and their movement, apart from my
conception of the conflict of characters, I have another, historical, conception which complicates my work in an extraordinary way and which
I am evidently not coping with. As a result I was concerned in the first
part with the historical side, and the character stood still and did not

36 ibid. 231.
37 Letter to A. A. Fet, 10 ... 20 May 1866, J.E. LXI. 138.

move. And this was a fault which I clearly understood from your letter, and I hope I have corrected it. . . .[38]

In revising the already published first part of *1805*, Tolstoy was really only continuing to do what he had already done in discarding some of these earlier draft versions relating to Prince Andrei, namely, imparting more momentum to the action at the sacrifice of static interest and creating greater internal plausibility of character. As a result the definitive portrait of Prince Andrei, for all his coldness, sense of superiority and bored irritability, is both rather more sympathetic and rather more consistent than that of the churlish, ill-mannered, jealous and opinionated talker who coexists with the aloof *homme comme il faut* in some earlier drafts.

Speaking in his old age to Goldenweiser, Tolstoy emphasized that 'when psychological mistakes are made, when the characters in novels and stories do what, from their spiritual nature, they are unable to do, it is a terrible thing . . .'.[39] Something of this desire for consistency and inner plausibility can be felt in the rejection of certain draft scenes concerning the Rostov brothers, Nikolai and Petya. Nikolai emerges in *War and Peace* as a very clearly defined character, ordinary with ordinary virtues, and an unquestioning acceptance of the way of life and the habits of mind to which his environment and education have conditioned him. In one draft version, however, he is shown as a blasé, disillusioned young man:

Disillusioned in the possibility of heroism in war, in the possibility of waging war without suffering and without being humiliated, disillusioned even in the reasonableness of the causes of wars, Nikolai was at the same time disillusioned in friendship, in love, in everything which he had not yet had time to experience.[40]

The Nikolai of *War and Peace* may be momentarily perplexed, even a little ashamed: but he is not the abject victim of disillusion. This Byronic pose is out of character, and no doubt for this reason the draft is discarded. Nikolai's brother Petya is the subject of a similar temporary aberration. In one draft Petya, having left his family after their departure from Moscow in 1812 and joined his regiment, speaks persistently of his disillusionment and the feeling of dissatisfaction with himself (the

[38] Letter to A. A. Fet, 7 November 1866, ibid. 149.
[39] A. B. Goldenweiser, *Vblizi Tolstogo*, Moscow-Leningrad, 1959, p. 113.
[40] J.E. XIII. 768.

identical expressions 'disillusionment' and 'dissatisfaction with himself' are repeated three times in the space of five sentences). But in the corresponding paragraph of the corresponding chapter of *War and Peace* he is shown on the contrary in a typical state of high spirits. Here is a translation of the two texts:

| *Draft* | *War and Peace* |
|---|---|
| Petya Rostov, having left his family after the departure from Moscow and having joined his regiment, was posted shortly afterwards as orderly to a general in charge of an important unit. Having joined the active army, Petya experienced a painful feeling, not so much of disillusionment as of dissatisfaction with himself which all sincere and ardent young men experience when they experience [sic] war in the flesh, about which they have, thanks to the false opinion current, a completely contrary notion. This disillusionment and dissatisfaction with oneself is always the stronger, the better the young man is at fighting. Petya was endowed with great ambition, strong nerves and a propensity for blood to flow to his head in such a way that he saw and understood nothing when he was angry. Otherwise he was almost a child. And so he was what is called foolhardy and so too, having joined the active army and been twice in action at Tarutino and Vyazma, he experienced a painful feeling of disillusionment and dissatisfaction with himself.[41] | Petya, having left his family after the departure from Moscow, joined his regiment and was taken on shortly afterwards as orderly by a general in charge of a large detachment. From the time he had received his commission and especially since he had joined the active army and taken part in the battle of Vyazma, Petya had been in a constant state of blissful excitement at being grown up, and in a perpetual ecstatic hurry not to miss any chance to do something really heroic. He was highly delighted with what he saw and experienced in the army, but at the same time it always seemed to him that the really heroic exploits were being performed just where he did not happen to be. And he was always in a hurry to be where he was not.[42] |

These two passages are markedly different, and in making his choice, Tolstoy was obviously guided by the fact that the second of the two was so much more a true reflection of that enthusiastic boyish *élan* which is the essence of Petya's non-introspective nature.

[41] J.E. XV. 102.    [42] *War and Peace*, IV. 3. 7.

In the process of writing the successive drafts of *War and Peace* Tolstoy sought not only to render the characters themselves more consistent but also to improve the account of their mutual relationships, especially those between a man and a woman, and to endow them with greater subtlety. For example, many of the draft versions of scenes describing the intimate relations between Hélène and Dolokhov, Sonya and Dolokhov, or Princess Marya and Nikolai are more banal and clumsy than the final ones. Dolokhov's liaison with Hélène is at first explicitly stated, blatant and crude. Dolokhov boasts to Nikolai that there are no women, countesses or cooks, who are not venal. He refers to Hélène as a 'fish'.[43] In the definitive version, on the other hand, the liaison, while clearly implied, and once alluded to inconspicuously by Dolokhov's mother, is never openly paraded. It is handled in the form of its repercussions, the suspicions of Pierre, the arrogance of Dolokhov, the duel, the breach. In this way it proves to be more disturbing. There is just the remote possibility, one feels, that Pierre is mistaken; just the chance that Hélène has been wronged; just the momentary suspicion that Pierre is making a fool of himself again.

Dolokhov's relations with Sonya are also better handled in the definitive than in the draft versions by saying as little about them as possible and by conveying the necessary information through third parties. Natasha tells Nikolai that Dolokhov has proposed to Sonya. Sonya tells Nikolai that she has refused Dolokhov. There is no scene between Dolokhov and Sonya themselves. Not that the episode is a particularly convincing one, although it is needed to motivate the gambling scene where Dolokhov ruins Nikolai at cards out of spite at his rejection. But at least it does avoid the embarrassing banalities of the early version, containing as it does the following love-letter from Dolokhov to Sonya:

Adored Sophie, I love you as no man ever loved a woman. My fate is in your hands. I do not dare to ask for your hand. I know that they will not give you, a pure angel, to me, a man with a reputation that is deserved. But from the moment I first knew you I have been a different man. I have seen heaven. If you love me even one hundredth part as much as I love you, you will have understood me. Sophie, give yourself to me and I will be your slave. If you love me, write yes, and I will find a time for a rendezvous.[44]

[43] J.E. XIII. 547.          [44] ibid. 577.

If there has to be a proposal, better let it be made by proxy than suffer the discomfort of this drivelling declaration. Not that Tolstoy could not write a good proposal scene. That between Boris and Julie is particularly interesting, because it is an example of a statement expanded into a scene, not a scene contracted into a statement. In one draft version, Tolstoy simply states: 'Boris, having decided that day to declare himself, made a proposal. The proposal . . . was accepted.'[45] In *War and Peace*, however, Julie has to resort to womanly wiles to extract the proposal (as Hélène had to try and draw Pierre out, or as Sonya Behrs had to write a pointed story for Tolstoy's own benefit). The situation of the woman proposing is handled by Tolstoy in time-honoured fashion by making Julie rouse Boris's jealousy by her own feigned attention to Anatole Kuragin.

There is much of the banal also in an early draft version of the ending of the Princess Marya-Nikolai relationship. The discovery is made that Prince Andrei's wound is not serious. It is assumed that he will recover and marry Natasha, in which case it will, according to the tables of affinity of the Orthodox Church, be impossible for Natasha's brother Nikolai to marry Prince Andrei's sister Marya. This version shows Nikolai as being rather relieved. He seems glad to get out of it. He winds up his business with Princess Marya amicably with a barely disguised sigh of relief. Here is the embarrassing finale:

'Oui, chère Marie, je vous ai aimé du moment que je vous ai vu [sic]. Mais il y a un obstacle et je suis heureux de ce que cela c'est arrangé comme cela est. Tant mieux, tant mieux . . .'
'Adieu, Nicolas', was all that Princess Marya said as she held out her hand, but she was so happy to say these words.
'Adieu, chère Marie, au revoir à la noce de Nathalie'—and kissing her hand he went out.[46]

Getting Nikolai married proved particularly difficult for Tolstoy. The problem was to get rid of Sonya. She had no money, and therefore it was impossible for Nikolai to marry her. In the first draft of the final parts of the novel Prince Andrei's life is spared, as we have seen, and Sonya's plan is to persuade him to marry Natasha. If he does, Nikolai will be unable to marry Princess Marya and Sonya will come into her own. But this is an impossible solution from Tolstoy's point of

45 ibid. 811.                    46 J.E. XV. 22.

view, for Sonya must not be allowed to marry Nikolai. Consequently in this early draft,[47] Prince Andrei is made to turn a
deaf ear to Sonya's persuasions; in his turn, he tells her that
there are considerations above one's own happiness, that his
sister Marya loves Nikolai, that she cannot marry him if he,
Andrei, marries Natasha, and that he does not intend to stand
in their way. Sonya is greatly moved by Andrei's sacrifice. She
resolves to make a similar sacrifice 'for his (Nikolai's) happiness,
for the happiness of the home, our home'. The dilemma is
solved in a few lines by two unselfish gestures.

With Prince Andrei seriously ill, however, and his recovery
in doubt, a different conclusion had to be sought. In another
draft,[48] Andrei, though gravely ill, is still alive. His life is in the
balance. He may recover or he may not. Nikolai and Princess
Marya meanwhile are at Voronezh. At this point the wife of
the Governor of Voronezh (Nikolai's aunt) takes the initiative.
She writes to Sonya in Moscow and appeals to her generosity to
release Nikolai and allow him to marry and retrieve the family
fortunes. Sonya is angry. She decides not to reply, but to wait
for Nikolai and not release him. Meanwhile, she hopes that
Prince Andrei will recover and so prevent the marriage anyway.

But, as Tolstoy eventually decided, Andrei was not to recover,
and so the problem of Sonya had to be thought out again.
Reluctant as ever to jettison completely a situation he had once
devised, Tolstoy does not abandon the Governor's wife. In the
final version she talks to Nikolai as before, in an effort to persuade him to renounce Sonya and marry Princess Marya. But
the significant improvement this time is that it is not she who
writes to Sonya (an unwarrantable outside interference), but
Sonya herself who writes to the hesitant Nikolai. True, the
Countess Rostova had implored her to do so as we are subsequently told; but like the letter from the Governor's wife,
these entreaties had only had the effect of making her more
stubborn. The overriding factor in her decision to write is the
conviction that Prince Andrei *will* live and thus negate the
consequences of her ostensible altruism.

The interesting thing about this final resolution of the
Nikolai-Sonya friendship—unsatisfactory as it is in some ways—
is that the letter from Sonya precedes Tolstoy's explanation of

[47] J.E. XIV. 149 ff.        [48] J.E. XV. 10, 15 ff.

the events which led up to it. The reader is first confronted with the text of the letter and with Nikolai's reaction to it, and has to wait until the next chapter to learn what prompted it. This is a constructional device which Tolstoy resorted to on several occasions as a more arresting and more thought provoking variation on his normal chronological narrative. Why did Sonya write the letter? Was it of her own free will? It is as if, in this instance, Tolstoy felt the weakness of the situation and strove to provide a little suspense, to stimulate a little curiosity until the not very convincing explanation had to be given.

### FIRST APPEARANCES AND IMPRESSIONS OF THE CHARACTERS

As a novelist Tolstoy took great pains over the introduction of his main heroes, and it will be noticed that several characters in his novels are first presented to the reader (or to each other) not as isolated entities but in terms of the impression they make on other people (or on each other). There are many interesting examples of the way in which Tolstoy altered his early versions because he was not satisfied that the all-important initial introduction had been properly made.

A careful study of the drafts of *War and Peace* throws light on this important side of Tolstoy's craft, namely the indirect or oblique presentation of a character. In one version of the opening chapters of the first part of the book, the viscount de Mortemart is telling his story in Anna Scherer's salon before an assembly of guests who have been given only a perfunctory introduction. Tolstoy intended to interrupt the viscount's story and tell the reader more about the main characters who form the audience. He began:

> Before recounting the viscount's story, which subsequently gained wide currency, I must describe some of his audience, the more so since these few people, as well as being remarkable in themselves, will come the reader's way many a time in the course of this story.[49]

But later these words are crossed out, and Tolstoy scribbled in the margin: 'who listens and how'. And so we find in the final text that Tolstoy, while cutting down the story itself from its first lengthy ramblings to a précis a mere paragraph long,

[49] J.E. XIII. 210.

devotes much more space to what the *audience* are doing—
Hélène glancing at her beautiful round arm or her still more
beautiful bosom, smoothing the folds of her dress, assuming as
required the expression assumed by her hostess; the Princes Lisa
getting on with her work; Hippolyte, eyes vacant, legs and arms
dangling, adjusting his lorgnette. The story itself fades right into
the background. Its reaction, or lack of reaction, on the people
who are listening comes to the fore.

The principle on which Tolstoy is working here is that in the
narrative exposition of a person or thing it is not the static
description of that person or thing which is of prime importance, but the description of the impression they make on, and
the reaction they provoke in other people. 'It seems to me',
observed Tolstoy at the age of 22, 'that it is really impossible
to *describe* a man, but it is possible to describe the effect he
produces on me.'[50] We can now apply these words to the introduction of Pierre in *War and Peace*. A comparison of the two
following texts brings out clearly Tolstoy's deliberate change of
emphasis in introducing for the first time his most important
character:

### Draft

'But why do you call Napoleon a lackey?' suddenly asked a stout
young man of a very shy and reticent appearance who had so far been
sitting in silence behind the ladies' backs.

All eyes turned on the young man. Prince Hippolyte snatched at the
lorgnette which had dropped from his hand, and as soon as he had
caught hold of it, quickly fixed his eyes on the young man.

He blushed, as only full-blooded young men blush, and went on with
an obvious struggle and effort, and as though fulfilling a duty:

'I consider him a great man'—and big beads of sweat stood out on the
young man's nose and brow. He looked round at everyone feeling that
he had committed a *gaffe* but evidently prepared to bear the full burden
of his blunder.

'Everyone has his own opinion, M. Pierre', took up Annette . . .[51]

Compare this now with Pierre's first appearance as it is described
in the final version of *War and Peace*. Three sentences explain
who Pierre is and where he has come from. Then follow the
words:

[50] J.E. XLVI. 67.          [51] J.E. XIII. 213

Anna Pavlovna greeted him with the nod she accorded to the lowest hier-
archy in her drawing room. But in spite of this lowest grade greeting,
a look of anxiety and fear, as at the sight of something too large and
unsuited to the place, came over her face when she saw Pierre enter. . . .

'It is very good of you, Monsieur Pierre, to come and visit a poor
invalid', said Anna Pavlovna, exchanging an alarmed glance with her
aunt as she conducted him to her. . . .[52]

This is sufficient to make the point that while Tolstoy originally describes what is happening to Pierre—his blushes, his
struggle with himself, the beads of sweat—he describes in the
final text what happens to other people when Pierre appears—
the condescending nod, the look of anxiety, the alarmed glance,
the dismay. The emphasis has been altogether shifted. This is
not to imply, of course, that Tolstoy uses this same device as an
habitual method of introducing his characters. When Prince
Andrei is introduced, *his* features, *his* bored expression, *his*
grimaces are described. When Andrei's wife Lisa first appears,
the description of her unusual upper lip is followed by the statement that everybody brightened up at the sight of her—a
combination of her distinctive features and the impression she
makes. Tolstoy's approach is varied, but he is always alive to
the possibilities of oblique characterization. We might mention
as further evidence the fact that in the early versions there is
much more narrative description of how Boris Drubetskoy talks
and behaves (for example in his meeting with Nikolai at Tilsit),
while in the finished work his unpleasantness is conveyed rather
through Nikolai's impressions of him.

The introduction of the minor character, Captain Tushin,
the eccentric pipe-smoking hero of Schöngraben, who makes
such a favourable impression on Prince Andrei in the novel,
is the outcome of much protracted labour. In one early version
Tolstoy gives a lengthy narrative description of him, and por-
trays him as a somewhat comic, un-military individual who is
at the same time a wealthy, educated and highly intelligent
member of the gentry:

By virtue of his wealth (he shared a thousand odd serfs with his two
brothers), his education (he was brought up by a French tutor and was
very well read), and his connections which he despised using, Tushin
was in an incomparably higher social position than the majority of
officers, infantry and cavalry, among whom he lived, but he so concealed

52 *War and Peace*, I. 1. 2.

this superiority that he not only did not arouse any envy, but indeed was on the most friendly terms with everybody. When arguments started about learned matters among the officer society in which he lived, everyone would turn to Tushin for an answer, and his words were taken as the infallible truth.[53]

These references to Tushin's wealth and social position are dropped in *War and Peace*; but this is not sufficient evidence for regarding him, as some Soviet critics do, as a representative of the common people, a sort of plebeian complement of the aristocratic Prince Andrei.

Another early version emphasizes, again in narrative form, the respect with which Captain Tushin was regarded because of his intellectual eminence: 'This officer was staff-captain Tushin, known to all his comrades as a quiet and gentle eccentric of singular intelligence and erudition, and fond of a drink.'[54]

The character is developed at some length in another draft version of the same chapter, although the name is temporarily changed to Anan'ev (a substitution in the manuscript for Timokhin, which is crossed out). Some of the thoughts ascribed to him are remarkably similar to those which Tolstoy later ascribes to Prince Andrei himself:

Anan'ev was known among his comrades as an absent-minded eccentric, a poor military man but a good comrade, a harmless eccentric, a freethinker, a bookworm and a philosopher. Anan'ev did indeed read a lot and think even more. He thought not because he wanted to think, but because he could not help thinking, although his thoughts often oppressed him. Now, standing by the guns, he thought that he would surely be killed that day and wondered what death would be like. 'Can there really be nothing left of me?' he asked himself. 'Golevsky will take over the division by right of seniority. And I shall not be here, and nothing will be left of me. But where shall I be at the moment I am killed? One second before I still was, I suffered, and suddenly I am no longer. No more me, but everything will go on without me. No, it's impossible. But I'll be killed—that's certain. Otherwise I would not have this feeling of depression which has been nagging at me for two days now. They say the soul will fly away to heaven! Supposing this is a superstition, that there is nothing but atmosphere in heaven; what they mean is that the soul will not perish, but will return to God, the creator of all. But if that is so, why does this soul, my soul within me, fear death so much now, since death will only liberate it from this covering of flesh? It ought to be glad. But it suffers and is afraid. I—my soul—is afraid, it is sick with fear. What does it mean?'[55]

[53] J.E. XIII. 376.          [54] ibid. 404.          [55] ibid. 451.

The chapter continues in the same vein, as Anan'ev ponders over the problem of the immortality of the soul.

Other versions of the same chapter take the form largely of conversations between Tushin (or Anan'ev) and a certain fellow-officer Belkin, who does not appear in *War and Peace*. Here the predominant theme is the immortality of the soul, but a new feature is introduced in the form of an article by Herder which Tushin is reading or has read. In one text Tushin outlines what he says is Herder's idea of a ladder of living things, a progression from plants and animals to man; the idea that every living organism turns into another living organism and so never disappears, and that therefore man will never disappear, but will also turn into a higher organism. But why, Tushin is asked, a *higher* organism? The question prompts him to ask himself in what way men are higher than the grass and the worms, and he continues:

'Why do we all love everything: the grass, a little insect, people, even your colonel? Sometimes you lie in the grass and feel like becoming grass; you look at the clouds or the water, and you want to be water or a cloud; you even feel you want to be a worm. . . . You know, it's all because we've been everything already. I always think that we've been living millions and millions of years already, and have been everything.'[56]

In yet another version, the conversation is integrated more closely into the novel by the substitution of Prince Andrei for Belkin, and the relegation of Belkin to the rôle of a third party. The introduction of Anan'ev is here very similar to the introduction of Tushin in *War and Peace*—that is, through the impression he makes on Prince Andrei, on the eve of the battle of Schöngraben. Andrei sees him for a moment in his tent without his boots on, and is struck at once by his shy, awkward manner, his friendly voice and his simple, intelligent speech. He sees him a second time shortly afterwards and is invited to take a meal in the captain's tent. Andrei accepts:

He agreed to go into the captain's tent. But he agreed not so much because he had nothing to do, as because he wanted to be with this man and to talk to him. Apart from the fact that this man was unusually sympathetic to him, his pride seldom gave him the opportunity to mix with people as man to man, with no element of calculation, no *arrière pensée*, as he could with this unknown little officer whom he would

[56] ibid 368.

probably never see again and who did not even know his name. What Mikhail Ivanovich, the architect, was for his father, this officer was for Prince Andrei.[57]

There is a preliminary exchange between the two men, and Prince Andrei thinks to himself: 'Ma parole d'honneur, je voudrais bien que beaucoup de mes camarades ayent des idées de cet individu.' Andrei then asks Anan'ev for his opinions about war. They are forthright in the extreme: 'War in my opinion is the ultimate degree of human folly, the manifestation of the most inane side of human nature. People who have no reason whatsoever to do so, murder each other.' Then Anan'ev is questioned about the Herder article which he has been reading and marking extensively in the margin, and gives a cautious, non-committal reply.

What emerges from these first attempts to launch Captain Tushin is that he is clearly envisaged in the beginning as an Andrei-type character in the sense that he is an intellectual and a 'seeker'. At the same time he is unworldly, simple, unaffected and awkward: that is to say he shares features in common with Pierre Bezukhov. It is particularly interesting therefore that in *War and Peace* Tolstoy should eventually transfer the conversations on Herder, on the links between lower and higher beings and on the immortality of the soul, to Prince Andrei and Pierre themselves, as they cross the ferry on their journey to Bald Hills.[58]

The first introduction of Captain Tushin in the novel[59] is of the oblique variety, as in the draft version quoted above. He is first seen being reprimanded by a staff officer for slovenliness, and uttering some embarrassed reply. Nothing is said about his background, but Prince Andrei, who witnesses the reprimand, is attracted by his large, kindly and intelligent *eyes*, and his unsoldierly, somewhat comic figure. On his next appearance Prince Andrei recognizes him by his *voice*, and overhears a conversation in which Tushin has a mere two or three sentences on the soul and the fear of death—all that remains of his original eloquence. This time it is Tushin's sincerity of tone which captures Prince Andrei's interest. Taken together the two scenes provide a good example of the indirect introduction of a character through the medium of the impression created by his eyes and voice, and his stance and bearing.

[57] J.E. XIII. 405 ff.    [58] *War and Peace*, II. 2. 12.    [59] ibid. I. 2. 15.

Just as important as a character's first introduction to the reader is the first meeting between two people whose fate is to be closely linked. This is especially apparent in the case of Prince Andrei and Natasha. The description of their first meeting at Otradnoe did not come easily to Tolstoy, as a perusal of several different versions shows. In one early draft[60] Andrei is virtually swept off his feet. He is infatuated by the sight and sound of the little girl dressed up as a man (a detail not included in the end). When she looked at him at supper 'he felt the blood rushing to his face, his lips and eyes felt strange, he blushed and felt as embarrassed as a little boy'. This is in marked contrast to the unfavourable impression made by Natasha in a later text.[61] This time Prince Andrei, on arriving at Otradnoe, sees and hears a girl who takes no notice of him. Later that day he sees the same girl at dinner, but pays not the slightest attention to her, dismissing her as 'provincial'. Tolstoy then intended that Prince Andrei should leave the same evening, his business completed, but this phrase is crossed out and the text continues, with Andrei, as in the final version, overhearing Natasha and Sonya talking in the moonlight, and leaving next morning before the girls are up. The final version,[62] although it follows the night scene closely, expands, and deepens the first impression which Natasha made on Andrei. When he first sees and hears her he asks himself—'What is she so glad about?' 'What is she thinking of?' 'Why is she so happy?' The sight of her disturbs him and stimulates thought and feeling. But it does not overwhelm him. This is a compromise, but an effective and convincing one.

As for Natasha's impressions of Prince Andrei, Tolstoy was equally uncertain how best to represent them. The first version is a compromise between a positive and a negative reaction, both of which were recorded and then deleted. The positive reaction read: 'In the evening Natasha told Sonya as she recounted to her friend her impressions of the day that Prince Bolkonsky was such a charming creature that she had never seen nor could ever imagine anyone comparable. He and Nicolas, nobody else.'[63] The negative reaction, likewise crossed out, was: ' "No, I don't like him, I don't like him," said Natasha

---

[60] J.E. XIII. 625 ff.
[62] *War and Peace*, II. 3. 2.
[61] ibid. 756.
[63] J.E. XIII. 627 n.

that evening about Prince Andrei. "There is something proud,
something dry about him." ' This version as amended sticks to
the middle of the road and Tolstoy is content to let Natasha
tell her mother that Prince Andrei is the sort of man she likes.

In the final version, Tolstoy changes his mind again and there
is no reference at all to the impression Prince Andrei makes on
Natasha. After all she is very young, and still, as she thinks, in
love with Boris; and Andrei, depressed and preoccupied as he
is, hardly appears as a gallant cavalier. Without wishing to
argue that Tolstoy's last thoughts are always better than his
first, one may well agree that psychologically speaking the
final solution of the problem of the first meeting of this pair of
future lovers is an improvement over the tentative essays.

### LOVE RELATIONSHIPS

A study of the rough work of *War and Peace* shows the difficulties Tolstoy experienced in getting the love relationships of
Natasha right—both her conflicting feelings for Prince Andrei
and Anatole Kuragin, and the growth of her love for Pierre.
Natasha's relations with Anatole and the attempted abduction
scene were written and rewritten a score of times. Tolstoy later
referred to this particular episode as 'the most difficult passage
and the keypoint of the whole novel'.[64] Apart from the psychological difficulties, there were many technical problems which
confronted Tolstoy. How was Natasha to react to Anatole's first
advances at the soirée? How should she respond to his letter?
How should Sonya find out about it? What should she do?
How should Pierre get to know about it and what part should
he play? It hardly seems to matter whether Sonya finds out by
picking up the letter from the table (in one version) or taking
it from Natasha's hands when she is asleep (in another). But the
question of Pierre is more important, because in the final text
this scene is really the starting-point of his intimate relationship
with Natasha. In one draft[65] Sonya informs Pierre of what has
happened by sending him Natasha's unfinished letter to Prince
Andrei. In another[66] he comes to dinner and Sonya takes him
aside to show him Anatole's letter. In a third[67] old Count

[64] Letter to P. I. Bartenev, 1 November 1867, J.E. LXI. 180.
[65] J.E. XIII. 851.          [66] ibid. 857.          [67] ibid. 855.

Rostov, to whom Natasha has confided her secret, goes round to Pierre's house himself in search of Anatole, and breaks the news to Pierre. In the final version[68] Akhrosimova, with whom the girls are staying, sends for Pierre herself. There are similar technical choppings and changings over the details of the attempted abduction. For the most part they are not important. But what does emerge more clearly in the end is the fact that Natasha thinks that she loves *both* men (one recalls the first plan and the note on Natasha: 'needs a husband—two even!'). She can't be happy, she says, without either of them. It is not that Anatole has ousted Prince Andrei; it is the impasse created by the necessity and at the same time the impossibility of choosing between them which is the essential psychological dilemma which in the definitive version Tolstoy is better able to convey.

As for the relations between Natasha and Pierre, Tolstoy is at pains in revising his work to defer for as long as possible the first mention of the feelings of love for each other which are to mature after Prince Andrei's death. In one draft[69] Natasha actually confesses to her brother Nikolai as early as the beginning of the second volume that she is in love with the married Bezukhov, but understandably enough this scene is later discarded. In revising the first part of *1805* Tolstoy considerably reduced his account of the impression Natasha made on Pierre. Later, in the proofs of the Natasha-Anatole relationship, Pierre is described, as he sees Natasha sobbing like a child, as experiencing a feeling of 'pity, tenderness and *love*' for her; but this phrase is eventually replaced by the single word 'pity'.[70] The moment is not quite ripe. The discarded words 'pity, tenderness and *love*' are held back until the final chapter of the second volume, just exactly half-way through the novel, when they are followed almost immediately by Pierre's words: 'If I were not myself, but the handsomest, cleverest and best man in the world and if I were free, I would this moment ask on my knees for your hand and your *love*.'[71] Shedding tears of gratitude and emotion (but not love) Natasha hastily departs. Once again it is the definitive version which displays the surer touch in portraying an emotional crisis.

[68] *War and Peace*, II. 5. 19.    [69] J.E. XIII. 555.
[70] See Zaidenshnur, J.E. XVI. 109.    [71] *War and Peace*, II. 5. 22.

## DEATH SCENES

On reading the revisions which Tolstoy made in the scenes where the death of a character is reported or described, one is struck by several features which seem to be typical of Tolstoy's technique as a novelist. One such feature is the restraint he imposes upon himself in handling emotional scenes. A good example is the episode in which the Rostov family learn of the death of their youngest son Petya. In a draft version[72] Natasha sees her father coming out of her mother's room. She asks him what is the matter. 'Petya . . . my son . . . Go . . . She is calling you . . .' he stammers out. As she enters her mother's room she sees Princess Marya. 'Marie, what? Is he killed?' she asks. Her physical suffering is shown by the fact that 'her chin quivered from time to time'. As amended later[73] this same text puts more emphasis on the physical signs of Natasha's grief: 'her chin began to quiver rapidly'; she is 'as white as chalk'. Compare this now with the corresponding passage in *War and Peace*.[74] Natasha's questions have been cut out. Neither before nor after her father's words does she say anything. By allowing her to be warned of bad news by a servant Tolstoy removes the necessity for any words, and none are spoken during the scene except the broken utterances of old Count Rostov. The other change which Tolstoy makes is to transfer the visible physical signs of weakness from Natasha to Princess Marya. It is Princess Marya who is pale. It is she whose chin quivers. And this is an important emendation. For the essence of this scene is that Natasha, at this critical moment, finds a release, a new strength, a new love for her mother. She embraces her 'with unsuspected strength'. The blow that nearly kills her mother restores Natasha to life. No doubt for this reason the physical marks of weakness, tears apart, are removed, and Natasha, for all her inner pain and anguish, shows outwardly the inner strength she has found.

The final version of the death scene of Lisa in childbirth contains a small but significant emendation:

| *Draft* | *War and Peace* |
|---|---|
| Suddenly a terrible cry—not her cry—she could not cry like that— | Suddenly a terrible cry—not her cry—she could not cry like that— |

---

[72] J.E. XV. 149.    [73] ibid. 173.    [74] *War and Peace*, IV. 4. 2.

| *Draft—contd.* | *War and Peace—contd.* |
|---|---|
| came from the next room. He ran to the door; the cry ceased and he heard the cry of a baby. 'What have they taken a baby in there for?' thought Prince Andrei. The door opened and the *accoucheur* came out, his sleeves rolled up, wearing no coat, pale and with a trembling jaw. Prince Andrei turned to him but the *accoucheur* gave him a bewildered look and went out without a word. A frightened woman ran out and, seeing Prince Andrei, stopped short in the doorway. He went into his wife's room. She was lying dead, in the same position he had seen her in five minutes before, and despite the fixed eyes and the pallor of her cheeks, the same expression was on her charming childlike face with its upper lip covered with tiny black hairs.[75] | came from the next room. Prince Andrei ran to the door; the cry ceased and he heard the cry of a baby. <br><br>'What have they taken a baby in there for?' thought Prince Andrei for a second. 'A baby? What baby? Why is there a baby there? Or has the baby been born?' <br><br>When he suddenly realised the joyful significance of that cry, tears choked him, and leaning both elbows on the windowsill, he began to cry, sobbing like a child. The door opened. The doctor came out of the room, his shirt sleeves rolled up, wearing no coat, pale with a trembling jaw. Prince Andrei turned to him, but the doctor gave him a bewildered look and passed by without a word. A woman ran out and, seeing Prince Andrei, stopped short in the doorway. (The rest of the passage is identical.)[76] |

In the final text Tolstoy induces a change of mood in Prince Andrei. He is made to believe for a moment that all has gone well, and a feeling of joy and relief, suddenly and ironically overwhelms him, before he discovers the truth. This rapid juxtaposition of joy and sorrow, of a state of emotional light and darkness, is a common device in Tolstoy's novels, especially in the context of death, and reference to it will be made again elsewhere.

The scene of the death of Platon Karataev also underwent some interesting changes before it reached its final form:

| *Draft* | *War and Peace* |
|---|---|
| Pierre set off again up the hill, limping more than before. He had hurt his right foot badly. He heard the German officer's orders, and saw one of the soldiers of the convoy turn back, examining his | When the prisoners moved off again, Pierre looked round. Karataev was sitting at the side of the road by the birch tree and two Frenchmen were standing over him and saying something. Pierre |

[75] J.E. XIII. 574.

[76] *War and Peace*, II. I. 9.

*Draft—contd.*

gun; he walked on without looking round.

'Look, it's started snowing', said a prisoner who was walking beside Pierre.

Only then did Pierre notice that the ground was covered with white spots. He glanced at the billowing white muslin curtain dangling on every side. Suddenly a shot rang out from behind. 'It can't be!', thought Pierre.

He looked round: there was smoke in the place where Karataev had been sitting. Something white was rising over the road, and a German soldier was running back along the road with a smoking gun.

The snow grew heavier and heavier. The wounds on his feet ached and throbbed so much in the snow that Pierre could not think. Suddenly he heard a terrible cry from the same place behind the hill. 'Who is it?' It was the dog howling over Platon's dead body.

'Well, go on snowing, go on, cover the whole ground, go on throbbing, go on', said Pierre to the snow and to his feet.[77]

*War and Peace—contd.*

did not look round again. He walked on limping up the hill.

Suddenly a shot rang out from behind from the place where Karataev had been sitting. Pierre heard the shot plainly, but at the very moment that he heard it Pierre remembered that he had not yet finished the calculation he had begun before the marshal went by—namely how many stages there were still to go to Smolensk. And he started counting. Two French soldiers, one of them carrying a lowered and smoking gun, ran past Pierre. They were both pale, and in the expressions on their faces—one of them glanced timidly at Pierre—there was something resembling what he had seen on the young soldier's face at the execution. Pierre looked at the soldier and remembered that this very soldier had burnt his shirt two days ago while drying it by the fire, and that they had laughed at him.

Behind him, where Karataev had been sitting, the dog began to howl. 'The stupid thing, what's she howling about?' thought Pierre.

Like Pierre, his soldier comrades walking beside him avoided looking back at the place where the noise of the shot and the howling of the dog had come from; but there was a set look on all their faces.[78]

It is characteristic of Tolstoy to introduce some recollections—and especially mundane recollections such as that of the soldier burning his shirt in front of the fire—at a moment of heightened tension. In describing the murder of Karataev, he is mainly concerned to expound the thoughts of Pierre as he looks first forward to the journey to Smolensk, and then back to recent

[77] J.E. XV. 138.      [78] *War and Peace.* IV. 3. 14.

events and a recent murder. While retaining from the first version the oblique approach to Karataev's murder, the smoking gun and the howling of Karataev's dog, Tolstoy significantly adds an allusion to the expression on the guilty soldiers' faces.

The reason for dispensing with the snowstorm in the final text was no doubt the very simple fact that on the day in question, 22 October, 1812, winter had not yet set in, as Tolstoy's historical sources told him. In this chapter in *War and Peace* it is the rain which is emphasized, and Pierre's thoughts about the weather, suitably altered to fit the occasion, are removed to an earlier paragraph: addressing himself to the rain, Pierre kept on saying mentally 'now then, go on pouring, go on!'

It is vain to speculate on the reasons which may have prompted Tolstoy to shift the blame for Karataev's murder from a German to a Frenchman. In view of the fact that Tolstoy despised Germans much more than he despised Frenchmen, one might have expected precisely the reverse procedure. But this is a small point. It is the change in the nature of Pierre's thought processes which is the most important difference between the two versions quoted, and it is this change which gives the clearest evidence of Tolstoy's approach—unsentimental, restrained, but highly moving—to the construction of those scenes in his novel in which his characters have to die.

## DRAMATIZATION

It is noticeable that Tolstoy uses his revisions for another purpose also, namely, to increase the dramatic elements in an episode at the expense of the static or narrative. In several cases the definitive version has, in comparison with the draft, more action and less exposition. For example, early texts of Pierre's encounter with the freemasons contain an undue amount of formal statement of the masonic teaching. In *War and Peace,* however, the exposition in Pierre's study is reduced and the live description of his reception at the Masonic Lodge is correspondingly increased. The same purpose can be detected in Tolstoy's lengthy grapplings with the character of Platon Karataev, although here the greater dramatic element which Tolstoy introduces into his final version by giving Karataev more to say and saying less about him is somewhat countered by the 'bookish' nature of the peasant speech—carefully culled on the evidence of Tolstoy's notes and drafts from Dal's *Proverbs of the Russian People* and retailed in an improbably concentrated form. Karataev, it will be remembered, did not figure in *All's Well That Ends Well*, the first draft ending we have of *War and Peace*. Pierre undergoes his regeneration in captivity. He comes to feel freer than before, freer from luxuries and pre-judices; he arrives at a greater understanding of love, joy, pity, the sun, singing. But there is at first no agency by which this regeneration takes place.

In a later draft of the action after Borodino,[79] we find Pierre on his retreat from the battlefield towards Moscow encountering an old man. He is briefly described as 'the personification of old age—tranquillity, renunciation of earthly life, equanimity'. He speaks a little about God's mercies, invites Pierre to his hut for food and drink and eventually arranges for him to be escorted to the Mozhaisk road. This is clearly the first hint of Karataev, but it is not at this stage followed up. (In *War and Peace*, it may be recalled, it is some soldiers whom Pierre meets on the road eastward who share their meal with him and escort him to Mozhaisk.) When Tolstoy returns to the Karataev theme he has several unsuccessful attempts to launch him. In one version[80] he is introduced abruptly; the roundness theme is developed, and the character of the man enlarged upon, mainly in narrative form; and at first the proverbs too form part of the author's narrative and do not come from Karataev's lips. The impression is given that Tolstoy is putting down as concisely as possible all he wants to say about Karataev as a sort of *aide-mémoire* to be worked up later.

In another version[81] Karataev is first pointed out to Pierre; then his name is mentioned. There is a sentence about him and then he speaks. A little more narrative description of him follows and then he speaks again, this time using a popular saying. The impression he makes on Pierre and the roundness theme are developed last of all. In yet another version[82] Karataev speaks before any mention is made of him. Pierre looks round to see who is speaking. There is a brief narrative description and then he speaks again, using the same popular saying as above. Only then do Pierre's impressions follow.

[79] J.E. XIV. 356 ff.     [80] J.E. XV. 26 ff.     [81] ibid. 41.     [82] ibid. 44.

But in the final text[83] Tolstoy introduces Karataev through the *effect* he has on Pierre, the overriding impression being one of a strong smell of sweat. There is a better balance struck between Tolstoy's narrative description and Karataev's spoken words. And all the proverbs come directly from Karataev's lips. Not everybody will find the Karataev episode a satisfactory one, schematic and didactic as it is, but it is probably true to say that the final version is an improvement over the earlier ones in the direction of greater immediacy and dramatic impact.

### CHANGES DICTATED BY REASONS OF PROPRIETY

Among the significant omissions in the final text one can group together several which can be explained by feelings of propriety—on Tolstoy's, or his wife's, or his publisher's part?— that is to say 'naturalistic' scenes of a rather indecent nature referring to sex and sexual perversion, and vulgar or unseemly words and phrases. Anatole appears in one draft version as a pervert in love with his sister Hélène and discovered by his mother in Hélène's bedroom, holding her hand.[84] All the details of this scene eventually go out and only a brief allusion remains when Pierre thinks to himself 'I've been told that her brother Anatole was in love with her'. But in the drafts nothing is too bad for Anatole. 'You know,' his father says, 'that at the age of 15 he seduced his sister's governess and spent all his pocket money on wine and cigars.' He even teaches two parrots to swear! Another scene to disappear is that in which Nikolai and Denisov visit a brothel where Nikolai is tempted and falls;[85] as for Hélène, her liaisons are much more openly bruited at first than in the final version.

Crudities of language are also expunged. The reference to Hélène as 'a beautiful bit of meat in a skirt'; the allusions to the 'belly' of the pregnant Lisa; old Prince Bolkonsky's reputed answer to the Emperor Paul's suggestion that he marry a certain lady: 'Go and find someone else to marry your whore'—all these and similar characteristic instances of Tolstoy's bluntness of speech disappear. He cut out the remark that Anatole did not squander money on women because 'he was so spoiled by women

[83] *War and Peace*, IV. 1. 12.     [84] J.E. XIII. 479.     [85] ibid. 497 ff.

that he could not understand that it was possible to pay them for something they wanted so much'.[86] He cut out Dolokhov's reply to Julie when she asked him what a girl could do to prove her love for him: 'very simple: give herself to me before she is married, then I'll marry her. Would you like to?'[87] He cut out the joke about the King of Prussia's wife: 'If I were Napoleon I wouldn't refuse her anything,' said one officer, knowing that she was dining with the Emperor of France. 'Yes, providing she didn't refuse him anything', said another.[88]

Tolstoy both modified and made more acceptable that coarseness and directness of language which we recall especially from Gorky's excellent reminiscences of him, and also resisted the temptation to try his hand at naturalistic brothel and bedroom scenes.

### STYLISTIC CHANGES

Many of the changes made in the process of writing *War and Peace* concern style in a narrower sense—language, vocabulary and syntax. Perhaps the best way to illustrate some of these changes is to make a comparison between three fairly close versions of a single, important incident in order to see how Tolstoy worked within the limits imposed by the restricted context of that incident. The example chosen here describes Prince Andrei on the eve of Borodino. The first version is a draft beginning of Volume III, Part 2, Chapter 24 (italic denotes that the same words occur in all three versions; capitals that they occur in two; italic capitals that almost the same words occur in two).

*On that bright evening of August 25 Prince Andrei lay* on a rug *in a broken-down shed* IN THE VILLAGE OF KNYAZKOVO. THIS SHED WAS ON THE OUTSKIRTS OF THE VILLAGE above the sloping pastureland on which the soldiers of his battalion stood. THE ROOF had been *TORN OFF THE SHED,* AND ONE SIDE which looked out over the steep ground WAS BROKEN away so that Prince Andrei had a distant and wonderful view animated by the view [sic] of soldiers, horses and columns of smoke rising up from camp fires on different sides. The remains of a barn could be seen on the outskirts of the village near the shed, and between the barn and the shed was *a row of* trees—aspens and *30-year-old birches* WHOSE *branches had been lopped,* ONE FELLED and several notched. Prince Andrei had caught his soldiers felling this little wood or grove which had evidently been

[86] J.E. XIII. 842.          [87] ibid. 841.          [88] ibid. 641.

planted by an industrious peasant-owner, and had forbidden them to go on felling, letting them cart off the shed and planks instead. The reprieved birches with their FOLIAGE TURNING YELLOW HERE AND THERE STOOD BRIGHT AND BUSHY above his head, NOT A SINGLE LEAF STIRRING in the evening quiet. Prince Andrei pitied and loved all that was alive and looked with joy at these birches. THE YELLOW LEAVES LITTERED THE GROUND BENEATH THEM, BUT THEY HAD FALLEN EARLIER; NOTHING WAS FALLING NOW. THEY SHONE IN the bright light, THE BRILLIANT LIGHT WHICH WAS BREAKING THROUGH FROM BEHIND THE CLOUDS. Sparrows flew down from the birch trees on to the remaining part of the fence and flew back again. *Prince Andrei lay leaning on his elbow* with his eyes closed. All THE ORDERS HAD BEEN GIVEN, THE NEXT DAY THE BATTLE WOULD TAKE PLACE. He had already visited the captain of his column, had eaten with the company and battalion commanders and now WANTED TO be alone and THINK, THINK AS HE HAD THOUGHT ON THE EVE OF AUSTERLITZ. HOWEVER MUCH TIME HAD PASSED SINCE THEN, HOWEVER MUCH HAD BEEN ENDURED SINCE THEN, *however* BORING, *burdensome and useless to anyone his life seemed to him, he felt now as he had done seven years before—on the eve of battle,* THE TERRIBLE BATTLE WHICH HE FORESAW FOR THE MORROW—*agitated, irritable* AND OBLIGED, NOW AS THEN, TO SQUARE ACCOUNTS WITH HIMSELF AND ASK—WHAT AND WHY AM I?[89]

## The second version of this chapter reads as follows:

*On that bright evening of August 25 Prince Andrei lay in a broken-down shed* in the village of Psarevo where the artillery shell boxes were. THIS SHED WAS ON THE OUTSKIRTS OF THE VILLAGE; fences ran round several acres of ploughland on which lay beaten down unharvested SHOCKS of OATS. ALONG *ONE OF THESE FENCES* ran *a row of 30-year-old birches with* THEIR LOWER *branches lopped* by the soldiers.

ONE BIRCH TREE HAD BEEN FELLED and carted off; in its place could be seen a new stump and a ring of little twigs and leaves. The other BIRCHES WITH THEIR autumn LEAVES TURNING YELLOW HERE AND THERE STOOD BRIGHT AND BUSHY, NO LEAF STIRRING, and shining green and yellow in the bright evening light. YELLOW LEAVES LITTERED THE GROUND BENEATH THEM, BUT THEY HAD FALLEN EARLIER; NOTHING WAS FALLING NOW. THEY SHONE IN THE BRILLIANT LIGHT WHICH WAS BREAKING THROUGH FROM BEHIND THE CLOUDS.

Beyond the ploughland were SOME BUSHES ALONGSIDE WHICH ROSE THE SMOKE OF CAMPFIRES—THE SOLDIERS' STOVES. THE ROOF AND ONE SIDE OF THE SHED WERE BROKEN and Prince Andrei could see, as in a frame, soldiers, campfires, green waggons of shell boxes and picket lines near a stream in a wood.

*Prince Andrei lay leaning on his elbow,* now looking straight in front of him, now closing his eyes.

THE NEXT DAY THE BATTLE WOULD TAKE PLACE AND HE WANTED TO THINK, THINK AS HE HAD THOUGHT ON THE EVE OF AUSTERLITZ. HOWEVER MUCH . . . ETC. (text as above).[90]

[89] J.E. XIV. 102.          [90] ibid. 333.

*On that bright evening of August 25 Prince Andrei lay leaning on his elbow in a broken-down shed* IN THE VILLAGE OF KNYAZKOVO at the further end of his regiment's encampment. Through a gap in the broken wall he could see *a row of 30-year-old birches* RUNNING ALONG THE FENCE *with their* LOWER *branches lopped off*, a field with BEATEN DOWN SHOCKS OF OATS in it and SOME BUSHES ALONGSIDE WHICH ROSE THE SMOKE OF CAMPFIRES—THE SOLDIERS' STOVES.

*However* narrow, *burdensome and useless to anyone his life now seemed, Prince Andrei felt, as he had done seven years before at Austerlitz, agitated and irritable on the eve of battle.*

THE ORDERS FOR next day's BATTLE HAD BEEN received and GIVEN . . .

There is nothing of any substance in the final version which is not already present in the drafts. It tells where Prince Andrei is, what he is doing, what he can see, what he is feeling. But what is most important for Tolstoy's purpose is that Prince Andrei should at the crucial moment in his life contemplate the *world of nature*. The details of the vantage point—the condition of the roof of the shed and of its walls—are irrelevant, and are readily dispensed with in the final version. It is nature which means so much to Prince Andrei now—not glory or love or social esteem. And so it is the birches, the oats, the bushes on which his attention focuses, and not the soldiers, the picket lines, the shell boxes or the remains of a barn. It will be noticed that Tolstoy, in singling out the objects of nature for Prince Andrei's contemplation, resorted to his favourite threefold division (he looked at A . . . at B . . . at C . . . ), and achieved a condensed and balanced effect which is not found in the draft versions. It will also be noticed that the two epithets at first applied to the birch trees ('bright' and 'bushy') are eventually discarded. The first is a translation of *vesëly*, 'bright' or 'happy', which might suggest the slight conceit of attributing to inanimate objects the properties of joy and happiness; the second is a poor rendering of *kurchavy*—literally 'curly-headed'—which is very much a stock epithet. One further fact we should mention is that the reference to the green and yellow foliage and the bright evening sunshine, which is missing from the final version, is not discarded but held back until later in the chapter when Tolstoy returns to the theme of the birch trees and the thoughts they evoke in Prince Andrei. This is another happy touch which distinguishes the final text. The crux of the whole chapter (of which we have quoted only the beginning), which will occur in all three versions alike, is to be the anguished reflections of Prince Andrei: 'to die . . . to be killed tomorrow . . . that I should not exist . . . that all this should exist, but not me.' In the drafts these thoughts are preceded by the paragraph:

He [Andrei] looked at the sparrows which had flown down in a flock from the fence to the ground. 'What can people decide? Everything obeys those eternal laws by which this sparrow dropped behind the others and later caught them up.'

'What do I want? To die . . . to be killed tomorrow . . . ?' etc.[91]

The interesting point about this is that it suggests that Tolstoy wanted at this crucial moment to hark back to an image already used in the beginning of the same chapter in the draft versions, namely the flight of the sparrows. But as it turns out the thought connection is not a happy one. In the final text Tolstoy follows the same principle of reverting to an image already used in the beginning of the chapter (the definitive chapter)—namely the birch trees—and by combining it with the images of light and colour borrowed from the *draft* opening of the chapter, establishes the right antithesis between life, the sun and light on the one hand and death on the other: 'He looked at the row of birches shining in the sunlight with their motionless green and yellow foliage and their white bark. To die . . . to be killed tomorrow . . .' etc. Readers of Anna Karenina will remember that this contrast between light and darkness, life and death is a favourite one with Tolstoy, and we need only recall the juxtaposition of Levin's brother's death and Kitty's pregnancy or the image of the bright light flaring up and going out in the scene of Anna's suicide.

Before leaving this important scene in *War and Peace* we can illustrate another feature of Tolstoy's technique which perhaps belongs more strictly to the criticism of the novel as a finished product than to this chapter on the processes by which the rough became the smooth. This feature is the carefully sought balance and symmetry which is evident especially in passages of great psychological or emotional importance. It is a thing which is very largely lost in translation, however accurate the translation may be. Take for example the third paragraph of the chapter

[91] J.E. XIV. 104.

we have just been discussing. This is how the Maudes' translation reads:

He had received and given the orders for next day's battle, and had nothing more to do. But his thoughts—the simplest, clearest and therefore most terrible thoughts—would give him no peace. He knew that tomorrow's battle would be the most terrible of all he had taken part in, and for the first time in his life the possibility of death presented itself to him—not in relation to any worldly matter or with reference to its effect on others, but simply in relation to himself, to his own soul—vividly, plainly, terribly and almost as a certainty.

What this English version does not fully reproduce is the parallelism and harmony of the endings of nouns and adjectives. Where English says 'thoughts—the simplest, clearest and therefore most terrible thoughts'—Russian says 'mysli—samye prostye, yasnye, i poetomu strashnye mysli'. Nor does the translation adequately convey the careful and consistent pairing of prepositions and adverbs. To do so it would have to read something like this:

. . . (the possibility of death presented itself to him) *without* relation to any worldly matter, *without* thought of how it might affect others, but only in relation *to* himself, *to* his soul, *with* vividness, *with* certainty, simp*ly* and terrib*ly* (bez . . . bez . . . k . . . k . . . s . . . s . . . –o . . . –o . . . ).

One can best appreciate the balance and rhythm of Tolstoy's prose by contrasting the polished with the unpolished material. The context of the following example is the aftermath of Borodino, and Tolstoy is considering the respective positions and policies of the French and the Russians after the battle. He writes in a draft version:

The French, with the help of the memory of all their former victories during fifteen years, with the full assurance of Napoleon's invincibility, with the help of the knowledge that, having killed nearly all the Russians on the Semenovsk *flèches* and the mound battery, having directed superior forces against these points, the knowledge that they had captured part of the battlefield, and with the knowledge that the still intact Guards, 20,000 strong, stood behind them, no longer being attacked since there was no one to attack them—might easily have held out from after two o'clock until evening at this precarious point of the issue of a victory which neither results in the flight of the vanquished nor the triumph of the victor: but for the Russians, their numbers dwindled to half, driven from their positions, without a single unbroken division—to refrain from flight at this precarious point seemed impossible.[92]

In the final version he considers the same positions and policies from the slightly different standpoint that neither army made the one more effort which would have been decisive. The text reads (my underlinings):

The French, with the memory of their former victories during fifteen years, with the assurance of Napoleon's invincibility, with the knowledge that they had captured part of the battlefield, that they had lost only a quarter of their men, and that they still had their Guards intact, might easily have made that effort. The French who had attacked the Russian army in order to drive it from its position ought to have made that effort, for as long as the Russians continued to block the road to Moscow as before, the aim of the French had not been attained and all their efforts and losses were in vain. But the French did not make that effort . . .[93]

'With . . . with . . . with . . .; that . . . that . . . that . . .; might have made . . . ought to have made . . . did not make the effort'—a characteristically Tolstoyan sequence. The one enormous draft sentence is reduced in content, lightened and broken down into three parts; the superfluous words in the first version—'*with the help of the* memory', '*with the help of* the knowledge', 'with the *full* assurance'—are eliminated.

As for the Russian position, the final version reverses the order and examines it in the preceding, instead of the succeeding paragraph:

The Russians did not make that effort because it was not they who were attacking the French. At the beginning of the battle they simply stood blocking the way to Moscow and they continued to stand there at the end of the battle as they had done at the beginning. But even if it had been the aim of the Russians to drive the French from their positions, they could not have made the last effort because all the Russian troops had been broken up, there was no part of the army which had not suffered in the battle, and although holding their positions the Russians had lost one HALF of their army.

Read consecutively in the right order these two paragraphs display a sentence balance which is as marked as that of the

[92] J.E. XIV. 220.    [93] *War and Peace*, III. 2. 39.

parts of speech. A short sentence ('The Russians did not make that effort . . . '), a medium sentence, a long sentence; a long sentence, a slightly shorter sentence, a short sentence ('But the French did not make that effort'). It is like the circumference of a circle composed of a series of arcs lengthening as they move away from the point of origin and shortening as they return to it. We shall have more to say about balance in the chapter on Tolstoy's language. These few remarks are included here because they arise directly from the fact that the properties of the finished product only really become apparent against the background of the unfinished.

Continuing the subject of verbal changes and improvements which do not directly concern characterization, we may now mention Tolstoy's trials and errors over the introduction into his novel of *mots* and puns. While reading through the historical sources for the period he was struck by the expression '*un archiduc vaut l'autre*', originating in diplomatic circles during the Napoleonic war against Austria in 1805 when the question arose which archduke to appoint to command the army. He liked it and decided to use it. By comparing the preliminary and the final texts we can follow his attempts to work it in most effectively. In one draft version the *mot* is simply recounted as part of the author's (ironical) narrative: 'Andrei even knew a *mot* spoken in Vienna and appearing for some reason very funny on that account. When they were talking about which archduke to appoint, some diplomat said: '*un archiduc vaut l'autre*', and everyone repeated this *mot*.'[94] In another version the *mot* is worked into a conversation between Bilibin and an Austrian diplomat at Brünn. The diplomat speaks first:

. . . la mort du pauvre Schmidt a été péniblement ressenti. Nous n'avons personne pour le remplacer. L'archiduc Ferdinand . . .
'Un archiduc vaut l'autre, n'est-ce pas?', said Bilibin, laughing and alluding to the words spoken by somebody in Vienna at the time when, in order to reconcile the wishes of the Russian government about the appointment as commander-in-chief of Kutuzov, being senior in rank, and the wishes of the Austrian government to appoint Mack, of junior rank, the archduke Ferdinand, a young man of no promise, was made fieldmarshal.[95]

Compare this with the final text where Bilibin, holding an important diplomatic post in Vienna, is talking to Prince Andrei

[94] J.E. XIII. 320.          [95] ibid. 337.

at Brünn: ' "Bring us nice news of a victory by the Arch-duke Karl or Ferdinand—*un archiduc vaut l'autre*, you know—and even if it's only a fire-brigade of Napoleon's it doesn't matter, we'll fire off some cannon." '[96] Since the *mot* is a diplomatic *mot* emanating from Vienna, it goes most naturally into the mouth of a diplomat accredited to the Viennese court. But poor as it is, it has to arise naturally from the conversation and stand in its own right without the need for lengthy comment and ex-planation. In this respect the final version is clearly the most successful of the three quoted.

Bilibin's verbal wit is given the chance to shine again on the subject of the French deception of the Austrian commander, Prince Auersperg, as a result of which the French crossed the Danube without a shot being fired. Once again the pun is allowed to do the work and the laborious explanation which followed it at first is eventually pruned. Compare the following draft version with the final text:

| Draft | War and Peace |
|---|---|
| 'Mon cher, nous sommes Mackés, comme à Ulm,' concluded Bilibin, getting in his *mot* consisting in the fact that the behaviour of Auers-perg was as foolish and inexplic-able as that of Mack, and that it was impossible to define this con-duct otherwise than by making a verb from the word Mack.[97] | (Bilibin is speaking): 'Ce n'est ni trahison, ni lâcheté, ni bêtise; c'est comme à Ulm . . .' he seemed to be searching for the right expres-sion . . . 'c'est du Mack. Nous sommes mackés,' he concluded . . .[98] |

In both these cases the improvement depends in part on the reduction of the text. In revising his raw material Tolstoy strove more commonly to prune and to reduce, less often to expand (unless the material was only down in note form in the first place). A comparison of the first volume of the canonical text of *War and Peace* with the text of *1805* as published in *The Russian Messenger* shows that while a few short scenes have been omitted altogether, the greatest changes involve the con-traction of scenes which are retained. The long argument be-tween Pierre and the viscount at Anna Scherer's is scaled down, as is the lengthy anecdote originally told by the viscount. A tedious description of a hostess's function and her thoughts on the placing of her guests is cut out, and only the image of the

[96] *War and Peace*, I. 2. 10.    [97] J.E. XIII. 343.    [98] *War and Peace*, I. 2. 12.

spinning-mill, and the simile of the hostess and the mill foreman are retained. The account of the orgy at Anatole's is reduced. The description of the Rostovs' name-day party is shortened. In the second part, much detail is cut out of the camp and battle scenes and the text of the Schöngraben encounter is pruned. Intrusions and comments by the author are considerably reduced, though not eliminated.

It is not true, however, to say that all Tolstoy's emendations were the result of pruning and discarding. The reverse process of extension and amplification can be observed also. For example, Tolstoy was anxious to include the witticisms credited to Balashev at the expense of Napoleon, which were quoted in the historical sources used by him. At first [99] he did so by tabulating them one after another, in two paragraphs of author's narrative and reported speech. Subsequently,[1] one at least of the jibes is expanded into the form of question and answer at the dinner-table, taking up more space in the chapter, but at the same time losing its quality of an entry in a memorandum. In almost all cases where puns or witticisms are introduced it is Tolstoy's aim to dramatize the situation, cut the explanation as much as possible and expand, if necessary, the spoken word. A close examination of the ironical scene at the opera where the performance is seen through Natasha's eyes as something unnatural and even grotesque shows in numerous small details the care Tolstoy lavished on the revisions and the small stylistic amendments which he was continually finding it desirable to make. The chapter opens in its final form with a typically Tolstoyan balanced, tripartite sentence.

'On the middle of the stage were smooth boards, at the sides was painted cardboard representing trees, and at the back was a cloth stretched over boards.'[2]

Here there are merely three finite verbs and three adverbial expressions indicating three different locations. But the corresponding section of one of the drafts reads as follows:

In the middle were smooth boards, at the sides was cardboard painted green, intended to represent trees, from behind the cardboard underneath lamps protruded men in frock coats and some women or other, and at the back was some very badly painted town such as you always get in the theatre and never in real life. Cloths were stretched out on top.[3]

[99] J.E. XIV. 32.          [1] *War and Peace*, III. 1. 7.          [2] ibid. II. 5. 9.
[3] J.E. XIII. 828.

Without going any further than this, one can guess at the
thought sequence in Tolstoy's mind. Since the cardboard did
in fact represent trees, why say it was intended to? If it repre-
sented trees it would normally be green, so why say so? The
author's comment about what is true in the theatre but not in
real life is too much like a gratuitous *ex cathedra* generalization.
The much-abused pronoun 'some one or other' (*kakoi-to*) can
well be spared. The long sentence with four finite verbs and the
short sentence with one achieve much more neatness and
balance by being combined into a single sentence with the
favourite threefold division. These are the sort of thoughts that
must have occurred to Tolstoy as he wrote and rewrote this
important scene.

It is not always possible to render in good accurate English
the little stylistic changes which Tolstoy introduced when tidy-
ing up his rough material. One example will have to suffice.
When Tolstoy described Anatole Kuragin as a male Magdalene,
he added that male and female alike share the same feeling of
innocence based on the same hope of forgiveness, and continued
his manuscript—reproducing Anatole's thoughts—with the
following words: 'All will be forgiven her for she loved much.
And all will be forgiven him for he enjoyed himself and did
nobody any harm.'[4] The antithesis 'loved much' (*mnogo
lyubila*) and 'enjoyed himself and did nobody any harm'
(*veselilsya i nikomu vreda ne delal*) is sharpened in the final
version[5] to 'loved much' (*mnogo lyubila*) and 'enjoyed himself
much' (*mnogo veselilsya*). The balance and rhythm of the
Russian which, when compared with the earlier version, is clearly
seen to be deliberate, cannot be adequately conveyed in English.
The biblical 'loved much' can stand, but the second phrase is
stylistically inadmissible. This is a problem for the translator.
Here we merely observe that such difficulties frequently obscure
the effects of the stylistic changes so diligently made by Tolstoy
whether in the direction of achieving equilibrium between one
part of a sentence and another, of striving after verbal harmony
and rhythm, or simply of modifying word order. This side of
Tolstoy's work has not, perhaps, received sufficient recognition.

Much labour was spent over the concluding sections of *War
and Peace*—the two epilogues in which the subsequent fate of

---

[4] ibid. 842.            [5] *War and Peace*, II. 5. 11.

the main heroes is reported and the author's views on history and philosophy systematized. Not that the material they contain was radically altered. The fate of the heroes was by this time fairly clear in Tolstoy's mind, and the relevant chapters were written without undue difficulty. The views on history and the role of the individual are fundamentally the same in the final version of the epilogue as in the numerous drafts of it, although many alterations were made in the choice of imagery, the order, systematization and classification of material, and the expression of ideas—despite which it would hardly be regarded as a model of lucid, well-ordered or stylistically felicitous prose. It should be mentioned here that in all but the definitive text of *War and Peace* the order of the two epilogues was reversed, the second or philosophical epilogue coming first. It is not known when or why the final order was decided upon. Perhaps Tolstoy wished to bring the sequence of these epilogues into line with the general sequence of the novel in which 'peace' scenes are followed by 'war' scenes (theoretical as well as actual). Perhaps he wished to spare the reader the necessity of reading what is now the second epilogue by making it a sort of self-sufficient appendage. Certainly he makes some interesting comments in one of the draft versions[6] on the effect his theorizing will probably have on his readers, whom he divides into two classes. The first (the majority) are those who 'when they come to the historical, and especially the philosophical arguments, will say—what again! How dull!—and will look and see where the argument ends, turn over the pages and go on reading. This sort of reader is the one who is dearest to me. His criticism I value most of all. . . .' Tolstoy adds that he feels he has wronged these readers in that he has disfigured his book by the insertion of these philosophical passages, but says (rather weakly) in justification that he is writing about the past and that the past has been misrepresented. The second group of readers are those who are primarily interested in the historical side of the book, and they will no doubt be dissatisfied at his blackening of accepted reputations and his failure to portray acknowledged heroes. To his own charge Tolstoy replies: 'I have been trying to write a history of the people [*narod*].' Bearing in mind these two categories of reader he may have wished to spare

[6] J.E. XV. 241.

their feelings by delaying to the very end what was bound to displease them most. Another no less plausible reason for the final order is that at the time of writing the epilogues Tolstoy regarded the 'philosophy' as the most important part of his work, the culminating idea to which everything else was only a prelude and an illustration. None of these reasons is adequate in itself, but taken together they provide enough grounds for thinking that the decision to leave the philosophical epilogue to the end was the right one.

There is a tendency among academic critics to assume that Tolstoy's second thoughts were always best. This is not invariably so. Some changes appear clumsy, capricious and unnecessary. In his old age Tolstoy is quoted as saying:

'Usually when one begins a new book one is very pleased with oneself and works with great interest. But as the book goes on you become more and more bored and often in revising it you cross out something and substitute something new not because the new thing is better but because you get tired of the old. You often strike out what is vivid and replace it by something colourless and inferior.'[7]

On another occasion he said: 'I don't understand how one can write and not revise everything innumerable times. I hardly ever re-read my published things, but if I happen to come across any page by chance, it always seems to me that it all needs revising.'[8] This is a warning against regarding Tolstoy's critical judgement as infallible or his conscientiousness as unfailing. Nevertheless it is in the belief that the great majority of Tolstoy's changes were in the right direction that this chapter has been written.

To round off our study of the drafts we quote the opinion, based on a scholarly examination of the published and unpublished manuscripts of *War and Peace* that: 'As a rule the description of the way of life of the gentry, war episodes, descriptions of battles and scenes with soldiers and officers came easily to Tolstoy. The historical part, the beginning of the novel, the development of the plot [*sujet*], the characterization of the main heroes and the conclusion of the novel came with difficulty.'[9] While agreeing with this opinion, we have had to be highly selective in this chapter and have chosen to devote our

[7] Goldenweiser, op. cit. p. 148.
[8] ibid. p. 53.
[9] G. Volkov, *Literaturnoe Nasledstvo 35/36*, Moscow 1939, p. 289.

space to the beginning of the novel, certain aspects of characterization and certain stylistic emendations. This is not the whole
story. But it is, we hope, sufficient to show that a glance into
Tolstoy's kitchen and a smell of his cooking (to use a metaphor
he liked to use himself) increases our enjoyment of the meal he
eventually serves up.

# II: USE OF SOURCES

WHEN we speak about the sources of *War and Peace* we generally think about two different things. We think first of the numerous histories, biographies, memoirs, diaries and letters which Tolstoy consulted for the social and historical background of the Napoleonic wars, the tactics and strategy of the major battles, the personalities of the leading historical figures—in fact those sources which Tolstoy used for the ostensibly non-fictional part of his narrative. On the other hand we think of Tolstoy's own family, his wife, his sister-in-law, his aunts, his cousins and his grandparents, people he knew intimately at Yasnaya Polyana, people he could remember from childhood, or people he could conjure up from the family archives or from family hearsay—men and women whose passions, ideals, weaknesses and whims are embodied in the fictional characters of *War and Peace*. Of these two different types of sources the English reader knows less about the first than about the second, and it is to the historical and memoir literature that we shall now turn.

### HISTORICAL SOURCES

A glance at the contents of Tolstoy's own library at Yasnaya Polyana[1] shows that the works of the Russian historian Mikhailovsky-Danilevsky, the official historian of the wars of 1805, 1806–7 and 1812 and a participant in the 1812 campaign, are more numerous than those of any other author. The three-volumed history of 1812 by Bogdanovich, also a royal commission, and Thiers's *Histoire de l'Empire*, as pro-Bonapartist as the Russians are anti-Bonapartist, are also to be found on the shelves. There are numerous memoirs of Russians and foreigners: of Sergei Glinka, the jingoistic editor of *The Russian Messenger*, who himself gets a brief mention in *War and Peace*; Radozhitsky, an artillery officer; Zhikharev, a young student; Joseph de Maistre, the Savoyard ambassador to St. Petersburg;

[1]For the contents see J.E. XVI. 141 ff.

Bernhardi's four-volumed *Denkwürdigkeiten aus dem Leben des kaiserl-russ. Generals von der Infanterie Karl Friedrich Grafen von Toll*. There are copies of early nineteenth-century periodicals and of patriotic novels about Napoleon and 1812 by the minor Russian novelists Zotov and Zagoskin. Not actually in the Yasnaya Polyana library, but known to have been used as source material by Tolstoy, are the memoirs of the partisan poet and hero of 1812, Denis Davydov, the works of Count Rostopchin, Governor-General of Moscow in 1812; Korf's *Life of Speransky*, the most influential of Alexander I's ministers in the early years of his reign; the memoirs of Napoleon's aide-de-camp General Rapp and of the duc de Raguse.

There is about all the Russian source literature mentioned a very strong patriotic flavour. It all stands firmly for king and country. It is imbued with the same chauvinistic, militaristic, sentiments which Tolstoy was later to repudiate vehemently and with compelling logic. We must remember that in 1863 when Tolstoy began his novel (then called *1805*) there was a marked revival of interest in the period of Russia's greatest national glory. Bogdanovich's book came out in 1859–60. 1862 was the fiftieth anniversary of the battle of Borodino. 1863 saw the publication of a new Russian journal, *The Russian Archives*, which devoted much space to biographical literature and memoirs and which made available (among other things) to the reading public source material on the Napoleonic wars. In the same year the Polish war began and Tolstoy even thought for a moment of leaving his newly married wife and going off again to fight. But the fact that Tolstoy was given to moments of patriotic fervour and the fact that his sources for the novel were, as is only to be expected, somewhat crudely nationalistic, does not mean that he chose these sources simply because they were patriotic or that he used them as material to bolster up his own sentiments. He chose the historians because he thought that theirs were the standard works on the subject. He probably knew Mikhailovsky-Danilevsky better than his other sources, and in his rough notes for the epilogue he rates him higher than Thiers or Bernhardi.[2] He had read him as a young man as his diaries for 1852 tell us, and that, coupled with the fact that the historian had himself taken part in the campaign of

[2]J.E. XV. 240.

1812, would account for Tolstoy drawing heavily on him for background detail. The many memoirs which he consulted of people who were also there are further evidence of the value he attached to eye-witness accounts. There is no doubt that Mikhailovsky-Danilevsky and other historians he used irritated him. But it is difficult to agree with the opinion that they were chosen precisely because they acted as a useful irritant and that they provided him with polemical material. 'He needed a man, a point of view which would call forth a protest in him', says one Soviet critic.[3] But many books which Tolstoy read provoked him to protest. It is wrong to think of him deliberately choosing his sources for historical information in order that they should fit in to a preconceived purpose. A century later the scholar can look back and say—if Tolstoy had been an impartial historian he would have used this source and not that, or that he would have read much more widely than he did. But then Tolstoy was not an academic research worker, as the same scholars now admit. This is no proof, however, that in the early stages of writing *War and Peace* he wilfully selected biased sources to lend support to a fixed point of view, although there is ample proof that he did not set about his task in the way a modern historian would. Nor would one expect him to, and he himself is wrong to try and pretend that he did, as for example when he says . . . 'whenever historical persons speak or act in my novel I have invented nothing, but have used historical material of which I have accumulated a whole library during my work'.[4]

It is interesting to see how the critics' views on Tolstoy's scholarly activity as a historical novelist have changed again and again. In a caricature in *The Spark* in 1868 the author is shown at work among his sources for *War and Peace*, prominent among which are romantic historical novels of the Napoleonic period by Zagoskin and Zotov, clearly inspired by, and clearly inferior to the Waverley novels. The implication of the drawing is that Tolstoy did not search much further for his historical material than the fictional works of these conventional, naive and chauvinistic authors. Certainly Tolstoy read these authors. He seems to have done so enthusiastically judging by the remark

[3] V. Shklovsky, *Material i stil' v romane L'va Tolstogo 'Voina i Mir'*, Moscow, 1928, p. 44.
[4] *Neskol'ko slov po povodu knigi 'Voina i Mir'*, J.E. XVI. 13.

he made in a letter to his wife in November 1864 where he speaks of reading Zagoskin's *Roslavlev* 'with a delight which nobody except an author can understand'.[5] *Roslavlev* is a novel about the invasion of 1812, prefabricated, jingoistic and sentimental. It has some superficial resemblances to Tolstoy's novel which are inevitable in view of the similarity of their subjects. For example, the early conversation about Napoleon in the presence of a foreign traveller in a salon in St. Petersburg with a hostess who spoke Russian badly reminds one of the scene in Mlle Scherer's salon with which *War and Peace* opens. There are one or two situations which Tolstoy might possibly have had suggested to him by Zagoskin—the hero Roslavlev agrees to wait for one year before marrying his fiancée as Prince Andrei does with Natasha, although with Roslavlev the request was hers not his. (Incidentally Tolstoy's sister-in-law Tanya Behrs, claims to have been the victim of a similar decision by Tolstoy and his wife when Tolstoy's brother Sergei proposed to her.) But the implication of *The Spark's* caricature, that Tolstoy had written a patriotic historical novel with Zagoskin, Zotov and the popular Russian 'Waverley' novels of the 1830's to inspire him, could not be further from the truth. Only when one reads *Roslavlev* and *War and Peace* in that order can one fully appreciate the significance and originality of Tolstoy's achievement.

Later critics built up the theory that Tolstoy had assiduously consulted the main source materials in the interests of historical fullness and accuracy, and they made much of every visit to the library and every request for a book or periodical. This is equally far from the truth. Tolstoy did not comb through the material like a conscientious post-graduate student. Nor can it be proved that he deliberately and artificially selected his source material, either in order to confirm his own theories or in order to attack and demolish the theories of others. He read his history as an ordinary well-educated dilettante might, trying to go to standard sources and rating highly biographies of people close to the events he describes and memoirs of people living through and taking part in them.

What use did Tolstoy make of the sources he had at his disposal? Much work has been done on the subject of Tolstoy's 'borrowing' and it is possible to compile long lists of episodes

[5] J.E. LXXXIII. 59.

in *War and Peace* which one can trace back to one or other of the major sources used. For example it has been shown[6] that material for the following episodes and details of Parts 2 and 3 of Volume I of *War and Peace* can be found in Mikhailovsky-Danilevsky's book *Description of the First War, 1805*: General Mack; the burning of the bridge at Enns; the allusion to the actions at Lambach, Amstetten and Melk; the Russians at Krems; the scouts' report of Napoleon's crossing of the Danube; Kutuzov's parting with Bagration and the latter's march to Hollabrunn; Schöngraben; Tushin's firing of the village; the Olmütz review; Alexander's letter *au chef du gouvernement français*; the lack of provisions at Olmütz; Alexander and the Wischau action; Savary's visit to Alexander; Dolgorukov's description of his interview with Napoleon; Napoleon's inspection of the army; Nikolai at the enemy's advance posts; the morning fog at Austerlitz; the Austrian column-guides among the Russian troops; Kutuzov's conversation with Alexander; Miloradovich about to go into action; Prince Andrei and the standard; the cavalry guard's attack; the disaster on the frozen ponds at Augesd; Alexander after Austerlitz; Napoleon's conversation with Repnin and Sukhtelen.

This is not a list of borrowings. It is an indication of those incidents in a section of Mikhailovsky-Danilevsky's narrative which Tolstoy made use of in one way or another—and it should be added in parenthesis that he followed closely the general lines of the historian's account of 1805. But how did he make use of them? We must answer this question within the wider framework of the sources as a whole and not simply on the basis of one work by one author.

Generally speaking the amount of verbatim borrowing by Tolstoy is small. It occurs as one would expect when he is giving the text of letters which passed between important people: letters or statements, for example, by Alexander or Napoleon. It occurs with certain documents or communiqués such as the instructions given by General Barclay to Baron Asch, the Governor-General of Smolensk (taken word for word from Mikhailovsky-Danilevsky's *Patriotic War of 1812*). From the

[6] See K. V. Pokrovsky, *Istochniki romana 'Voina i Mir'* in *'Voina i Mir': sbornik pamyati L. Tolstogo* edited by T. I. Polner and V. P. Obninsky, Moscow, 1912, pp. 113-28.

same source comes the complete text of the prayer specially composed in the Synod for the deliverance of Russia from the enemy invasion—the prayer Natasha hears in church with such emotion. There are examples of a virtually word for word reproduction of certain conversations, such as the one between Napoleon on the one hand and Repnin and Sukhtelen on the other which ends up with Napoleon complimenting the latter on his assertion that 'youth is no hindrance to courage' and assuring him 'young man, you will go far!' Tolstoy has taken this from Mikhailovsky-Danilevsky's 1805 volume, the latter having translated it from the French of Prince Repnin's own memoirs. The description of Paulucci's intervention in the debate of the Russian General Staff at Drissa is reproduced almost verbatim from a letter by Joseph de Maistre. Examples of this sort can be multiplied, but are of limited interest.

Of rather more interest are the near literal borrowings of short narrative passages, descriptions, conversations, *mots* and images. We give some examples of this type of close borrowing where Tolstoy's version shows some slight changes compared with the original, although these changes are rarely of much significance:

| *Mikhailovsky-Danilevsky* | *Tolstoy* |
|---|---|
| Napoleon rode along the bivouacs and inspected our fires. The French camp began to stir. The soldiers held up lighted wisps of straw . . . [7] | The shouts and fires in the enemy camp arose because the Emperor Napoleon was riding round his bivouacs while his orders were read to the troops. On seeing the Emperor the soldiers set light to wisps of straw . . . [8] |

**Again:**

| *Mikhailovsky-Danilevsky* | *Tolstoy* |
|---|---|
| Then the emperor sent for Shishkov, the Secretary of State, and said to him: 'It is necessary to write an order to the army immediately, and also to Count Saltykov in Petersburg, telling him of the | [Returning home from the ball] the Emperor sent for Shishkov, the Secretary of State, at 2 a.m. and commanded him to write an order to the army and a rescript to Field Marshal Prince Saltykov |

[7] A. I. Mikhailovsky-Danilevsky, *Opisanie Pervoi Voiny Imperatora Aleksandra s Napoleonom v 1805 godu*, St. Petersburg, 1844, p. 172. (Subsequently referred to as *War of 1805*.)

[8] *War and Peace*, I. 3. 13.

| *Mikhailovsky-Danilevsky—contd.* | *Tolstoy—contd.* |
|---|---|
| enemy's invasion. Say that I will not make peace as long as a single enemy soldier remains on our soil.'[9] | in which he insisted that he include the words that he would never make peace as long as a single armed Frenchman remained on Russian soil.[10] |

The following example is taken from Denis Davydov's *Diary of the Partisan Operations in 1812*:

| *Davydov* | *Tolstoy* |
|---|---|
| Ermolov said to the Prince [Kutuzov] 'It's not too late yet, Your Highness, the enemy has not gone away; now, Your Highness, it's up to us to make a rapid advance, otherwise the Guards won't so much as see any smoke.' Kutuzov ordered an advance, though at every 100 paces the troops stopped for nearly three quarters of an hour.[11] | Soon after this Ermolov went up to Kutuzov and remarked respectfully: 'It's not too late yet, your Highness, the enemy has not gone away. Will you order an attack? Otherwise the Guards won't so much as see any smoke.' Kutuzov did not reply, but when they reported to him that Murat's troops were in retreat he ordered an advance, though at every 100 paces he halted for three quarters of an hour.[12] |

The next passage contains two slight variations on the original which again is Mikhailovsky-Danilevsky:

| *Mikhailovsky-Danilevsky* | *Tolstoy* |
|---|---|
| It was getting dark; clouds covered the sky. The weather was dry but the ground was damp, so that the troops made no noise as they marched; even the artillery could not be heard. It was forbidden to talk aloud, smoke pipes or strike a light; they tried to prevent the horses from neighing.[13] | It was an autumn night with purply-black clouds, but with no rain. The ground was damp but there was no mud, and the troops made no noise as they marched; only the faint clattering of the artillery could be heard from time to time. It was forbidden to talk aloud, smoke pipes or strike a light; they tried to prevent the horses from neighing.[14] |

Here Tolstoy introduces the colourful compound adjective 'purply-black' (*cherno-lilovaty*) as if to give a little variety to

[9] A. I. Mikhailovsky-Danilevsky, *Opisanie Otechestvennoi Voiny v 1812 godu*, St. Petersburg, 1843, p. 157. (Subsequently referred to as *War of 1812*.)
[10] *War and Peace*, III. 1. 3.     [11] Quoted by Pokrovsky in op. cit.
[12] *War and Peace*, IV. 2. 7.     [13] Quoted by Shklovsky, in op. cit. p. 203.
[14] *War and Peace*, IV. 2. 6.

the historian's rather flat prosaic narrative. Perhaps a strong strain of common sense made him think that if the artillery were on the move there was no reason why in the given weather conditions, they should not be heard. Hence, no doubt, the other significant amendment.

A common example of a literal or near literal borrowing is the witticism put in the mouth of one or other of the characters in *War and Peace*. In nearly all cases these *mots* can be traced back to a written source. Zhikharev's *Diary of a Student,* covering the years 1805–7 when he was in his late 'teens, and recounting in letter form St. Petersburg and Moscow social gossip, theatre and opera news and a variety of period detail, provided Tolstoy with some ready-made conversational titbits. He tells, for example,[15] how the old men referred to Mme Aubert-Chalmé, the fashionable French dressmaker in Moscow, as Mme Ober-Shelma, or 'arch-rogue'. When Marya Dmitrievna Akhrosimova (whom Tolstoy 'created' from a historical prototype vividly described by the same Zhikharev) is entertaining Natasha and Sonya in her town house in Moscow, she tells Natasha that she will take her round to visit the 'arch-rogue's', giving no explanation of her pun which, at the time, we assume was readily understood. Describing Russian reactions to the defeat at Austerlitz, Zhikharev says that the old people who exercised control over public opinion argued that it was impossible for the Russians to go on having successes all the time. 'If you keep on modelling, you're bound to get smeared with clay', they said, 'and we've been modelling for over 40 years. . . .'[16] Tolstoy borrows this popular saying (*Lepya, lepya i oblepish'sya*) and uses it to describe the impression made on Moscow opinion by the Austerlitz defeat, attributing the words to Prince Dolgorukov and adding somewhat gratuitously by way of explanation that they were intended to suggest consolation for the Russian defeat by the memory of former victories. Most of Tolstoy's sources provided him with at least one memorable saying. His own copy of Bernhardi's *Denkwürdigkeiten aus dem Leben des kaiserl. russ. Generals von der Infanterie Karl Friedrich Grafen von Toll* has the page turned down at the place where the author describes Napoleon writing

[15] S. P. Zhikharev, *Zapiski Sovremennika, Pt. I, Dnevnik Studenta,* Moscow-Leningrad, 1955, p. 12.     [16] ibid. 135.

to one of his Marshals on the day after Borodino and saying 'le champ de bataille a été superbe'.[17] Tolstoy did not forget the phrase. Writing about the aftermath of Borodino he says of Napoleon: 'It was not merely that he wrote on that day in a letter to Paris that "le champ de bataille a été superbe" because 50,000 dead bodies lay there; even on St. Helena . . . he wrote . . . etc.'[18] (and here follow many more quotations from the French).

The literal or near literal reproduction of famous sayings can easily be detected in *War and Peace* and there is no need for any further illustrations. What is not so easy to detect is the extent to which the choice of words and images of a given source are faithfully reflected in Tolstoy's own style. Boris Eykhenbaum has some interesting things to say about this. He quotes the words of Thiers that Napoleon's armies *'semblaient couler comme trois torrents inépuisables'*.[19] He shows how Tolstoy takes this casual comparison and rings the changes on the basic words *couler, torrents, inépuisables,* not even forgetting the *trois.* Thus 'he was looking through his field glasses at his troops as they *swept* like *torrents* out of . . . the wood and *poured* across the *three* bridges . . . one after another, *inexhaustibly* they continued to *stream* out of the wood. . . .'[20] The French *torrent* is literally rendered by the Russian *potok*; the adjective *inépuisable,* inexhaustible, becomes a gerund *ne istoshchayas' inexhaustibly*; the simple verb *couler* suggests to Tolstoy three compound verbs of cognate meaning, *vyplyvat', razlivat'sya, vytekat',* which add weight and variety to the original. The figure three is transferred from the torrents to the bridges. Thiers provides other good passages to which Tolstoy applied this method, which is not literal translation, but magnification of the original image through the translation and permutation of the roots of the original words. He also suggests colourful images and odd little dramatic touches which Tolstoy reproduces by a more or less literal translation of the sense if not the actual words. As the French approach the Kremlin in 1812 they hear a strange sound above their heads. They heard according to Thiers, *'des milliers d'oiseaux noirs, corbeaux et*

---

[17] See L. M. Myshkovskaya, *Masterstvo L. N. Tolstogo*, Moscow, 1958, p. 171.
[18] *War and Peace*, III. 2. 38.      [19] Eykhenbaum, op. cit. p. 339.
[20] *War and Peace*, III. 1. 2.

*corneilles*.[21] Tolstoy calls them 'a huge flock of jackdaws',[22] perhaps translating *corneilles d'église*. Thiers's words provide him with his portentous image of the birds cawing and flapping their wings and circling over the Kremlin towers as the French march in and a solitary Russian peasant fires a despairing shot at them.

We have dealt so far with extremely close correspondences between Tolstoy's text and that of his sources. We can now consider cases where the correspondence is not so close and the hand of the novelist is more apparent as he shapes and expands his material. Our first example, from Mikhailovsky-Danilevsky, refers to the eve of the battle of Austerlitz:

| *Mikhailovsky-Danilevsky* | *Tolstoy* |
|---|---|
| Riding up to Kutuzov and seeing that the rifles stood stacked, the Emperor Alexander asked him: 'Mikhail Larionovich, why aren't you advancing?' 'I'm waiting', answered Kutuzov, 'for all the columns to be formed up'. The Emperor said 'you know, we are not on the Empress's Field where a parade does not begin until all the troops are assembled'. 'Sir,' answered Kutuzov, 'that is just why I'm not starting because we are not on the Empress's Field. However, if you order it . . .'[23] | 'Why aren't you starting, Mikhail Larionovich?' said the Emperor hurriedly to Kutuzov, glancing courteously at the same time at the Emperor Francis. 'I'm waiting, Your Majesty', answered Kutuzov, bowing respectfully. The Emperor, frowning slightly, bent his ear forward to show that he had not quite heard. 'Waiting, Your Majesty' repeated Kutuzov (Prince Andrei noticed that Kutuzov's upper lip twitched unnaturally as he said the word 'waiting'). 'Not all the columns have formed up yet, Your Majesty.' The tsar heard but obviously did not like the reply; he shrugged his rather round shoulders and glanced at Novosiltsev who stood by him, as if complaining of Kutuzov. 'You know, Mikhail Larionovich, we are not on the Empress's Field where a parade does not begin until all the troops are assembled', said the tsar with another glance at the Emperor Francis, as if inviting him, if not to join in, at least to listen to what he was saying. But the |

---

[21] Quoted by Pokrovsky in op. cit.      [22] *War and Peace*, III. 3. 26.
[23] Mikhailovsky-Danilevsky, *War of 1805*, p. 181.

*Tolstoy—contd.*

Emperor Francis continued to look about him and did not listen. 'That is just why I'm not starting, Sir,' said Kutuzov in a resounding voice, apparently to preclude the possibility of not being heard and again something in his face twitched. 'That is just why I'm not starting, Sir, because we are not on parade on the Empress's Field' he said clearly and distinctly . . . [2 paragraphs]. However, if you order it . . .'.[24]

Here all the original is repeated more or less verbatim. What Tolstoy adds are the 'stage directions' for the characters— 'hurriedly', 'courteously', 'respectfully',—and the typically Tolstoyan physical gestures—the twitching of the upper lip (repeated, it need hardly be said)[25] and the shrugging of the rather round shoulders. Tolstoy in fact reproduces Mikhailovsky-Danilevsky's dialogue exactly, but at the same time fills in the reactions of the speakers to what is being said, describes what they did with their eyes, their lips, their bodies, and indicates what poses they adopted.

The scene in the Sloboda Palace in July 1812 when the nobles and the merchants both assembled to hear the Emperor's manifesto[26] is pieced together by Tolstoy largely on the basis of the account left by S. N. Glinka in his *Notes on 1812*.[27] Glinka was present at the assembly and he is himself introduced into Tolstoy's account of the occasion as well as providing the material for it. The process of converting Glinka into Tolstoy is worth recording in outline since it is fairly typical of the way Tolstoy used a source which he drew on very largely. After setting the scene, Glinka records a heated conversation in front of the Hall of the Nobility. 'One of the nobles said: "We should ask the Emperor how many troops we have and where our army is." ' In Tolstoy these words are ascribed more or less verbatim to Pierre, who was present at the assembly. ' "We should ask the Emperor', continued Pierre, 'most respectfully ask His

[24] *War and Peace*, I. 3. 15.          [25] See Chapter V.
[26] *War and Peace*, III. 1. 22 ff.
[27] S. N. Glinka, *Zapiski o 1812 gode*, St. Petersburg, 1836, p. 17 ff.

Majesty to communicate to us how many troops we have and the position in which our army and our forces now find themselves, and then . . ." ' But in Pierre's case, the two questions of the size and location of the army are put in a typically hesitant, awkward and embarrassed manner in keeping with Pierre's character and his feelings on this occasion. The heavy verb 'to communicate' (*komyunikirovat'*) and the clumsy twist given to the end of the sentence are Tolstoy's contributions to the task of working up his source material. (Incidentally the Maudes' translation renders the verb as 'to let us know' and neutralizes what seems to me the intended effect.)

Glinka carries on:

Stepan Stepanovich Apraksin retorted: 'Even if we had the right to question the Emperor about it, the Emperor could not give us a satisfactory answer. Our troops move in accordance with the enemy's movements which are liable to change every hour; the number of the troops is subject to the same change.'

Tolstoy now inserts an explanatory paragraph introducing an old acquaintance of Pierre's, one Stepan Stepanovitch Adraskin. (This change of a single letter in the surname of a historical character is a very frequent device of Tolstoy's). Adraskin shouts at Pierre: ' "In the first place, I tell you we have no right to question the Emperor about it, and in the second place if the Russian nobility had that right, the Emperor could not answer us. The troops move in accordance with the enemy's movements—their numbers increase and decrease. . . . " ' Here the only points of note are Tolstoy's rhetorical fondness for 'in the first place' and 'in the second place' and the rather greater precision of the second sentence. Glinka's version continues:

After this a tall broad-shouldered well built man of about forty, fine-looking and fluent of speech . . . said . . . 'It is not the time now for discussion: we need to act. War is raging, an exceptional war, a war of invasion, a war in our own country. It will dig graves for our towns and people. Russia will have to face a great struggle; and the struggle requires unprecedented measures. Let us advance in hundreds of thousands; lets us arm ourselves as best we can. Let us quickly advance into the enemy's rear; let us form cavalry cohorts; let us harass Napoleon everywhere; let us cut him off from Europe and show Europe that Russia is rising to the defence of Russia.'

Tolstoy carries on by ascribing a similar oration to 'a man of medium height and about 40 years of age, whom Pierre had

formerly met at the gipsies' and knew as a bad card player . . . '.
These qualifications are not in Glinka. Tolstoy's speaker is not
honoured with the flattering epithets which Glinka bestows.
He is an ordinary man, a real person whom Pierre knew, and
whose way of life was no better than Pierre's. But at this critical
moment he is carried away on a wave of patriotism, and Tolstoy
adds to Glinka's original text poses and gestures in keeping with
the rhetoric and the near-hysteria of the occasion:

'Yes, it is not the time for discussion—we need to act: there is war in
Russia. The enemy is advancing to destroy Russia, to desecrate the
tombs of our fathers, to carry off our wives and children.' The nobleman smote his breast. 'We will all arise, we will all go every one of us,
all for our dear Tsar!' he shouted, rolling his bloodshot eyes. Several
voices were heard in the crowd. 'We are Russians and will not spare our
blood in defence of our faith, the throne and the Fatherland! We must
stop raving if we are sons of our Fatherland. We will show Europe how
Russia is rising to the defence of Europe.'

Glinka's version now switches to the first person:

Amid the heat and fervour my voice rang out too: I exclaimed: 'Hell
must be repulsed by hell. I once saw a child smiling as the lightning
flashed and the thunder rolled: but it was a child. We are not children:
we see, we understand danger: we must resist danger.' My words cut
like a flame through the general silence. All the time I was being pushed
further into the assembly hall where along both sides of a table covered
with green cloth, sat more than seventy magnates wearing their
sashes. . . . Finally I said: 'we must not be afraid: Moscow will be
surrendered.'

This passage becomes in *War and Peace*:

'Glinka, the editor of *The Russian Messenger*, who was recognised (cries
of author! author! were heard in the crowd) said that hell must be
repulsed by hell, that he had seen a child smiling as the lightning
flashed and the thunder rolled, but that we would not be that child.
'Yes, yes, as the thunder rolled!' the back benches repeated approvingly.
The crowd advanced to the large table at which sat grey-haired or bald
seventy year old magnates, wearing uniform and sashes, almost all of
whom Pierre had seen in their own homes with their buffoons or playing
boston in their clubs . . . [nine sentences]. 'Yes Moscow will be surrendered! She will be our expiation!' shouted one man. 'He is the
enemy of mankind!' cried another. 'Let me speak . . . Gentlemen,
you are crushing me!'

Glinka's words are faithfully translated into indirect speech and
their rhetorical and boastful effect is thus diminished. Whereas
in Glinka they are central, in Tolstoy they are marginal—just

one person's opinion. The ominous prophecy 'Moscow will be surrendered' is moreover transferred from Glinka to an anonymous man in the crowd. Possibly Tolstoy thought that it was unbecoming and defeatist in the mouth of the fervent patriot. Glinka in his memoirs is careful to give reasons for this unpopular opinion, among them being that Moscow was accustomed to suffer on behalf of Russia, and that the surrender of Moscow would be the salvation of Russia and Europe. But Tolstoy may have found the first reason an exaggeration and the second not a reason at all.

There is one other curious factual change which Tolstoy makes in the text of his source. Glinka's seventy odd magnates become seventy year old magnates. There is no point in this alteration, and one can only assume that Tolstoy mistook the meaning of the figure seventy in his notes and taking it to refer to age, added the epithets 'grey-haired' and 'bald' to make it seem more plausible.

In his memoirs Glinka records how his speech was interrupted by the arrival of Rostopchin. Then the Emperor Alexander himself began to address the merchants in their assembly hall. With tears in his eyes he resurrects the spirit of Minin, although his actual words are not recorded. Glinka continues:

as one voice the words rang out: 'Sir, take everything, our property and our lives'

The Emperor moves on to the nobles' assembly hall and here Glinka listens to his words:

Here are the Emperor's words: 'I never doubted the devotion of the Russian nobility; but today it has surpassed my expectations. I thank you in the name of the Fatherland. Gentlemen! let us act: time is most precious'.

In *War and Peace* Tolstoy reverses the proceedings. That is to say the Emperor first visits the hall of the nobility. Presumably Glinka, as an eye-witness, recorded the events in their correct sequence and it is possible that Tolstoy's pride in his own class and lack of sympathy for those who earned their living by buying and selling persuaded him that whatever Glinka might say to the contrary, the Emperor must surely have honoured the nobles first with his presence. Tolstoy reproduces the Emperor's words to the nobles verbatim (merely

changing 'expectation' to 'expectations'). He does not invent a
speech for the Emperor to make to the merchants. But he does
make a curious variation on the unanimous reply which Glinka
says the merchants made to their Emperor. He attributes the
words not to the assembly as a whole but to one individual, a
fat *otkupshchik*. The word *otkupshchik* means technically a
man who leased from the Government the monopoly of the
sales of a certain commodity—often spirits—for a particular
area. It had an unpleasant connotation. Combined with the
adjective 'fat' it was far from complimentary. Why did Tolstoy
put these generous sentiments 'take our lives and our property!'
into the mouth of a fat dealer in spirits? Presumably to make
Pierre feel more ashamed that for all his aristocratic disdain for
such men, he himself had not been more generous, and to sting
him into making his offer to give and maintain a thousand
men.

It would take up too much space to multiply examples of the
sort just given from Mikhailovsky-Danilevsky and Glinka.
Perhaps enough has been said to show that Tolstoy's use of his
sources was far from mechanical. It may be appropriate at this
point to mention another fairly common variation which Tolstoy
introduced in his near-literal reproduction of source materials,
namely the taking over verbatim of a phrase or sentence applied
originally to one person or thing and the application of the
identical words to somebody or something else. Mikhailovsky-
Danilevsky narrates how Kutuzov, wounded at Austerlitz, says
to the doctor sent to him by the Emperor Alexander: ' "Thank
the Emperor and tell him that my wound is not serious, but
that the fatal wound is there" pointing to the French.'[28] Tolstoy
obviously liked the comparison, but he gave it a slight twist:
' "The wound is not here, it is there!" said Kutuzov, pressing
the handkerchief to his wounded cheek and pointing to the
fleeing [Russian] soldiers.'[29] In the same author's account of
Balashev's mission to Napoleon before the start of operations
in 1812 there is much detailed material which Tolstoy borrows
and works up.[30] This is the source among other things for
Tolstoy's amplification of Balashev's two famous witticisms

[28] Mikhailovsky-Danilevsky, *War of 1805*, p. 184.
[29] *War and Peace*, I. 3. 16.
[30] Mikhailovsky-Danilevsky, *War of 1812*, pp. 210 ff.

at dinner. But once again there is a twist given to some of Mikhailovsky-Danilevsky's words. Mikhailovsky-Danilevsky writes that Napoleon boasted to Balashev that his troops 'fight like lions'.[31] Tolstoy in repeating the same conversation and the same simile[32] applies it not to Napoleon's army as a whole, but only to his allies the Poles. Is Tolstoy attributing to Napoleon his own suspicion as a Slav that his fellow Slavs are the bravest part of Napoleon's army? Are the events of 1863 uppermost in his mind? Is the change merely accidental? There is no means of knowing. But a careful study of all such minor alterations to the texts of Tolstoy's historical source material (and there are very many of them) would certainly provide interesting evidence of the working of the author's mind which is not apparent when one confines one's attention to the finished text.

As a generalization it is probably true to say that the most numerous examples of 'borrowing' in *War and Peace* are those where a scene or episode is written very largely on the basis of an original, but with a limited amount of verbatim correspondence, where in fact the whole gist of the original reappears and many or most of the details, but where the literal correspondence of the two texts is less close than it is in the examples so far quoted. The description of the reception and banquet in honour of Bagration at the English Club in Moscow[33] is an expansion of Zhikharev's entry in his diary for 4 March 1806,[34] Zhikharev being one of the guests on this occasion, and his account as an eyewitness being all the more valued by Tolstoy for that reason. Tolstoy takes from Zhikharev such details as the number of people present at the banquet (250 club members and 50 guests); the clumsy embarrassed movements of Bagration as he entered the club; the verses presented to him on a silver salver: the verbatim text of these verses; the band striking up its patriotic strains; the seating of the guest of honour (between two Alexanders, as an allusion to the Emperor's name); the toasts and the hurrahs, the choir singing a special cantata in Bagration's honour: and the words of the cantata. Tolstoy adds in his much fuller version the characteristic image likening the conversation in the club to the hum of bees swarming in springtime. He describes the footmen as well as the guests. He fills in

---

[31] Mikhailovsky-Danilevsky, *War of 1812*, p. 211.
[32] *War and Peace*, III. 1. 6.     [33] ibid. II. 1. 12.
[34] Zhikharev, op. cit. p. 195.

the conversation of the various groups standing and waiting for Bagration to arrive. He describes Bagration's physical appearance in much greater detail and makes rather more of his shyness and gaucherie. And finally he gives some space to the reactions of Count Rostov and his son to the occasion.

Zhikharev also provides Tolstoy with his material for the character of Marya Dmitrievna Akhrosimova in his *obiter dicta* on the celebrated personality of the day, Nastasya Dmitrievna Ofrosimova, a woman, as he says, 'remarkable for her common sense, frankness and absolute devotion to the Government',[35] a woman who never minced her words; and one has to discount Tolstoy's statement[36] that the choice of Akhrosimova's name was quite involuntary and that nothing resembling the actual facts of Ofrosimova's life is ascribed to Akhrosimova in his novel.

Tolstoy's extensive use of de Maistre's *Correspondance diplomatique* and his *Soirées de St. Pétersbourg* has been noted from time to time by scholars. Professor Berlin has conveniently collected a few examples which we quote from *The Hedgehog and the Fox*:

. . . the celebrated description of Paulucci's intervention in the debate of the Russian General Staff at Drissa is reproduced almost verbatim from a letter by Maistre. Similarly Prince Vassili's conversation at Mme Scherer's reception with the *homme de beaucoup de mérite* about Kutuzov is obviously based on a letter by Maistre, in which all the French phrases with which the conversation is sprinkled are to be found. There is, moreover, a note in one of Tolstoy's early rough drafts, 'at Anna Pavlovna's Maistre-Vicomte', which refers to the raconteur who tells the beautiful Hélène and an admiring circle of listeners the idiotic anecdote about the meeting of Napoleon with the Duc d'Enghien at supper with the celebrated actress Mlle Georges. Again old Prince Bolkonsky's habit of shifting his bed from one room to another is probably taken from a story which Maistre tells about the similar habit of Count Stroganov. Finally the name of Maistre occurs in the novel itself, as being among those who agree that it would be embarrassing and senseless to capture the more eminent princes and marshals of Napoleon's army, since this would merely create diplomatic difficulties.[37]

Other examples could be added. In one of the draft versions of the conversation between Prince Andrei and Pierre when Pierre visits his friend at Bogucharovo, Tolstoy puts the following words into Prince Andrei's mouth: 'J[oseph] M[aistre] said

[35] ibid. p. 126.                    [36] J.E. XVI. 9.
[37] Isaiah Berlin, *The Hedgehog and the Fox*, London, 1953, p. 50.

rightly: "Il n'est dans la vie que deux maux bien réels: c'est le remords et la maladie. Et il n'est de bien que l'absence de ces maux." '[38] Virtually the identical words are attributed to Prince Andrei in *War and Peace*,[39] but no acknowledgement is made of their origin. Less easily verifiable is the nevertheless plausible suggestion that Tolstoy's reasons for deciding to start the description of the war of 1805 from the beginning of the campaign and not from the eve of the battle of Austerlitz was connected with de Maistre's emphasis on Kutuzov's brilliance in the battles preceding Austerlitz, about which Russian sources had little or nothing to say.[40]

Besides de Maistre, many of Tolstoy's other sources have been explored from time to time by scholars. Perovsky's account[41] of his own interrogation by Davoût and his last minute reprieve forms the gist of the scene in *War and Peace*[42] where Pierre is likewise interrogated by Davoût in Moscow, 1812, with his life hanging delicately in the balance. The correspondence between the two accounts is very close. Bogdanovich's story[43] of the daring exploit of the partisan hero Figner and a young lieutenant who dressed up in French uniform and penetrated the enemy camp during the French retreat from Moscow—a few laconic sentences is all the space Bogdanovich devotes to it—is magnified and dramatized by Tolstoy and attributed to Dolokhov and Petya Rostov.[44] In the same way Tolstoy adds dialogue and incidental detail to a simple episode narrated by Radozhitsky[45] about a doctor and his wife sheltering from the rain in a tavern, and the result is the chapter in which Nikolai Rostov and his friends tease and joke with Marya Hendrikhovna, the plump blonde German wife of a regimental doctor, as they too dry off in a tavern from the rain.[46]

Bernhardi's biography of General Toll is another of the books which Tolstoy had in his library at Yasnaya Polyana and which he named in his rough work on the epilogue as one of his three main sources (the others being Mikhailovsky-Danilevsky and

[38] J.E. XIII. 611.                          [39] *War and Peace*, II. 2. 11.
[40] E. E. Zaidenshnur, J.E. XVI. 66.
[41] *Iz Zapisok pokoinogo grafa V. A. Perovskogo, Russkii Arkhiv* 1865, pp. 1031–1058.                              [42] *War and Peace*, IV. 1. 10.
[43] Quoted by Pokrovsky op. cit.        [44] *War and Peace*, IV. 3. 9.
[45] I. Radozhitsky, *Pokhodnye Zapiski Artillerista s 1812 po 1816 god*, Moscow, 1835. Quoted by Pokrovsky, op. cit.
[46] *War and Peace*, III. 1. 3.

Thiers).[47] According to a Soviet scholar[48] who has examined the text closely, the book, which is rather a history of the period of Napoleon's wars with Russia than a collection of memoirs, and which, understandably enough, is pro-German but not pro-French, was used by Tolstoy for backstage information in particular—what went on behind the scenes on the eve of Austerlitz, what opinions were expressed by the different parties in the discussion on tactics and strategy. In his own copy Tolstoy marked passages which concerned Weyrother, Kutuzov and Alexander. Weyrother is given the credit for playing the main part in the preparations for Austerlitz. Kutuzov's role, apart from objecting to the battle, is completely passive. Tolstoy made use of this material in describing the Council of War which preceded the battle of Austerlitz. Bernhardi also emphasized some negative features of the Emperor Alexander, unlikely to be recorded in Russian sources—his vanity for example, his evasiveness, his irresolution. Tolstoy borrowed from Bernhardi the scene on the battlefield at Austerlitz where the Emperor Alexander feels ill, sits down under a tree, takes out his handkerchief, weeps and is comforted by von Toll. His version reproduces Bernhardi almost literally (the tree becomes an apple tree!), with this addition that Nikolai Rostov witnesses the scene and wishes that he could have been in Toll's place.[49]

In his diary for 1865,[50] Tolstoy noted that he found the memoirs of Raguse very useful. The *Mémoires du maréchal Marmont, duc de Raguse,* one of Napoleon's marshals who had been jointly responsible for surrendering Paris to the allies in 1814, were published in 1857 in nine volumes, and Tolstoy read them, or parts of them, while writing *War and Peace.* Among the small details which he seems to have derived from this source are the fact that Napoleon was a poor rider. Raguse also describes Napoleon's habit of riding round the field of battle when the day is over, observing the dead and wounded and experiencing a sense of joy. Tolstoy comments on these features in his diary when mentioning Raguse's memoirs and later incorporates them into his description of the aftermath of the battle of Austerlitz.[51]

[47] J.E. XV. 240.
[49] *War and Peace,* I. 3. 18.
[51] *War and Peace,* I. 3. 19.

[48] Myshkovskaya, op. cit. pp. 162 ff.
[50] J.E. XLVIII. 473.

Many episodes in *War and Peace* are based on Mikhailovsky-Danilevsky's books, especially his *Description of the First War, 1805*. We will mention only two. The story[52] of how Murat, having mistakenly overestimated Kutuzov's strength, tried to deceive him and negotiate a truce and how Kutuzov gratefully accepted the offer and made capital out of it, is fairly closely followed in *War and Peace*[53]—in contrast, incidentally, to the version of the same story which Thiers gives,[54] where the initiative for duping the French is credited to Kutuzov; while at a later stage[55] Tolstoy reproduces the gist of the Russian historian's description[56] of the collapse of the ice on the dam near Augesd and the disastrous consequences for the Russian troops retreating after Austerlitz. Both these episodes had dramatic possibilities and Tolstoy accordingly incorporated them, in all their essentials, in his narrative. Mikhailovsky-Danilevsky's books are fairly rich in anecdote, fanciful as well as factual. That is no doubt why Tolstoy took them as his main source. By contrast, Thiers's narrative is more sober. Yet Tolstoy for all his understandable indignation at Thiers's Napoleon worship and his superior and condescending attitudes to the Russians ('the Russian troops have learned the art of war by waging it with us'; 'the Russian army plundered, ravaged, even murdered, behaving like downright barbarians')[57] nevertheless used him a good deal for those parts of *War and Peace* in which Napoleon plays a prominent role. Needless to say he interpreted the material in his own way, concerned as he was to belittle the French emperor. Where Thiers eulogizes, Tolstoy satirizes. Somewhat similar is the novelist's treatment of Baron Korf's *Life of Speransky*.[58] This is a sympathetic account of the great would-be reformer of Alexander's reign, an admirable man of many virtues as his contemporaries saw him. Tolstoy is ready enough to use the details of Speransky's domestic life which he finds in Korf's biography—details quoted there by Speransky's daughter about her father's dinner table, his regular guests, their personalities, and idiosyncracies (e.g. Stolypin's stammer), their after dinner talk, their

---

[52] Mikhailovsky-Danilevsky, *War of 1805*, p. 125.
[53] *War and Peace*, I. 2. 14.
[54] M. A. Thiers, *Histoire du Consulat et de l'Empire*, Vol. 6, Paris, 1847, p. 271.                      [55] *War and Peace*, I. 3. 18.
[56] Mikhailovsky-Danilevsky, *War of 1805*, p. 204.
[57] Thiers, op, cit. pp. 232 and 249.
[58] M. A. Korf, *Zhizn' grafa Speranskogo*, St. Petersburg, 1861.

witticisms. These details all reappear when Tolstoy describes the dinner party at Speransky's house at which Prince Andrei is present.[59] But the sympathetic attitude which Korf displays towards the subject of his biography is no more acceptable to Tolstoy than Thiers's eulogies of his hero. Tolstoy's appreciation of the work of these great men is inevitably coloured by his own independent outlook on 'great men' and the work they profess to be doing. He is temperamentally hostile to the politician, the political reformer, the constitution maker in the abstract. Therefore the concrete figure of Speransky, for all his private virtues, is bound to appear to him cold, bureaucratic, unsympathetic. He is not wilfully distorting his sources. He is simply applying his own moral and ethical standards to the behaviour of the men he is writing about, taking the 'facts' of their behaviour from his sources, but putting a different construction on these 'facts' than the one put on them by well disposed biographers.

We have given sufficient examples of how Tolstoy reproduces the gist of a scene without necessarily borrowing literally from his sources, without a virtual word for word correspondence between the text of the original and the text of the novel. We can now mention one or two examples of how a bare sentence or two in a source work gives Tolstoy a hint for constructing a scene which may extend over several chapters. Mikhailovsky-Danilevsky writes about the early stages of the war of 1805, making the following short statement:

Not having succeeded in his intention, Murat approached the river Enns almost at the same time as Prince Bagration, in an effort to capture the bridge. A detachment of the Pavlograd hussars which had been in the rear dismounted and under grape-shot fire set fire to the bridge which had been covered in advance with inflammable material; the detachment was commanded by Colonel O'Rourke.[60]

This is the cue for the very vivid chapter in *War and Peace*[61] where Nikolai Rostov's squadron of the Pavlograd Hussars and the regimental Colonel Schubert fire the bridge across the Enns and Nikolai has his first taste of action—and of fear. Mikhailovsky-Danilevsky has little to say about the action of Schöngraben which fills several chapters of *War and Peace*. Three or four pages about troop dispositions and the curt remark

59 *War and Peace*, II. 3. 18.
60 Mikhailovsky-Danilevsky, *War of 1805*, p. 89.
61 *War and Peace*, I. 2. 8.

that our artillery set fire to the village of Schöngraben and that the fire quickly spread—that is all. But this simple statement captured Tolstoy's imagination and gave him the impetus to write the long episode of Tushin's heroic exploits culminating in the firing of Schöngraben.

There is no doubt that the germ of the idea for certain important episodes in *War and Peace* is contained in the letters written by M. A. Volkova to V. I. Lanskaya during the years 1812–18.[62] Tolstoy had access to these letters before they were published. Their style and their sentiments are well imitated in the correspondence between Princess Marya and Julie Karagina in the novel. It is almost certain that we owe the name Prince Andrei to Volkova's correspondence. In a letter dated 24 June 1812 she writes to her friend that 'Prince Andrei has decided to set off for the war and is leaving his wife to cope with her childbirth as best she can'. The identical decision of Prince Andrei in *War and Peace* and his wife's death in childbirth must surely have their origin in this letter which we know Tolstoy was able to consult in 1863. Again we read in her letter of 11 November 1812 that 'Prince Vyazemsky had the temerity to take part in the battle of Borodino as an ordinary spectator'— just as Pierre himself did. Vyazemsky has left his recollections of 1812 (published 1869) and his situation at Borodino resembles Pierre's in many ways. It is possible that Tolstoy had heard Vyazemsky's anecdotes before they were published. It is possible that Volkova's letter suggested the situation to him. It is equally possible that Stendhal, whose *La Chartreuse de Parme* was much admired by Tolstoy, put into his head the idea of describing the battle of Borodino from the point of view of a non-combatant who happened to turn up on a battlefield for the first time, as Fabrice happened to turn up at Waterloo. With three people to drop the hint it is unlikely that Tolstoy invented the situation out of his own head.

### MISUSE OF SOURCE MATERIAL

Tolstoy's extensive use of written sources for his work on *War and Peace* not surprisingly led him into occasional errors —trivial errors for the most part, which will hardly be noticed

[62] See *Vestnik Evropy*, 1874, No. 8, 572 ff: *Griboedovskaya Moskva v pis'makh M. A. Volkovoi k V. I. Lanskoi.*

by any but the most careful readers. One fairly common mistake he makes is the failure to synchronize dates given in Western European sources according to the Gregorian calendar with the Julian calendar chronology of his Russian sources. When Tolstoy says[63] that Napoleon left Dresden on 29 May 1812 and reached the Russian frontier on 12 June, we know that inadvertently the first date is given in the new style (from Thiers) and the second in the old style (from Bogdanovich), since Napoleon took not twelve but twenty-four days on his journey. Mistakes of this sort occur several times and are invariably due to the simultaneous use of several sources. Rather different are the careless mistakes sometimes made in matching historical and fictional chronology. It is said, for example, of the dying Prince Bolkonsky,[64] that he had been stricken with paralysis for three weeks, whereas in the novel only ten days elapse between the bombardment of Smolensk on 5 August 1812 when he was still in perfect health and his death on 15 August. Or again, in the chapters after the Battle of Borodino,[65] Kutuzov is described as sending a report from Tatarinova with the news of the battle and the death of Prince Bagration, and other Russian generals. In fact his report from Tatarinova was sent off on 25 August after the first action at the Shevardino Redoubt and on the day before the battle of Borodino in which Bagration lost his life. The news of Borodino only reached St. Petersburg on 30 August and not on 27 August as Tolstoy says in the novel—clearly a physical impossibility. One could mention other minor inconsistencies in *War and Peace* such as the fact that Boris Drubetskoy's regiment is at first called the Semenov Guards and later the Izmaylov Regiment, or the reference Tolstoy makes[66] to the cloudless June night in St. Petersburg very shortly after the soirée at Anna Scherer's which, we are told, took place in July 1805. It is perhaps surprising that there are so few of these inconsistencies in a work of such dimensions. But to return to the sources—we also notice that Tolstoy is liable to quote incorrectly. To Thiers he attributed the statement that Napoleon ordered his army to be paid in forged Russian money of his own manufacture,[67] whereas in fact the French historian's words are merely that the army was to be

---

[63] *War and Peace*, III. 1. 2.
[64] ibid. III. 2. 8.    [65] ibid. IV. 1. 2.    [66] ibid. I. 1. 6.    [67] ibid. IV 2. 9.

paid 'in Russian roubles'. To Glinka he attributed a whole episode which is not mentioned by him at all (Tolstoy asserted in writing on at least two separate occasions that the somewhat undignified scene of the Emperor Alexander tossing biscuits to the crowd from the palace balcony[68] was borrowed by him from Glinka, although no trace of it can be found there). Again his account of Napoleon taking the Russian envoy Balashev by the ear[69] seems to be a misquotation from the source in which Caulaincourt, the French Ambassador to Russia, was the victim of this friendly gesture. Tolstoy was not exempt from confusion over proper names. When Bartenev, who was undertaking the publication and correcting the proofs of the novel, wrote to him to say that he had replaced the name of Count A. Uvarov (who didn't exist) by that of F. P. Uvarov, and had substituted the word 'author' for the name Nikolev who, being blind, would have been unable to read the verses at the English Club banquet as Tolstoy had him do, Tolstoy retorted that he (Tolstoy) was right in both cases because his information came from Zhikharev. Unfortunately his reply only raised further doubts about his accuracy, for he made yet another mistake in his letter, writing Balashev instead of Uvarov! The corrections were duly made.[70]

There is no doubt in my mind that Tolstoy's errors, whether in wrongly transmitting material from written sources or in failing to adhere consistently to his own facts, are due entirely to carelessness. It is necessary to say this because some scholars have thought otherwise. It has been suggested,[71] for example, that in 'quoting' Thiers but in fact misquoting him, Tolstoy was deliberately trying to discredit the French historian! It has also been suggested that certain illogicalities which may be detected by the very careful reader of *War and Peace* were deliberately introduced in order to provide a variation in an alleged conventional narrative pattern.[72] An apparent example of this is the remark made in the opening chapter of the novel by Anna Scherer who says angrily: 'Oh don't speak to me about Austria!' although no mention has been made of Austria. In fact in the printed version of *1805*, later revised by the author,

[68] *War and Peace*, III. 1. 21.     [69] ibid. III. 1. 7.
[70] Letter to P. I. Bartenev, 16 ... 18 August, 1867, J.E. LXI. 176.
[71] Shklovsky, op. cit. pp. 177 ff.     [72] ibid. p. 104.

a joke was made about Austria which annoyed Anna Scherer and prompted her angry exclamation. Although one can argue that Tolstoy failed to take account of the fact that the cut he made in one place might have logical repercussions in another, there is no need to do so, since in *War and Peace* it is expressly stated that Anna Scherer's remark was made in the course of a conversation on political affairs, and one naturally assumes that Austria had been mentioned. In a work of such great length it is indeed remarkable that so few lapses can be detected.

### SOURCES FOR NON-HISTORICAL CHARACTERS

So far we have dealt with Tolstoy's use and occasional misuse of historical and memoir sources. Much has been written on the cognate subject of the sources for his non-historical characters. The English reader, unfamiliar with Biryukov's biography of Tolstoy[73] or Tolstoy's own son's article on his father's mother and grandfather,[74] may nevertheless know the English transla-tion of the memoirs of Tatyana Kuzminskaya (*née* Behrs),[75] Tolstoy's sister-in-law and the principal prototype of Natasha. Much of the information from these and other sources has been gathered together and condensed in a recent Soviet article,[76] and since this provides the most compact and convenient résumé of the subject, we give a translation of the relevant part of it, the sentences in square brackets being our additions:

It may be said with the greatest probability that Tolstoy's immediate forbears who were alive during the period 1805–1812 suggested the characters of the Bolkonskys and the old Rostovs. The characteristic features of Tolstoy's grandfather on his mother's side, Nikolai Sergeevich Volkonsky (1753–1812)—'a clever, proud and gifted man'[77]—and many details of his life, were used for the old Prince Bolkonsky. [It has been pointed out[78] that Prince Bolkonsky perhaps owes more to Field Marshal M. F. Kamensky than to Tolstoy's own grandfather—an illustration of the composite nature of prototypes of which *War and Peace* provides many examples.] Tolstoy's mother, Marya Nikolaevna Volkonskaya (1790–1830), who lost *her* mother when she was two years old, and who lived partly in Moscow and partly in the country with her father who

[73] P. I. Biryukov, *L. N. Tolstoy, Biografiya*, Moscow, 1906.
[74] S. L. Tolstoy, *Mat' i Ded L. N. Tolstogo*, Moscow, 1928.
[75] T. A. Kuzminskaya, *Tolstoy as I knew him: My life at home and at Yasnaya Polyana*, New York, 1948.
[76] E. E. Zaidenshnur, J.E. XVI. 136 ff.
[77] Quoted from Tolstoy's *Vospominaniya*, J.E. XXXIV. 351.
[78] Eykhenbaum, op. cit. *Kniga vtoraya*, p. 262.

looked after her education, provided material for the character of Princess Marya. In a draft version Tolstoy actually indicated her exact age in 1811— 21. Her relations with her father and the tenor of their life are also reflected in *War and Peace*. [One may add that the text of Princess Marya's diary in *War and Peace* is very similar to the notes Tolstoy's mother kept about her own children.] Individual features of Tolstoy's aunt A. I. Osten-Saken (1797–1841) who is also described in Tolstoy's *Memoirs*—especially her religious faith—are introduced in part into the character of Princess Marya. Tolstoy's mother's companion, the Frenchwoman Louise Henissienne, is portrayed in Mlle Bourienne, the companion of Princess Marya. To describe the Bolkonsky's way of life, Tolstoy made use of stories told by his mother's cousin, V. A. Volkonskaya, according to his eldest son Sergey.

In the character of the old Count Rostov, Tolstoy incorporated several features of his grandfather on his father's side. Count Ilya Andreevich Tolstoy (1757–1820), in Tolstoy's description 'a man of limited intelligence, very kind, jolly, not merely generous but extravagant to the point of folly, and above all trusting'—is very likely the exact prototype of the old Count Rostov. [It may be remembered by the way that one of the names originally given to Rostov in the draft version was Prostoy 'Simple'.] His wife, Tolstoy's grandmother, Pelageya Nikolaevna Tolstaya (1762–1838)—'a rather stupid, poorly educated and very spoiled woman'—is reflected in Countess Rostova. According to T. A. Kuzminskaya, certain features of Countess Rostova remind one of L. A. Behrs, Tolstoy's wife's mother. Some features of Tolstoy's father who took part in the war of 1812 are reflected in Nikolai Rostov.

Unlike the people so far mentioned, the prototypes of Count Rostov's daughters, Natasha and Vera, were not alive in 1812 but were Tolstoy's own contemporaries who helped him to copy *War and Peace*—Sofia Andreevna's sisters and she herself. On 11th November 1862 Sofia Andreevna wrote to her sisters: 'Girls, I'm going to tell you a secret, and don't mention it: perhaps Levochka will describe us when he's fifty! . . .' As for Natasha, Tolstoy said 'I took Tanya, beat her up with Sonya, and the result was Natasha'. Natasha's characteristic features, however, make her much more like Tanya Behrs than Sofia Andreevna. Tolstoy wrote in his diary on 15th January 1863: 'Tanya is a charming creature of naiveté, egoism and sensibility.' Later he wrote of her as 'a kind, madly uninhibited energetic nature'. These attributes coincide with the description of Natasha as envisaged in the original plan. Natasha's outward appearance as Tolstoy imagined it also coincided with that of Tanya Behrs. He wrote about this to M. S. Bashilov in connection with a drawing for the first part of the novel. 'In the kiss can't you model Natasha on Tanya Behrs? . . . I'm sure that you, as an artist, having seen a daguerreotype of Tanya when she was twelve, then her picture in a white blouse when she was sixteen and then her big portrait last year won't fail to make use of this model and its stages of development which are so very close to those of my model.' Tolstoy's young wife, the mother of several young children by the time the novel was complete, was a model for Natasha as a mother in the epilogue of the novel.

[Tanya Behrs-Kuzminskaya not surprisingly has a good deal to say in her memoirs about scenes and characters in *War and Peace* which reproduce the Yasnaya Polyana experiences of herself and her friends. For example the scene in the conservatory where Natasha persuades Boris to kiss her instead of her doll Mimi is a faithful copy of Tanya Behrs' own experience with her future husband Kuzminsky. Natasha's first ball owes much to Behrs' description of her own first ball at Tula in the presence of the heir to the throne, when, as with Natasha, loneliness and despondency were crowned by triumph and bliss. Prince Andrei is made to suffer from the same delirium as Behrs herself experienced and recounted to Tolstoy. The story of Behrs' cousin's courtship by a man who saw her at the theatre and vowed 'das soll mein Weib werden' has its echoes in the courtship of Berg and Vera Rostova when the identical German words are used by Berg. There is little doubt that Natasha is an exalted and poeticized version of her model, but there is no need to explain this embellishment by the suggestion of one of Tolstoy's sons that his father was in love with Tanya Behrs. There is no suggestion that the corresponding impoverishment of Sonya as compared with her partial model T. A. Ergolskaya—see below—was due to any ill feeling on the author's part towards his guardian.]

Vera Rostova has features closely resembling Elisaveta Andreevna Behrs [another of Tolstoy's sisters-in-law]; in one plan Vera is even called Lisa. Some outward (but not inward) features, and in part the fate of Tolstoy's guardian T. A. Ergolskaya (1792–1874) were used by him in the character of Sonya; her relations with Tolstoy's father are partly reflected in the relations between Sonya and Nikolai Rostov. [Ergolskaya (Sonya) refused to marry Tolstoy's father (Nikolai Rostov) to allow him to marry a wealthy heiress (Princess Marya) and so retrieve the family fortunes. After Tolstoy's mother's death his father proposed to Ergolskaya, she refused, but agreed to act as mother to his children.] For the character of Boris Drubetskoy, Tolstoy used some features of Polivanov, his wife's brother's friend and some features of his wife's cousin, Kuzminsky, whom Tanya later married. The Natasha-Anatole episode is based on a real episode from the life of Tanya Behrs and Anatole Shostak of which Kuzminskaya tells in detail in her memoirs.

Marya Dmitrievna Akhrosimova, in appearance, in manners and in many details of her life, closely resembles N. D. Ofrosimova (1753-1826), described in Zhikharev's *Diary of a Student* which Tolstoy used as a source work for his novel. One must also take into account Tanya Behrs's letter to Polivanov in 1865, immediately after the first part of the novel had been read at the Perfilevs'; it contains evidence that Akhrosimova reminded the audience both of A. S. Perfileva and M. A. Volkova. Some features of [the soldier and poet] D. V. Davydov are reflected in Denisov. For Dolokhov, Tolstoy used features of A. S. Figner, a partisan hero of 1812, and also of Tolstoy's uncle, Fedor Ivanovich Tolstoy, whose description is contained in Tolstoy's *Memoirs* [The name may well have been derived in typically Tolstoyan fashion from another of the partisans of 1812—Dorokhov.] Staff Captain Y. I. Sudakov is portrayed in the character of Captain Tushin. . . .

In creating the character of the little Princess Lisa Ivanovna Bolkonskaya Tolstoy used features of Princess Louisa Ivanovna Volkonskaya, the wife of a second cousin of Tolstoy. After the publication of the final part of the novel in *The Russian Messenger*, L. I. Volkonskaya wrote to Tolstoy and asked who was the prototype of Prince Andrei. Tolstoy replied (3 May 1865): . . . 'Andrei Bolkonsky is nobody—the same as any character by a novelist as opposed to a writer of memoirs or personalities. I would be ashamed to appear in print if all my work consisted of copying portraits, making enquiries and memorising.'

This is a convenient place to end the quotation. But the fact remains that Tolstoy had many models to copy, made extensive enquiries and carried a notebook round with him at Yasnaya Polyana to aid his memory, jotting down conversations, descriptions, traits of character, scenes from life. Most novelists have done the same. It is a typical procedure of the realistic novelist. Tolstoy's mind was exercised not in creating characters out of the void or in trying to portray individuals from a very different background to his own but in selecting and rejecting from the real life models of people near and dear to him, adding here, subtracting there, blending one trait with another, emphasizing, exaggerating, idealizing, distorting. Invention was almost a term of abuse with Tolstoy. How often in his letters and diaries does he make the adverse criticism of a piece of writing he does not like—'it's all made up! (*vse vydumano*)—a remark which contrasts sharply with Dostoevsky's 'I am a novelist so that I can invent' (*chtoby vydumyvat'*).[79] For Tolstoy it was not the product of the imagination but the reality of life which presented the writer with his most difficult challenge—a thought which he expressed as a young man of 23 when he wrote: 'the word is far from adequate to convey the things of the imagination, but to express real life is harder still.'[80] Tolstoy created people; but he did not invent characters and situations out of his head. He brought to life in his novel the material he had assembled from the lives of real people. He was no Emily Brontë. His was an intensifying, not an inventive genius.

[79] F. M. Dostoevsky, *Dnevnik Pisatelya, Polnoe Sobranie Sochinenii*, Vol. 10, St. Petersburg, 1895, p. 18.  •  [80] *Zapiski o Kavkaze*, J.E. III. 216.

IDEOLOGICAL INFLUENCES

The source material which we have been considering in this chapter did not provide Tolstoy with any ideological pabulum. It cannot be held responsible for the extreme positions he came to adopt in the later stages of *War and Peace* on questions of the philosophy of history and the philosophy of war. It is interesting to us for the light it sheds on Tolstoy's style, his assimilation of other people's words and phrases and his technique of composition. But the same interest does not attach, in this work at least, to the sources from which he may have borrowed his ideas on the philosophy of history and the philosophy of war as they were expressed in the later volumes of *War and Peace*. This is an independent field of study and a most difficult one, and we shall only trespass here on the very edge of it.

It is common knowledge that Tolstoy admitted himself to have been indebted above all to the writings of two men— Rousseau and Stendhal. But there would be little point in looking for a confirmation of Tolstoy's views on history in Rousseau. And Tolstoy had already evolved his characteristic style of military narrative without the help of *La Chartreuse de Parme,* as we shall see later. Boris Eykhenbaum, one of the most original Soviet literary critics, made out what on first reading seemed a plausible case for the influence of Proudhon on the writing of *War and Peace*. This case, as expounded by Eykhenbaum,[81] starts with the assertion that the title of Tolstoy's novel, *War and Peace,* is not an accurate description of its content in that there is no 'peace' but only war and family relationships during wartime. The title looks different, however, when one remembers that Proudhon wrote a book called *La Guerre et la Paix: recherches sur le principe et la constitution du droit des gens*. For Tolstoy had visited Proudhon in Brussels in 1861 at the time when Proudhon was finishing the introduction to his book. And the book, says Eykhenbaum, embraces a theory that war and peace are inseparable, that the one presupposes the other, that war is a phenomenon of life, that if it did not exist poetry would have invented it, that every people has its epic poetry and that epic poetry is based on war. War is part of the divine order of things,

---

[81] Eykhenbaum, op. cit. see Part 4, Chapters 1 and 2, pp. 281 ff. and also *Kniga pervaya,* 1928, Part 3, Chapter 4.

says Proudhon, quoting de Maistre (it is only fair to add
Proudhon's conclusion that it is nevertheless a terrible thing
and that the only sensible thing to do is to direct man's basic
combative instincts into channels of peaceful emulation and
competition). Eykhenbaum's contention is that Tolstoy was
much impressed by Prouhon's views and was inspired to write
a military epic for which he borrowed the title from Proudhon,
inflating what was at first conceived as a family novel into a
novel of epic proportions. To add weight to an argument seeking to link Tolstoy's name with Proudhon's, it is emphasized
that both writers wrote on many common themes, notably war,
the 'woman question', art and the gospels. There is more to
Eykhenbaum's case than this, but we do not expound it more
fully because we are convinced that it cannot be substantiated. It
is easy to see points of contact between the two men—their
hostility towards the State, their disbelief in the value of
political action, their belief in the need for an inner revolution,
a revolution within the minds and the hearts of men. But this
similarity in outlook and the fact that they wrote on some
common subjects (they were both prolific writers) has nothing
to do with the concrete question of the direct influence of
Proudhon's book on *War and Peace*. Nobody has yet succeeded
in showing precisely what this influence was. As for the title,
if it did come from this source—and in the absence of any
evidence either way it is a completely open question—that fact
in itself does not appear to have any significance for the novel.

The case for the influence of de Maistre on Tolstoy's views in
*War and Peace,* which Eykhenbaum also stated, is much more
plausible, and has been admirably put by Professor Berlin.[82] He
makes it quite clear that the positive beliefs of the Catholic
reactionary Savoyard diplomat were utterly alien to Tolstoy.
Yet at the same time he shows that de Maistre shared Tolstoy's
belief that those who think they control events, whether generals
or statesmen, are the greatest fools; that both men reacted
against 'the liberal, optimistic belief in human goodness, human
reason and the value and inevitability of material progress: both
deny that mankind can be made for ever happy and virtuous by
rational and scientific means'. Both men, he says were cynical,
sardonic, highly sceptical of the liberal reformers, pessimistic

[82] Isaiah Berlin, op. cit. pp. 48 ff.

about the fate of the western world. 'Both looked for a harmonious universe and found chaos, and offered to throw away the weapons of criticism in favour of the single great vision.' These parallels are interesting in their own right, and since they are available to English readers there is no need to enlarge on the argument here. Berlin says that 'the striking resemblance between their views can hardly be put down either to accident, or the mysterious operation of the *Zeitgeist*'. Perhaps future scholars will establish direct influence as well as resemblance. As yet, however, it does not seem to me that there is quite sufficient evidence for saying that some of the views Tolstoy expressed in *War and Peace* were derived from de Maistre, any *more* than for saying that Tolstoy found in de Maistre a like-minded man in some ways, and in his writings a welcome confirmation of ideas he held as a result of his reading, thinking and observation—particularly so in the case of his attitude to war and the conduct of battles, which stemmed directly from his own experience in the Crimean campaign.

The Russian 'Formalist' critics in the early years of the Soviet Union made much of the alleged influence on Tolstoy of his circle of Slavophile or near Slavophile friends of a conservative, medievalist outlook—Pogodin, Yur'ev, Samarin, Urusov. In particular Eykhenbaum mentions the work of the historian Pogodin.[83] He emphasizes Pogodin's preoccupation with problems of cause and effect, freedom and necessity. He draws attention to the comparisons he makes with phenomena from the world of physics, mechanics, mathematics. He mentions the correspondence going on between the two men in 1868 on problems of the philosophy of history. He notes Tolstoy's acknowledgement of Pogodin's *Historical Aphorisms* (1836) which he received in 1868. He states that Tolstoy's conversations with Pogodin and the reading of his book were one of the main sources and stimuli for his chapters on the philosophy of history. As an illustration he adds that Tolstoy's term 'the differential of history' was apparently borrowed from Pogodin, who speaks of history having its own logarithms, its own differentials. In the case of Urusov, the suggestion is made that Urusov's views and his book on the campaigns of 1812–13,[84]

[83] Eykhenbaum, op. cit. see Part 4 Chapter 3, pp. 329 ff.
[84] ibid. pp. 341 ff.

based on an attempt to discover the laws of war with the help
of mathematical analysis, had a great influence on Tolstoy. It
allegedly helped him considerably in the sections of *War and
Peace* which have to do with the theory of war. Urusov's defence
of Kutuzov against the lukewarmness or even hostility towards
him of many historical sources, may have influenced Tolstoy, it
is argued, in his positive attitude to the Russian Commander-
in-Chief. As with Pogodin so with Urusov the affinity is stressed
between certain of his images and similes and those of Tolstoy—
'all these parallelograms of forces, squares of distances, algebraic
equations, all this Urusovism'— as Eykhenbaum put it. Indeed
he quotes a letter of Turgenev of 1869 in which the novelist
says that he is looking forward to the final volume of *War and
Peace* and expresses the hope that Tolstoy will have 'got Urusov
out of his system a bit'[85]—which is roughly the meaning of the
verb *razurusit'sya* which he coins.

Eykhenbaum does a great service in drawing attention to
Tolstoy's friendship, correspondence and exchange of ideas with
these unconventional thinkers, with their roots, generally speaking, in the past. They were undoubtedly more sympathetic to
the novelist than the forward-looking believers in progress and
the perfectibility of State and society by social and political
means, the realists, nihilists, natural scientists and evolutionists
who were his contemporaries. But again is the case of direct influence proved? Tolstoy, it is true, consulted Pogodin for information about 1812 when he first began *War and Peace* in 1863.
But the book from which Eykhenbaum draws his examples,
Pogodin's *Historical Aphorisms,* was only lent on Pogodin's
suggestion in 1868 after much of *War and Peace* had already
been written and after the celebrated *A Few Words about War
and Peace,* with its defence of Tolstoy's views about historians
and about the role of so-called great men in history, had
appeared in print.[86] Pogodin sent it to Tolstoy because he
thought, from what he knew and had read of Tolstoy's ideas,
that his book would provide him with material to support them.
And Tolstoy in his reply said that he would read it and was

[85] Eykhenbaum, op. cit. see Part 4 Chapter 3, p. 342.
[86] For a discussion of Eykhenbaum's views on Pogodin's and Urosov's influence on Tolstoy, see A. Skaftymov, *Obraz Kutuzova i filosofiya istorii
v romane L. Tolstogo 'Voina i Mir',* *Russkaya Literatura,* 2, Leningrad,
1959, pp. 73–94.

sure that he would find confirmation of his views there. There is no suggestion that Tolstoy had previously read the work and borrowed from it, or that his ideas were not already substantially formed by 1868 when Pogodin's book arrived. Another interesting piece of evidence put forward by those who doubt Eykhenbaum's hypothesis is a letter Tolstoy wrote to his wife early in 1869, saying, 'my historical views very much surprised Yur'ev and Urusov and were highly thought of by them.'[87] Finally one further fact of importance is that Urusov's book on the campaigns of 1812–13, which came out in 1868, says in its introduction that the investigation is written in connexion with the publication of *War and Peace* and that Tolstoy's opinions 'about the causes of the war of 1812 and his views on military events inspired me with the idea of searching for historical laws, especially the laws of war, with the help of mathematical analysis.' Some of these views of Tolstoy are quoted in Urusov's work.

And yet the evidence against is not really any more telling than the evidence for, if we are looking for proof of the direct influence of one book on another. What is important is that all these men were friends, met, talked, wrote and exchanged ideas and all drew something out of a common pool. The question of priority is irrelevant and impossible to determine. From our point of view, concerned as we are with style, language and the direct use of sources, what matters is that some of Tolstoy's imagery in the later part of *War and Peace* is demonstrably similar to that of Pogodin and Urusov in particular, and that it is only logical to infer that Tolstoy borrowed and assimilated the mathematics and physics (as much from conversation no doubt as from books) and not vice-versa.

Another name which has been mentioned in recent critical literature[88] as a probable source for certain of Tolstoy's ideas in *War and Peace* is that of Alexander Herzen, whose memoirs (translated into English as *My Past and Thoughts*) were greatly admired by Tolstoy and whose emigré writings in general were closely followed by him in Russia. One interesting fact which emerges from a study of the relations between Tolstoy and

[87] Quoted by Skaftymov, op. cit. p. 80.
[88] See for example A. A. Saburov, *'Voina i Mir' L. N. Tolstogo, Problematika i Poetika*, Moscow, 1959, pp. 13 ff.

Herzen is that the first part of the latter's memoirs was published in Russia in 1856 and read by the former at the very
time when his Decembrist novel was, as he says in the draft
foreword referred to in Chapter I, first conceived. This early
part of *My Past and Thoughts* touches on Napoleon, the 1812
campaign and the fire of Moscow. On this evidence a recent
Soviet scholar has made the following conjecture (the words in
quotation marks are from Herzen):

From my *Past and Thoughts* Tolstoy could not help but have learned
that 'the stories of the fire of Moscow, the battle of Borodino, the
Berezina, the capture of Paris' were 'the Iliad and Odyssey' of his older
contemporaries; or that 'the half savage bearded people in sheepskin
coats' speaking a language completely unknown to their masters, showed
a profound humanity in the darkest days of the flight from Moscow;
in *My Past and Thoughts* Tolstoy met for the first time that disrespect-
ful characterization of Napoleon which ran so counter to the generally
accepted opinion and which soon found its echo in his own work. And
Tolstoy, like Herzen, saw the direct link between the events of 1812
and the Decembrist movement.[89]

Herzen's negative attitude to Napoleon was strongly expressed too in his article on Robert Owen, the fifth section of
which is devoted to the French general. Tolstoy knew and
admired this article. His views on Napoleon are in many ways
close to those of Herzen. In more general terms the conjectured
influence of Herzen's thinking on Tolstoy's ideas in *War and
Peace* centres on certain common beliefs in their philosophies
of history. The two men opposed the idea of a purpose in
history, a predetermined path or aim. They refused to accept
the inevitability of progress. They saw history as a multitude
of mutually interacting causes, not a process directed by the
wills of individual men and women. Needless to say, the revolutionary atheism of Herzen was completely alien to Tolstoy. But
in questions of suspected influence it is similarities, not dissimil-
arities, which attract attention.

It has been suggested that a more direct influence on the
argument of *War and Peace* than the views of Tolstoy's Slavophile friends or those of Herzen may have been Hegel's
*Philosophy of History*, and more especially, the Introduction.[90]
We know that Tolstoy read Hegel and crossed swords with him
in his novel. We know that both men wrote on similar subjects

[89] A. A. Saburov, *'Voina i Mir'* L. N. *Tolstogo, Problematika i Poetika*,
Moscow, 1959, p. 16.                    [90] See Skaftymov, op. cit.

—on the role, for example, of great men in history, their isolation and unhappiness, their uselessness once their object has
been achieved—although the moral attitude of the two writers
to the conduct of great men was diametrically opposed, Hegel
admiring the Alexanders, Caesars and Napoleons because he
believed that they embodied the best thoughts and the best
deeds of their time, and that their actions should not be condemned by lesser men ignorant of the purpose they were serv-
ing, even if they had to 'trample down an innocent flower' or
'crush to pieces an object in their path'; Tolstoy belittling
Napoleon among other things, for his complete failure to understand truth, beauty and goodness, and condemning him by
absolute moral standards. Both men wrote on freedom and
necessity, on man as simultaneously a conscious free agent and
an unconscious tool of Providence, history or some higher
principle. Both men played down individual freedom and
played up objective necessity in one form or another. Tolstoy
said of people who take part in war that they imagine that they
know what they are doing and that they are doing it for themselves, but that in reality they are the involuntary tools of
history, performing a task which is concealed from them,
although comprehensible to us. Hegel said that individuals and
nations which strive after their own ends are at the same time
instruments and tools of some higher and broader purpose,
about which they know nothing and whose aims they are unconsciously fulfilling.

Is the use of the word 'influence' admissible here? Tolstoy
told Pogodin in 1868 (probably quite rightly), that his ideas on
the boundaries between freedom and necessity and his views on
history were the fruits of his life's intellectual work. This does
not mean that they were the fruits of his own unaided efforts.
All writers are inevitably influenced by what they read, and
originality of thought does not mean freedom from outside
influences, but a new combination of ideas (which may have
been expressed before by different people at different times) so
that in their new relationship these ideas express a new meaning. Tolstoy clearly found inspiration in de Maistre, Hegel,
Rousseau, Proudhon even, as he found inspiration of a different
sort in, say, Stendhal, Dickens, Thackeray and Sterne. There is
no doubt that he was swayed this way and that by everything

he read; that he seized avidly at any confirmation of his ideas in other people's work and even borrowed their examples. Many of the negative sides of his work, his criticims, prejudices, intolerance, are shared by one or other of the men he read and admired (admired, that is, for the force of their destructive criticism, not for their positive philosophies). His central negative thesis that individuals cannot consciously and rationally understand and guide the course of events was hardly an original thesis when Tolstoy expounded it. But his central positive thesis that the 'great' men are not those who think they are guiding the course of events, but men like the simple, intuitively wise Kutuzov who passively surrenders when he knows he is powerless to control; that the national 'heroes' are not the generals and statesmen but the numerous unobtrusive individuals, noblemen or peasants, Rostovs, Tushins or Karataevs, who by their simplicity, their absence of affectation and hypocrisy, and their innate natural goodness are true representatives of the Russian nation; and that the process of understanding history begins not with the exposition of 'great' men's deeds, but with the integration of an infinitely large number of infinitely small human actions—this thesis is Tolstoy's original contribution to the novel. The apotheosis of Kutuzov, the demonstration of the workings of the unconscious spirit of the nation and the attempted integration of the differentials of history are the unique fruits of Tolstoy's own thought and art —even if, as seems likely, the term 'differentials of history' was itself the product of another mind.

# III: IDEA AND GENRE

THE title of this chapter embraces two closely connected subjects—the idea or complex of ideas which Tolstoy wished to express and actually did express on paper, and the literary medium through which he chose to express them. What is the basic idea of *War and Peace*, and is the novel in fact an epic novel, as it has so often been called? It is likely that these two questions will always remain controversial, and open to widely differing interpretations. It is possible, however, to indicate the area of disagreement and to point to solutions which seem most plausible.

In the first chapter of this book the pre-history of *War and Peace* was sketched in, and with it Tolstoy's professed reasons for abandoning *The Decembrists*. We know how his interest in a Decembrist hero led on to a desire to write about the class from which the Decembrists came—the gentry—and the part it played in the national life of the times. The roots of the Decembrist rising lay in the Napoleonic wars; and it is a fair assumption that the story of 1812, the part played in it by the gentry and the causes of the tremendous upsurge of national feeling which swept through the whole of Russia offered Tolstoy far greater scope than the restricted theme of an abortive conspiracy.

Tolstoy was a lover of history. His interest in the subject centred in particular on the history of his own country. His reading had taught him that at certain periods of time, at moments of great danger to a country, a spirit of national unity transcending selfish interests is born, and that such a spirit was alive as never before in Russia in 1812. The more he read, the more he became convinced that the history of such periods cannot be confined to a catalogue of the conscious deeds of a few so-called great men, but is nothing short of the totality of unobtrusive and largely unconscious actions of the people as a whole.

Tolstoy was also an aristocrat. He was proud of his aristocratic lineage and conscious of the duties of his class, for all his awareness that in Russia class privileges had heavily outweighed class obligations. He was intensely patriotic, and his attachment to Russia and the Russians, for all their faults and failings, was accompanied by a certain antipathy towards foreign countries which his brief travels in Europe did nothing to dispel. He had also been a soldier, and cherished an involuntary respect for bravery and heroic deeds in battle which his later pacifism never quite eradicated. All these personal characteristics no doubt helped to induce Tolstoy to choose for his first novel a theme which was woven together from aristocratic, patriotic and heroic threads, and which would have for its climax the year 1812, the year of Russia's greatest national triumph.

It is not difficult to speculate on the reasons which steered Tolstoy in the direction of 1812 and of *War and Peace*. To the ones already mentioned could be added the desire to provide a broad national base for his novel which the conspiracy of the Decembrists could not have given. There are also some grounds, partly connected with the unpublished drafts and forewords, for believing that the novel might have been conceived as a sort of apologia for Tolstoy's own class, the gentry, and a defence against the criticisms being levelled by the 'new men' of the 1860's, whose radical, revolutionary and nihilistic sentiments were profoundly distasteful to Tolstoy. All these, and doubtless other factors must have weighed with Tolstoy as he moved back from 1856 to 1805, and forward again to 1812, and it would be wrong to single out any one of them and give it priority over the rest.

If it is not easy to be dogmatic about the exact reasons for Tolstoy's choice of his subject, it should be less difficult, given the finished work as we have it, to interpret the ideas which the author did in fact express in it, as distinct from the complex of motives which led to its being written. And yet it is precisely over the interpretation of the *idea* of *War and Peace* that critical opinion is so sharply divided.

There is a marked tendency among Soviet critics to interpret *War and Peace* very largely in terms of class and country. They see it on the one hand as showing the cleavage between the people (*narod*) and the aristocracy (*znat'*), and the moral superiority of the former over the latter. On the other hand they regard it as an expression of patriotic pride in the glorious achievements of the Russian nation and its moral superiority over the French invaders and the pro-French elements within its midst. Some typical generalizations from the most recent and exhaustive monograph on *War and Peace* will illustrate these views:

> The material procured for a novel about the Decembrists became at one of the later stages of the work organically woven into the fabric of the basic ideology of Tolstoy's writings as it had taken shape already in the 1850's: the aristocracy [*znat'*] and the people [*narod*] as the negative and positive poles of life and 'the best people from the gentry' moving from one pole to the other: and correspondingly, two moral-psychological planes of representation——a sphere of falsehood and a sphere of truth: the sphere of falsehood in the life and consciousness of the aristocracy, the sphere of truth in the life and consciousness of the simple people.

Again the same author writes, apropos of the idea of *War and Peace*:

> The treatment of the people [*narod*] leads in the course of its develop-ment to the apotheosis of popular [*narodny*] heroism and patriotism. A high appraisal of the role of the people in the historical process culminates in the posing and the negative solution of the problem of the role of personality in history. The problem of the role of personality in history and its solution grow into the problem of historical necessity and freedom of the will. At the same time the negative solution of the problem of the role of personality in history is a modification of the problem of the role and importance of those who place themselves above the people. The denunciation of Napoleon, Bennigsen and Rostopchin continues the denunciation of the Kuragin circle—Prince Vasily, Boris Drubetskoy and others. The links in the system of ideas are interlocked in many various and complex chains. Such is the basic system of ideas of *War and Peace*.[1]

Elsewhere he says that 'the basic idea of *War and Peace* is the affirmation that the people [*narod*] are the hero of a valiant feat of arms, and that this feat of arms is a great triumphant act of the people';[2] that 'this noble feat of arms of the Russian people [i.e. 1812], as a manifestation of the national [*natsional'ny*] character, is the basic and central theme of *War and Peace*';[3] and that the people are the collective hero of the novel.

> The people are the main hero of *War and Peace* not only because in the decisive episodes of the narrative representatives of the people, simple soldiers, partisans and militiamen are the main, decisive factor

[1] Saburov, op. cit. p. 243.          [2] ibid. p. 253.          [3] ibid. p. 37.

of victory. Perhaps of no less importance is the fact that the people are the central link of the work—the point of attraction for all the positive heroes whose fortunes develop in close association with the basic theme, the theme of the people . . . The positive heroes of *War and Peace* take the path of divorce from their own milieu and rapprochement with the people.[4]

The assumption underlying most modern Soviet interpretations of the ideas which Tolstoy is said to be expressing in his novel (leaving aside the theoretical digressions on war and the philosophy of history), can be stated briefly in general terms. Very simply it is this that the more the gentry subscribe to the simple, natural, 'popular' (*narodny*) way of life of the Russian nation, the more they narrow the gap between themselves and the *narod*, and the more they renounce the emptiness of society life for the full domestic round of work and family responsibilities —the more comprehensible to themselves and the more satisfying their lives become. It is part of this design that Pierre's spiritual transformation should be brought about by the peasant Karataev; that Prince Andrei should be a different and better man in the company of the allegedly simple 'Russian' Pierre or of the 'popular' captain Tushin than in the salons of St. Petersburg; that Natasha and Nikolai should both have the national love of song and dance and the ability to feel at home with 'uncle'; that Natasha and Pierre, Nikolai and Princess Marya, should find salvation in family life and in the country, the epitome for Tolstoy of all that is simple, 'popular' and good; that not only the untypical Karataev but numerous representatives of the common people should be treated with warmth and sympathy and should constitute a necessary and beneficial part of the lives of the gentry. It is part of the design also that many of the main heroes should be shown to advantage in the close company of the common people—Pierre and Karataev, Princess Marya and her 'God's folk', Nikolai and Lavrushka, Prince Bolkonsky and Tikhon. Finally it is Tolstoy's achievement to have equated what is 'popular' with what is Russian, and what is Russian with what is good; and conversely to have equated 'antipopular', foreign and bad.[5] The French are the invaders. They are alien. The Russians are their innocent victims. They are 'our people', nobly and successfully defending their mother-

---

[4] Saburov, op. cit. p. 52.
[5] See especially Ya Bilinkis, *O Tvorchestve L. N. Tolstogo*, Leningrad, 1959.

land against the nineteenth-century equivalent of the fascist aggressors. Kutuzov is simple, wise, 'Russian'—and successful. Napoleon is arrogant, stupid, 'French'—and unsuccessful.

The victory of the Russian army over the French culminates in the moral triumph of the Russian man; he is victorious not only by force of arms, but also by virtue of his moral superiority.[6] Similarly the Russian aristocracy is divided between the 'positive heroes', who, whatever their external façade, are at heart as Russian as Pushkin's Tatyana, and the 'negative' characters, the victims of Tolstoy's ironical denunciation—the Kuragins, Drubetskoys, and their ilk—who by their sophisticated way of life, their French speech, and their Frenchified salons belong unambiguously to the other camp.

These generalizations are the impressions formed from reading many Soviet works of criticism.[7] Presented as they are in this condensed and simplified form they have perhaps inevitably become a little distorted. Nevertheless it is no exaggeration to say that it is the opposition of aristocracy and people, of the two camps of Russians and non-Russians (actual and metaphorical) which is felt to be the main idea which Tolstoy succeeded in expressing in his novel, while extolling at the same time the heroism of the Russian nation and the glories of 1812.

This interpretation contains a mixture of truth and untruth, some factual errors and some errors of emphasis. The basic concept of the aristocracy as a negative, and the common people as a positive pole cannot be substantiated. The aristocracy as a class are not painted black. Some of its members are good people, others are bad, while others again have good and bad qualities equitably shared. Nor is it true to say that the 'positive' members of the aristocracy—Prince Andrei, Pierre, Princess Marya, Natasha—become better in proportion as their lives bring them into closer contact with the people. Prince Andrei's journey is not to the people through the people. He is made to see the folly of military and worldly success not just through his encounter with Captain Tushin, but through his experiences

6 See especially Saburov, op. cit.
7 Among recent Soviet works consulted were Bilinkis, op. cit.; S. P. Bychkov, L. N. Tolstoy, Moscow, 1954; Tvorchestvo L. N. Tolstogo, ed. M. B. Khrapchenko et. al., Moscow, 1954; Tvorchestvo L. N. Tolstogo, ed. D. D. Blagoi et. al., Leningrad, 1959; and 'Voina i Mir' L. N. Tolstogo. Sbornik statei, Gorky, 1959.

of the horrors of war and the uncertainties of love. His fluctuating moods and changing assessments of what is important and what is not, derive from his mature observations of war and the happiness, disappointment and renewed happiness of his association with Natasha—rational and emotional factors which have nothing to do with considerations of class. Similarly Pierre never becomes identified with the *narod*. There is nothing simple or traditionally Russian about his way of life. The peasant Karataev exerts a positive influence on him; but so too does Natasha, who, for all her love of national songs, games and dances, is hardly one of the common people.

The Russian-French polarity is also a false one. Pierre is not anti-French. He was educated in France, speaks French as well as, if not better than Russian and never talks disparagingly of French culture and civilization. He is even given a French name. He hates Napoleon, not because he is French, but because he is a fool and a *poseur*. He dislikes the salons of St. Petersburg and Moscow, not because of their imitation of French manners and their veneration for things foreign, but because of their artificiality and veneer. The use of French by native Russians is unnatural and unnecessary, and an obvious target for Tolstoy's satire. But this does not mean that the French language in itself is unnatural and artificial. The Rostov family, warmly and sympathetically presented as typically Russian gentry, are not anti-French, although they are all intensely patriotic in time of war. Prince Andrei is steeped in French culture, as any well educated man of his time was bound to be.

Tolstoy's attitude to the French in *War and Peace* (Napoleon and French militarism excepted) is friendly rather than hostile. He is ironical at the expense of the declamatory, rhetorical, complacent Frenchmen of whom Ramballe is an example, but he appreciates their cheerfulness and bravery. Ramballe is a naively vain and limited man, but he is not at all repugnant. 'They are also human beings', says a Russian soldier, looking at the French prisoner Morel.[8] Even Davoût spares Pierre's life, once human contact has been established between them; and it is the Russian Dolokhov, not a Frenchman, who is responsible after the death of Petya Rostov for the most brutal massacre assumed to have taken place in the novel.

[8] *War and Peace*, IV. 4. 9.

What strikes one in reading *War and Peace* is Tolstoy's deep dislike, not of the French, but of the Germans. Phull, Weyrother, Berg—every German in the book is marked by a conbination of pedantry, stolidity and spiritual coarseness. When Natasha is protesting against her mother's orders not to make room for the wounded on the Rostov carts, she says: 'This is so beastly, so disgusting, so . . . I don't know what. Are we Germans or something?'[9] In a similar tone of disgust, the old Prince Bolkonsky alludes to the Germans as soldiers:

> Bonaparte was born with a silver spoon in his mouth. He has splendid soldiers. And then the first people he attacked were the Germans. Only laggards have failed to beat the Germans. Ever since the world began, everybody has beaten the Germans. But they never beat anybody. Only one another. He made his reputation fighting them.[10]

It is an interesting fact that this quotation stopped at the end of the second sentence in the *Russian Messenger* version of *1805* and in the 1868 edition of *War and Peace*.[11] The rest of the paragraph was added later by Tolstoy, presumably with the Prusso-Austrian War of 1866 in mind. After the battle of Königgrätz there must have been Russians who wondered whether the Prussia of Bismarck and Moltke had become, or was about to become, a great military power. In making this late addition, Tolstoy is presumably scoffing (mistakenly) at this idea. In short, his anti-German sentiments in *War and Peace* are much stronger than his antipathy towards certain French shortcomings and foibles.

It is wrong, too, to regard St. Petersburg high society in general and the Kuragins in particular—vulgar, unprincipled and unprepossessing as they are—as the incarnation of all that is *anti-popular* and *un-Russian*. Anatole Kuragin, blackguard though he may be, is just as much a Russian as Pierre. He dies fighting for his country with just as much or just as little patriotism as the average private soldier. Hélène does not cease to be Russian because she is vain and debauched, and is never seen in the company of the lower classes.

Much of the difficulty of accepting current Soviet interpretations of *War and Peace* as the apotheosis of the *narod* is connected with the imprecise meaning and imprecise use of this

9 ibid. III. 3. 16.          10 ibid. I. 1. 24.
11 Professor D. P. Costello first drew my attention to this fact.

Russian word. Tolstoy's wife used a word from the same root as *narod* when she asserted that 'the idea of the people' had been dear to her husband in *War and Peace,* just as 'the idea of the family' was dear to him in *Anna Karenina.*[12] How are we to interpret this claim? If we equate *narod* with the peasantry, the overwhelming majority of Russia's nineteenth-century population, we can say with some certainty what Tolstoy's attitude towards them was when he *began* to write his novel. His school experiment at Yasnaya Polyana had ended in disillusion. He had devoted himself to the education of his peasants, lived among them, done all he could to help them. But he had not succeeded. In a letter of 1863, the year after he gave up teaching, he said: 'I must confess that my view of life, the people [*narod*] and society is now quite different from what it was when we last met. One can be sorry for them [sc. the people], but it is hard to understand how I could have loved them so much.'[13] It was no doubt this reaction which led him to write the words quoted in our first chapter, that the lives of civil servants, merchants, theological students and peasants were uninteresting and only half intelligible to him. The same sentiment is expressed in one of the draft versions, in which Tolstoy interrupts the narrative of the early chapters of Volume I to say:

Up to now I have been writing only about princes, counts, ministers, senators and their children, and I am afraid that there will be no other people in my story later on either.

Perhaps this is not a good thing and the public may not like it: perhaps a story of peasants, merchants and theological students would be more interesting and instructive for them; but for all my desire to have as many readers as possible, I cannot satisfy this taste for many reasons. In the first place because the historical monuments of the time I am writing about have survived only in the correspondence and memoirs of people of the highest circle—literate people; the interesting and clever stories which I have managed to hear, I also heard only from people of that circle. In the second place because the lives of merchants, coachmen, theological students, convicts and peasants seem to me boring and monotonous, and all the actions of these people seem to me to stem, for the most part, from one and the same motives: envy of the more fortunate orders, self-interest and the material passions. If all the actions of these people do not in fact stem from these motives, their actions are

[12] *Dnevniki S. A. Tolstoi 1860–1891*, Moscow, 1928, p. 37.
[13] Letter to A. A. Tolstoi 17 ... 31 October, 1863, J.E. LXI. 23.

so obscured by these impulses that it is difficult to understand them and therefore to describe them.

In the third place because the lives of these people (the lower orders) bear less of the imprint of the time.

In the fourth place because the lives of these people are ugly.

In the fifth place because I cannot understand what a policeman thinks as he stands by his box, or what a shopkeeper thinks and feels as he invites people to buy braces and ties, or what a theological student thinks when he is being taken to be flogged for the hundredth time etc. I cannot understand this any more than I can understand what a cow thinks when it is being milked or what a horse thinks when it is carrying a barrel.

Finally, in the sixth place (and this, I know, is the best reason) because I myself belong to the highest order of society and like it.

I am not a bourgeois [*meshchanin*], as Pushkin boldly said, and I say boldly that I am an aristocrat by birth, by habits and by position. I am an aristocrat because I am not only not ashamed, but positively glad to remember my ancestors—fathers, grandfathers, and great grandfathers. I am an aristocrat because I was brought up from childhood in love and respect for the highest orders of society and in love for the refined as expressed not only in Homer, Bach and Raphael but also in all the small things of life. I am an aristocrat because I was sufficiently fortunate that neither I, nor my father, nor my grandfather knew want or the struggle between conscience and want, nor had any necessity ever to envy anyone or sue for favours, nor knew the need to be educated for money or a position in society and so on—ordeals to which people in want are subjected. I see that this was a great fortune and I thank God for it, but if this fortune does not belong to everybody, I do not see any reason to renounce it or not to take advantage of it.

I am an aristocrat because I cannot believe in the high intellect, the refined taste or the absolute honesty of a man who picks his nose and whose soul converses with God.[14]

It would obviously be unfair in the light of other evidence to argue that this confession, which never reached the pages of *War and Peace*, settles the argument, and that Tolstoy was congenitally incapable of understanding, liking or writing about the common people. He could and did write with sympathy and humanity about the peasantry (his story *Polikushka* was published in the same year as *War and Peace* was begun), and he introduced into his novel men and women from the lowest orders of society—peasants who fought in the army, peasants who worked in the fields, peasants who waited on their masters in the great houses and estates of the gentry. But however sympathetic the representatives of the common people may

[14] J.E. XIII. 238.

seem in their brief appearances in *War and Peace*, they do not constitute the focal point of the novel, and it is a patent distortion of emphasis to group them together under the heading *narod* and to oppose them unambiguously to the aristocracy as the collective hero of *War and Peace*.

The word *narod*, however, can be understood in a much wider sense than 'the common people'. It can in fact be translated as 'nation'. Much of the implausibility of some Soviet interpretations of *War and Peace* would be removed if it were always made clear in what sense the word was being used. One can argue with conviction that Tolstoy's interest in 'the people' was not centred narrowly on the *muzhik*, whether as an object of affection or of dislike. It broadened out during the years of writing *War and Peace* until it reached the point where 'the people' came to be identified with 'the nation'—with all the men and women who consciously or unconsciously manifested the *spirit* of the Russian people, all the soldiers, conscripts and partisans, who embodied the *spirit* of the Russian army. One can argue convincingly that on Tolstoy's evidence in his novel selfish interests predominated in peace-time Russia, class divisions were pronounced, anti-national sentiments prevailed: but that under the impetus of an enemy invasion and a defensive war for the motherland, the discordant elements drew together, and a greater national unity was achieved than ever before. The gulf between the 'two nations', the gentry and the peasantry, and between the patriotic and unpatriotic elements of the gentry was greatly narrowed. The national heroism of 1812 was a truly *popular* phenomenon, popular in the widest and best sense of embracing all people, masters and men. Those leaders who instinctively understood the national spirit, allowed themselves to be led by it. Those who believed that they alone guided events came to grief.

This is a plausible point of view. But it is not, I think, the central idea of *War and Peace*. Goldenweiser quotes Tolstoy as saying:

> The most important thing in a work of art is that it should have a kind of focus—i.e. some place where all the rays meet or from which they issue. And this focus should not be capable of being completely explained in words. This, indeed, is the important thing about a good work of art, that its basic content can in its entirety be expressed only by itself.[15]

15 Goldenweiser. op. cit. p. 68.

It is not easy to express in words the focal point of Tolstoy's novel. Broadly speaking it is the contrast between two opposite states: on the one hand selfishness, self-indulgence, self-import-ance, and the attendant evils of careerism, nepotism, vanity, affectation and the pursuit of purely private pleasures; on the other hand a turning outwards from the self, a groping towards something bigger, an endeavour to surmount individualism, a recognition that the cult of the self is an unworthy alternative to the service of one's neighbours, one's family, the community and the country at large. Most people, Tolstoy appears to be saying, are preoccupied most of the time with their own selfish cares. Some are incorrigible careerists like Boris Drubetskoy or Napoleon, place-seekers and intriguers. Some such as Hélène or Anatole Kuragin think only of their own pleasure and are not restrained by any scruples of conscience from gratifying it. They are superb animals—handsome, graceful, lithe—with the senses and the appetite of an animal, and a total lack of consideration for human beings. What is more, they are not at all disturbed by their selfishness and would no doubt be offended if it were suggested that they were anything but normal, decent people—not saints certainly, but no worse than their neighbours. To this category of people belong the statesmen and military leaders who believe that their work is important and devoted to the public cause, but who are really only implementing their selfish desires for fame, power and decorations.

Others again such as Natasha and Nikolai Rostov are fond of themselves and of the normal round of upper class entertain-ment, the accepted and unquestioned way of life of the gentry. They are not troubled by profound thoughts; they are not moved to ask themselves difficult questions about the purpose of life in general or their own lives in particular. But although they may be a little vain, a little too complacent at times, they unquestionably create a favourable impression on the reader by virtue among other things of their simple, forthright characters, their ability to share in the universal pleasures and obligations of everyday life and their freedom from hypocrisy and intrigue.

Prince Andrei and Pierre are also endowed with their fair share of self-centredness and love of pleasure. But if they think about themselves a great deal, they are most emphatically not self-satisfied. Prince Andrei's early acceptance of the virtues of

social success, fame and military glory does not stand the test
of time and he is brought to see the folly of his cherished ideals.
Pierre is beset with doubts and torments, endlessly searching for
a way of life which will have some purpose beyond the mere
satisfaction of his instincts and desires. They are both seekers,
spiritually restless, changing and evolving, not content to accept
for long what is generally accepted. In a much smaller way, the
sympathetic Captain Tushin is also a man of independent mind,
a non-conformist, a 'Tolstoyan' character. It is not *necessary* to
to be a seeker in order to earn Tolstoy's commendation; but all
seekers are commended by him.

If the focal point of *War and Peace* is the problem of the
sublimation of the self, this problem is capable of being answered
in the way in which Tolstoy was himself trying to answer it as
he wrote his novel, and in which Pierre and Natasha, and
Nikolai and Princess Marya answer it in the closing chapters
of their story. The solution to the problem is the sober acceptance of family responsibility at the sacrifice to some extent of
the uninhibited individual personality, work which brings its
own reward, and the pursuit of simple pleasures accessible to
all; the recognition that it is right and natural that the sparkling,
vivacious Natasha should become a somewhat staid and lustre-
less mother of children, and that her husband and her brother
and her brother's wife should arrive at a happy state of active
and fruitful domesticity. Tolstoy has an unfortunate tendency
from time to time to call the virtues he admires specifically
Russian: he writes, for example, with reference to Pierre that
he felt a 'vague, exclusively Russian feeling of contempt for
everything conventional and artificial';[16] and he tells how the
diplomat Bilibin described a certain campaign with 'a fearless
self-censure and self-derision genuinely Russian'.[17] But since he
himself provides many examples of Russians who *are* conventional, artificial and egotistical, one must take these passing
observations of his with a grain of salt.

Tolstoy's treatment of the historical characters in *War and
Peace* illustrates the same general thesis of the superiority of
service to the group (in this case the country, not the family)
over the purely selfish cultivation of the individual personality.
This thesis is, however, expressed in the historically dubious

[16] *War and Peace*, III. 3. 27.          [17] ibid. II 2. 9.

form of a contrast between a general who passively submits to events in the knowledge that they are too big and too important for him to control, and an emperor who believes that he is clever enough and powerful enough to impose his personality on the course of history. If we examine the role assigned in *War and Peace to* Kutuzov and Napoleon against the historical evidence, as far as it can accurately be determined, it will not be difficult to show that Tolstoy's contrast between the simple, unaffected, wise, unselfish, 'popular' Russian general and the effeminate, arrogant, stupid French *poseur*—between the man who knows that he cannot lead and the man who thinks he is leading—lacks historical confirmation. Kutuzov is stripped in the novel of his more unprepossessing characteristics (some of which appear in the drafts but not in the final version) and his lechery and sloth are played down. Conversely, some of his well-authenticated positive qualities of generalship—his initiative and his conscious acts of leadership—are ignored. It has been convincingly argued[18] that, despite what Tolstoy said, Kutuzov deliberately chose the site for the battle of Borodino and that it was a good site; that Kutuzov's conduct in the Turkish war proved him to be an attacking general; that in the 1812 campaign he took strong measures on the left and right flanks at Borodino which Tolstoy chooses to ignore; that Uvarov's action at Borodino, which was taken on Kutuzov's orders, checked Napoleon and prevented him from bringing up reserves; that the position taken up by the Russians at Tarutino was deliberately chosen by Kutuzov; that the flank march on to the Kaluga road can be ascribed to the deliberate tactics of Kutuzov, as supported by his letters.

On the other hand, it is contended, Tolstoy turned a blind eye to Kutuzov's blunders. He failed to mention that Kutuzov forgot about 300 cannon he had at Borodino, and by failing to bring them into action caused the inequality between French and Russian casualties to be greater than it need have been.

In the attempt to present Kutuzov as a man of fixed and consistent views on the conduct of the war against Napoleon in 1812, Tolstoy even went so far as to remove a passage from the published version of the novel which suggested the contrary.

[18] See *inter alia*, V. Shklovsky *M. I. Kutuzov i Platon Karataev v romane 'Voina i Mir'*, Znamya, No. 5, 1948, pp. 137–45.

In the 1873 edition he struck out the words that before the council of war at Fili 'Kutuzov could not understand that it was possible to retreat beyond Moscow without a battle'.[19]

All this points clearly to the distortion or selective use of historical facts. But Tolstoy could argue that the official histories he used were also distorted—more so perhaps than his own version of events. He could argue that by emphasizing Kutuzov's services to his country he was correcting the impression given by the official historians and memoirists who for the most part discredited and even ridiculed him. Fortunately in order to appreciate *War and Peace* we do not have to depend on the historical accuracy of Tolstoy's alleged facts, some of which are demonstrably untrue, or the historical plausibility of his interpretations, some of which are at least as probable as those offered by professional historians. What matters is that the underlying artistic idea should be consistently and convincingly expressed. In the context of art, an artistic truth may be more valid than an historical truth. In order to sustain Tolstoy's thesis in *War and Peace* Kutuzov is given a definite part to play. Does he play it consistently, or is his role self-contradictory?

There is no doubt that the symbolically passive Kutuzov *acts* in *War and Peace*. He rescues his army from danger. He takes important decisions. He refuses to defend Vienna. He chooses between different courses (to retreat, not to make a stand at Krems). He *guides* the spirit of the army as far as he is able. And in this there is nothing incompatible with Tolstoy's central idea. The point is that he knows instinctively when events are beyond his control and he must submit. His impassivity on really important occasions is a logical, and consistent policy which in the event showed responsibility and wisdom. Whether in fact the real Kutuzov was such a wise and consistent man is beside the point. He is shown throughout as a man who is guided by events which he knows are too big for him and not as one seeking, like Napoleon, to impose his will upon them. Within the context of the novel his behaviour is entirely compatible with the purpose which the author wishes to make him serve.

A more serious charge against the inner consistency of *War and Peace* is that the truth which Tolstoy allegedly demonstrates

[19] Quoted by Bilinkis, op. cit. p. 242.

in the case of Kutuzov is not applicable in the case of the other great Russian general, Bagration. Bagration's role at Schöngraben, it is sometimes stated, is that of a general under whose command the battle is won, not by giving in to the situation and allowing it to retrieve itself in due course, but by personally dictating it. But is it a fact that the battle, as Tolstoy describes it, was won *because* Bagration was in command of it and *because* all the stages of it went according to his preconceived plan? Quite clearly not. It is the confusion, the disregard or ignorance of orders, the isolated and unpredictable acts of initiative and heroism on the part of obscure soldiers which remain in our minds from Tolstoy's description of the scene. There was always room in Tolstoy's philosophy for the personal initiative of little men, men who did not pretend that they foresaw or planned out the course of history, men like Captain Tushin at Schöngraben or Prince Andrei Bolkonsky at Austerlitz, whose spontaneous action in grasping a fallen standard and charging at the enemy turned a limited defeat into a limited victory in one corner of the field. Such actions are the individual manifestations of that mysterious spirit of the army which inspires groups and individuals within groups, but which is not created by the personality of any one great man, however much he may believe that he can influence the behaviour of the masses who obey him, or control the morale of his troops.

A further criticism levelled against Tolstoy's general thesis is that it cannot be squared with the positive and active role he assigns to the Russian partisans. Here again the criticism of inconsistency seems to be unfounded. The individual actions of small groups of brave Russian men played their part in the events of 1812. But they were not the *cause* of Napoleon's retreat from Moscow or the conscious agent of the destruction of his army, and Tolstoy does not make it appear that they were. In Tolstoy's philosophy the individual has freedom and control within a limited range of activity—whether in choosing to raise or not to raise his arm or in harassing and discomfiting an enemy. But in any activity which affects people other than himself he is only one of a very large number of factors which make up the totality of causes. In his description of the retreat and disintegration of the French army Tolstoy does not attribute the sole or main cause to the studied and deliberate tactics of the Russian partisans.

The *idea* of *War and Peace,* as well as being expressed through the fictional and the historical characters, is further developed in the philosophical discussions and the second epilogue. The key thesis of the limitation of man's conscious will in shaping history merely emphasizes in a different way Tolstoy's wish to deflate the importance of the self and to magnify the importance of other phenomena, irrational, intangible and incomprehensible, in comparison with which man must seem a puny creature and his display of self-importance a pathetic pose.

Whether or not this thesis is acceptable to the reader, it is neither absurd and contemptible as some critics have held it to be, nor inconsistent with the action of the novel. When Tolstoy has completed his work of demolition, man is left with a pitifully small field in which to exercise his free will. The fact that so many of Tolstoy's characters act with apparent freedom, exult in the spontaneous creative forces of life, choose their friends, their loves, their pleasures and their duties, act impulsively or accomplish deeds of heroism, does not in itself refute his theories. The life of these people can be rich, many-sided, apparently self-determined—without the conviction on their part that they are free agents life would be intolerable—and yet the consciousness of freedom which permeates it can still be an illusion. Men must have this consciousness to live, and through it they live more fully and more richly, but it is ultimately this very consciousness of freedom and not freedom itself which they enjoy. One does not have to agree with this belief to acknowledge that it is a legitimate inference to be drawn from the novel. Pierre's decision to marry Hélène is not a 'free' one; fate brings him and Natasha together; chance unites Princess Marya and Nikolai; Sonya is doomed to become an old maid. Nothing that the main characters do is inconsistent with their author's philosophy— although this does not mean that this philosophy is the correct one or the only one to explain the enigma of free will.

There is one other problem which is relevant to the subject of the idea or complex of ideas of *War and Peace*: the nature of war and the novelist's attitude towards it. Here again the concept of self enters into Tolstoy's judgement of the events of 1812. Napoleon is waging an aggressive war, a war of self-aggrandizement. The Russians display the utmost self-sacrifice in fighting to liberate their country from the aggressor. Here, surely, is a distinction between a 'just' and an 'unjust' war. And yet despite the very real admiration which Tolstoy shows for the altruism of the Russian people, their consideration for others, their readiness to sacrifice comfort, property and wealth in the interests of their country, one cannot agree with those critics who see *War and Peace* primarily as a hymn of praise to a great and glorious feat of arms. To Tolstoy no war—not even a 'just' defensive war—can be anything but a human tragedy. Prince Andrei's thoughts on the eve of Borodino on the indescribable horrors of war—its aim murder, its methods spying and treachery, its professional practitioners, the military class, ignorant, cruel, idle and debauched—are hardly the thoughts to grace a panegyric upon an epic victory. Nor is the behaviour of the Russian partisans, efficacious as it was and inspired by patriotic motives, an unqualified credit to the human race.

*War and Peace* is no more a patriotic tribute to 1812 than it is an encomium to the simple Russian people. It is a testimony of the way in which people live and behave. The greatness of the novel lies in its affirmation of life in all its bewildering variety. Some people are unselfish and idealistic: but they have their moments of frailty and fallibility. Others are selfish and nasty: but they are not condemned with that ruthlessness to which Tolstoy resorted a generation later. War is stupid and unpredictable: but people are brave and put on clean shirts to die.

Its greatness, too, lies in the fact that it has the power to convey the disturbing ambivalence of basic and apparently virtuous human instincts—love of life and personal courage. Why love life if the purpose of one's own life is not clear? Why value courage—even its highest expression in defence of one's native land—if it is manifested in such actions as the senseless slaughter of Borodino? These are questions which everyone sooner or later has to face. Tolstoy faces them and suggests his tentative answers—work, the family, responsibility 'to other people, the renunciation of physical violence—and with characteristic irony does so in the context of *le monde* and the field of battle. These tentative answers help to give the book a unity and focus. But since they are essentially prosaic, while the less worthy alternatives to them which the novel has to offer are glamorous, poetic and of an epic grandeur, *War and Peace* retains a balance and artistry markedly different from the overt didacticism and spiritual bullying of Tolstoy's last novel *Resurrection*.

## GENRE

Now that we have at last mentioned the words novel and epic in the same sentence, we can conveniently consider the question of the genre of *War and Peace*, and whether one or other of the conventional literary designations can be properly applied to it. As we have already seen, Tolstoy was most reluctant to call his work a novel. In 1865 he wrote to Katkov, the editor of the journal which was publishing the first instalments, and specifically asked him *'not to call the work a novel'*,[20] underlining the words for emphasis. Three years later he stated, somewhat unhelpfully, in his article in *The Russian Archives* that *War and Peace* 'is not a novel, even less is it a poem, and still less an historical chronicle. *War and Peace* is what the author wished and was able to express in the form in which it is expressed.' Many years later he said to Goldenweiser: 'I think that every great artist is bound also to create his own form. . . . Turgenev and I were once recalling all that was best in Russian literature and it proved to be the case that the form of all these works was completely original. Not to mention Pushkin, take Gogol's *Dead Souls*. What is it? Neither a novel nor a long short story. Something completely original. Then there is Turgenev's *Diary of a Sportsman*, the best thing he ever wrote, Dostoevsky's *House of the Dead*, my *Childhood*—sinner that I am—Herzen's *My Past and Thoughts* and Lermontov's *Hero of our Time*. . . .'[21] The same thought is expressed in the paragraph in Tolstoy's article just referred to: 'From Gogol's *Dead Souls* to Dostoevsky's *House of the Dead* there is not a single prose work rising at all above mediocrity in the recent period of Russian literature which quite fits in to the form of a novel, a poem or a story.'

Tolstoy denied that his work was a novel for the following reasons, which he put forward in the proposed introductions to *1805* which were never published:

[20] Letter to M. N. Katkov, 3 January 1865, J.E. LXI. 67.
[21] Goldenweiser, op. cit. p. 116.

In publishing one part of my work without a title and without a definition of the genre to which it belongs, that is in not calling it a poem, or a novel, or a long short story or a story, I consider it necessary to give a few words of explanation why this is so and why I cannot define what part of the whole is comprised by what is published here.

The proferred work most nearly approaches a novel or a long short story, but it is not a novel because I cannot and do not know how to set fixed limits to the characters I have invented, like marriage or death, after which the interest of the narrative would cease. I could not help realising that the death of one character only roused interest in others and that marriage was for the most part the start and not the finish of the plot's interest. Again, I cannot call my work a long short story because I simply cannot make my characters act merely with the object of providing or clarifying some idea or group of ideas.[22]

In another variant of the same introduction he qualifies what are substantially the same reasons with the words: 'We Russians generally speaking do not know how to write novels in the sense in which this genre is understood in Europe.'[23]

Although Tolstoy was concerned about the lack of an obvious climax to his work and the number of what might be called culminating points in it, the reasons he gives are hardly sufficient to disqualify it as a novel. It is impossible to define in the abstract what a novel *should* be like. One can only observe what *extended works of prose fiction* are like and have been like. And there is no doubt that *War and Peace* has many of the characteristic features of earlier European novels. It has its love stories, happily crowned by marriage. It has many standard situations of entertainment and adventure—a girl's first ball, an attempted abduction, a duel, a wager, a gambling scene, a hero believed dead but in fact alive, a heroine who attempts suicide in a moment of despair. It has to do with basic human emotions and conflicts—passion, jealousy, unrequited love, deep religious feeling, ambition, courage, thirst for adventure. It has its fair share of journeys, meetings and partings. Coincidences play an important part, as when Prince Andrei turns up in the Rostovs' yard in Moscow, Nikolai arrives at Bogucharovo in time to rescue Princess Marya, Natasha sees Pierre in deserted Moscow, Pierre is rescued among others by his enemy Dolokhov, or Prince Andrei and Anatole Kuragin, likewise the bitterest of foes, lie side by side in the operating tent after Borodino. This

[22] J.E. XIII. 55.          [23] ibid. 54. See Chapter I, p. 21.

is not to imply that *War and Peace* is like any novel in particular, but that it has enough recognizable thematic and other points of contact to establish it as belonging to that loose and ample genre called the novel.

What is perhaps not so obvious to the English reader is the extent to which earlier Russian literature has made its various contributions to *War and Peace*. Pushkin's 'novel in verse' *Eugene Onegin* is an outstanding example, and like many other Russian novelists Tolstoy drew inspiration for his themes from this rich source: the landowner's country estate and its simple, domestic pattern of life; rural recreations, hunting, guessing games, superstitions; devoted family retainers; a heroine, 'Russian at heart', familiar with the customs and traditions of popular Russian life; the round of high society, the ballroom, the salon, the tea-table; and finally the duel. Lermontov's *Hero of Our Time* may have provided, in the character of Pechorin, some of the features of the young Prince Andrei and of Dolokhov, as well as impressing and influencing Tolstoy by its extensive use of psychological introspection and interior monologue, and its ironical attitude to *poseurs*. Pierre has some traditional features of the 'superfluous man', out of harmony with his environment who, in one guise or another, made frequent appearances in the Russian literature of the first half of the nineteenth century. The main women characters fit into place in the portrait gallery of somewhat idealized Russian heroines created by Tolstoy's predecessors and older contemporaries. Princess Marya's deep sense of duty, unselfishness and profound religious feeling inevitably remind one of the similar characteristics of Turgenev's Lisa Kalitina. Above all, perhaps, one notices in *War and Peace* the humaneness, the philanthropic impulses, the moral earnestness and the feeling of antagonism towards hidebound social conventions which are to be found in much of the best Russian writing of the last century.

In reading *War and Peace* one is also aware of themes, aspects of characterization and the handling of situations which one is familiar with from the earlier writings of Tolstoy himself. The military side of the novel strongly recalls Tolstoy's early Caucasian stories and his Sevastopol sketches. The introduction to *The Raid* (first published in 1853 and suppressed, significantly

enough by the censors, and in which, incidentally, the germ of
Kutuzov has been seen in the character of Captain Khlopov)
already raises the question of war and courage in abstract terms,
the author declaring that he is more interested in the feelings
which impel one man to kill another than in the way in which
armies are drawn up on battlefields. Why *do* men kill each
other? Is courage always a virtue or are some people driven to
it by false motives? Can a horse which rushes down a steep
and dangerous slope be called brave, if it does so because it is
afraid of the whip? Can a man be called brave, if he exposes his
own life to kill another man out of vanity or the desire for glory?
Questions of this sort which are first adumbrated by Tolstoy in
*The Raid* become increasingly relevant to war on the scale on
which it is practised in his first novel.

The *Sevastopol Sketches* have a much closer connexion with
*War and Peace*. The first sketch is in many ways simply a conventional tribute to the spirit of the defenders of Sevastopol and
the strength of the Russian people, written after 'a bad attack
of patriotism'. But the second sketch has many more recognizable Tolstoyan characteristics. From having been a reporter,
Tolstoy elevates himself to the role of orator. The hero of his
story, he says, is truth, and truth is not at all lovely and not at
all reconcilable with the military communiqués of war corres-
pondents. The truth is that war is not what people think it is.
It is not as people describe it. Everything is unreal. Nobody
really knows what is happening or what will happen. In the
midst of superhuman bravery and endurance there is vanity,
hypocrisy and hankering after decorations. People are afraid in
battle and are then ashamed of it (e.g. Nikolai Rostov in his
first encounter with the enemy); they embellish their account
of battle with fictitious stories redounding to their own credit
(again one thinks of Nikolai). Death in battle is not a noble or
romantic thing. And the scene of the death of Praskukhin in
*Sevastopol in May* provides an early glimpse of the technique
which is seen in its maturity in those passages in *War and Peace*
where Prince Andrei is wounded: the emphasis on the contrast
between the simple, outward action of a few seconds and the
complex, inner life of those few seconds; the flood of reminiscences and questions; the ardent desire to go on living.

Turning to the domestic side of *War and Peace* we recognize

similarities of themes and treatment of themes between parts of
the novel and the earlier stories *Childhood* and *Family Happiness,* which in turn show marked traces of Tolstoy's own childhood and youth at Yasnaya Polyana. In *Childhood* one is made
aware of the conflict between that spontaneity of feelings and
the simultaneous urge to examine those feelings critically which
tormented Tolstoy and the great 'Tolstoyan' characters of his
novels. One is conscious of the cycle of love of self and hatred
of self which is repeated in *War and Peace* not only in the
person of Pierre. One even notices in the portrayal of character
the Tolstoyan preoccupation with physical idiosyncrasies. Some
years later *Family Happiness* elaborates the theme of selfish and
selfless love and seeks the ideal of family happiness not in the
satisfaction of personal desires but in the exercise of responsibility on the part of the parents towards the family as a unit,
the ideal attained by the two married couples at the end of
*War and Peace.* In *The Cossacks* Tolstoy attributes to his hero
Olenin the following words and thoughts which could belong
equally well to Pierre: ' "How must I live so as to be happy and
why was I not happy before?" And he remembered his previous
life and felt disgusted with himself. . . . And suddenly a new
light seemed to be revealed to him. "Happiness", he said to
himself, "consists in living for others. . . ." '

We shall have occasion in a later chapter to speak again of
the connexions between Tolstoy's early and mature styles of
writing. Here enough has been said to make the point that *War
and Peace* has close affinities both with earlier works of Russian
fiction and with Tolstoy's own youthful compositions—and in
the latter context, remembering the impact on Tolstoy's own
work of his life at home and in the army, we may quote the
opinion of Boris Eykhenbaum that the writing of *War and
Peace* was possible 'because its military background was the
Crimean campaign and its family background, life at Yasnaya
Polyana'.[24]

For all its affinities with other novels, *War and Peace* is a work
of such vast proportions and such heroic content that it is not
surprising to find the word 'epic' associated with it almost from
the very beginning, despite the author's assertion that his book

[24] B. M. Eykhenbaum, *Lev Tolstoy, Kniga Pervaya,* Leningrad-Moscow, 1928,
p. 151.

did not fit in to any recognizable genre. In a diary entry of the same year as the first drafts Tolstoy said that 'the epic manner is becoming the only natural one for me'.[25] There is a reference in one of the draft versions to the viscount at Anna Scherer's salon continuing his story about Napoleon and Mlle Georges 'in the epic manner'.[26] In Tolstoy's diary for 1865 there is a note about the poetry of the novelist being found 'in a picture of manners and customs based on an historical event: *The Odyssey, The Iliad, 1805*'.[27] Many years later Tolstoy told Gorky that 'without false modesty, *War and Peace* is like the *Iliad*'.[28]

How are we to understand 'epic' and Tolstoy's Homeric parallel? In a loose general sense the word was used, especially in the eighteenth and early nineteenth century, as a synonym for narrative—one spoke of a narrative or *epic* manner of telling a story. Byron used the word in *Don Juan* with the emphasis on length and therefore boredom:

> I feel this tediousness will never do,
> 'Tis being *too* epic.

To equate epic with an expansive narrative manner, however, is not the intention of those critics who use the word in the more precise sense of classical heroic poetry, and especially the Homeric poems. Some point to the lengthy and weighty 'Homeric' digressions in Tolstoy which are allegedly introduced to 'raise the tone'[29] and reflect on broad moral and philosophical issues. Others draw attention to his extended similes with their 'Homeric' comparisons. Others again dwell on the vast number of episodes in the novel, the predominance of battle scenes, the range of territory covered by the action, the variety of social groups depicted, the part allegedly played by the common people, the numerous scenes of traditional national life.[30] A useful summary of the features singled out by those who would call *War and Peace* an epic and link Tolstoy's name with Homer's may be provided by a quotation from the recent book by G. Steiner, *Tolstoy or Dostoevsky*: ' . . . the archaic and pastoral setting; the poetry of war and agriculture; the primacy

---

[25] 3 January 1863, J.E. XLVIII. 48.    [26] J.E. XIII. 216.
[27] 30 September 1865, J.E. XLVIII. 64.
[28] M. Gorky, *Reminiscences of Tolstoy, Chekhov and Andreev*, London, 1948, p. 57.
[29] e.g. Eykhenbaum.    [30] e.g. Saburov.

of the senses and of physical gesture; the luminous, all-reconciling background of the cycle of the year; the recognition that energy and aliveness are of themselves holy; the acceptance of a chain of being extending from brute matter to the stars and along which men have their apportioned places; deepest of all an essential sanity. . . .'[31] It is 'the affinity of temper and vision' between Tolstoy and Homer which Steiner, in my opinion rightly, emphasizes. The general similarities which he mentions, while interesting and for the most part valid, do not really get close enough to the essence of the Homeric epic as a genre and ignore vast and important areas where Tolstoy's subject matter, style and composition are utterly remote from Homer's. A rather different contribution to the question of the Homeric epic genre elements in *War and Peace* has been made by the Hungarian Marxist critic, G. Lukacs. Having defined his general approach by saying that '*War and Peace* is like an Iliad, the story of certain men, and an Aeneid, the story of a nation, compressed into one', he makes a serious attempt to give a precise meaning to the term epic and its use in the context of Tolstoy's novel. 'The description of Achilles' weapons', he says, following Lessing, 'is truly epic, not only because the poet describes their making and not their appearance, but also from the point of view of the composition as a whole, for it occurs exactly where these weapons of Achilles play a decisive part in the story, in the characterization and fate of the heroes. Thus these arms of Achilles are not objects independent of the characters in the story, but an integrating factor of the story itself.'[32] Inherent in the concept of epic (in the Homeric context) is the emphasis on making and doing, on the process and not the result. Inherent also is the recognition that each simple object is relevant to the story as a whole. Epic is defined not only by its heroic subject matter, but also by its mode of composition. With Tolstoy, Lukacs argues, every object necessary to make up a complete picture is present, and every object is directly related to the story as a whole. Every detail is an element of the plot. The placing of every detail is significant for the elaboration of character and plot—an example he gives is that of the Christmas visit of Nikolai, Sonya and Natasha by sleigh

[31] G. Steiner, *Tolstoy or Dostoevsky*, London, 1960, p. 74.
[32] G. Lukacs, *Studies in European Realism*, London, 1950, p. 152.

to Melyukova to dress up and play Christmas games; the costumes, make-up and other apparent incidentals are described in the greatest detail precisely because the episode as a whole represents a crisis in the lives of Nikolai and Sonya, when Nikolai resolves to marry his cousin despite all objections. What Lukacs says about the relevance and positioning of detail in *War and Peace* is convincing and revealing. At the same time it may be doubted whether it is the peculiar property of the classical heroic poems any more than of any well-ordered narrative prose tale.

An epic or heroic poem in the classical sense is essentially an adventure story told for entertainment, revolving round the superhuman deeds of men in battle. It normally abounds in speeches and descriptive detail, and is commonly written from a courtly point of view. It has supernatural elements in the form of gods, miracles and monsters. It lacks invective and didacticism. It is not concerned with the psychology of its heroes and shows little interest in their domestic relationships. Tolstoy himself had reservations about the value of the ancient heroic poems for a nineteenth-century author. As he said in *War and Peace*, the ancients 'have left us model heroic poems in which the heroes furnish the whole interest of the story, and we are still unable to accustom ourselves to the fact that for our age this sort of story is meaningless'.[33]

The comparison, then, of Tolstoy's novel with the *Iliad* in terms of genre is of dubious worth. Nevertheless it has more to recommend it than some Soviet attempts to find associations between the novel and Russia's own so-called heroic poem *The Lay of Igor's Host*, such astonishing statements as, for example, that 'the heroes of *War and Peace* are the direct descendants of the old Russian epic heroes', or such assertions that the image of 'drinking to the dregs the cup of death' in the name of country and freedom is common both to the ancient Russian epic and to *War and Peace*.[34] In the search for new things to say about Tolstoy's novel, the attempt has already been made to isolate features of it which recall the ancient Russian chronicles, and especially the *Primary Chronicle*. The late Boris Eykhenbaum wrote on this theme shortly before his death, and the gist of his thesis can be summarized in his own words:

[33] *War and Peace*, III. 2. 19.            [34] See Saburov, op. cit. pp. 350 ff.

In sum it transpires that there are inherent in *War and Peace* (especially in the second half, with the battle of Borodino as it centre) the same distinguishing features of thought, style and composition which are revealed in the *Primary Chronicle*: the construction of the work not on the plot basis usual in a novel, but on the temporal (annual) movement of events; the general fragmentariness of the narrative with frequent digressions of a philosophical character; the depiction of war as a 'terrible necessity'; the denial of the chain of cause and effect ('an event had to happen only because it had to happen', as is said at the beginning of the third volume of *War and Peace*); and side by side with this, the assertion of man's moral freedom and responsibility.[35]

Original as this juxtaposition may be, it is not convincing. One does not expect an historical chronicle to have a plot, and to liken *War and Peace* to the *Primary Chronicle* because they both lack a conventional plot and because they both narrate the events of successive years is not helpful. There is nothing to be gained by linking Tolstoy's famous philosophical digressions with the *Primary Chronicle* rather than with the *Iliad*. To say that both the novel and the chronicle depict war as 'a terrible necessity' does little more than confirm that Tolstoy was not unique in holding this view. When Eykhenbaum adduces a fairly close correspondence between the *bylina* of Danila Lovchanin and the character of Danila the hunter in *War and Peace*,[36] he is on firm ground and adding to the already extensive material on sources used or adapted by Tolstoy. For the rest, his tentative parallelisms are worth little.

To what genre, then, does *War and Peace* belong? The attempt to answer this question shows both the imprecise and utterly inadequate nature of literary classification and also the astonishing breadth of Tolstoy's book. *War and Peace* is a novel which has recognizable plot affinities with other Russian and Western European novels, an historical theme, an epic background of brave men and brave deeds, a family foreground in which the main characters are realistically portrayed and psychologically explored. And yet to call it an historical novel or an epic novel or a psychological novel or any other sort of novel is to obscure rather than to illuminate. Equally unsatisfactory is the argument that it transferred its allegiance, as it grew up,

[35] B. M. Eykhenbaum, *Cherty letopisnogo stilya v literature XIX veka*, in *Trudy otdela drevnerusskoi literatury*, XIV, Moscow-Leningrad, 1958, pp. 545–50.          [36] ibid p. 549 n.

from one genre to another. The theory that *War and Peace* began as 'a family novel in the English style' and ended as an epic novel on a national scale cannot be substantiated. From the very start there is evidence that Tolstoy's book was to be a story about certain fictitious and historical characters at the time of the Napoleonic Wars, whose lives and fates were to be affected by the movements of the armies of Alexander and Napoleon, uneasy rulers whose apparent greatness is to pale before the simple goodness of men and women who set the happiness of a quiet family life above social success and ego-centric pleasures. As for the non-domestic side of *War and Peace*, Napoleon, Austerlitz, Borodino, the fire of Moscow, the partisan warfare, the ironical attitude to official accounts of battles and kings, to historians, to so-called 'great men', to foreigners, to Russian high society—all these ingredients are alluded to in one form or another in the earliest plans and drafts of the novel and make nonsense of the suggestion that they—or some of them—were necessitated by a later elevation of genre.

In so far as *War and Peace* is a landmark in the history of the novel, it is not because it belongs to, or is the culminating point of this or that genre or because it is a hybrid of various genres. If there are any rules to which an author must conform if his work is to be assigned to a recognizable genre, Tolstoy did not know them and did not care. We can only say that *War and Peace* marks a new stage in the history of the Western European novel because of its concern with historical, social, ethical and religious problems on a scale never attempted in any previous novel. It has considerable psychological subtleties—but no more so than the novels of Stendhal. Turgenev or Jane Austen wrote more economically and with greater wit. Smollett, Fielding or Sterne had more humour, more entertainment value. Balzac had more historical colouring, more period detail. Emily Brontë had in my opinion greater depths of imagination. Many a second-rate author had extolled historical deeds of national heroism or created memorable characters. But in Tolstoy there was a unique combination of intelligence, imagination and seriousness of purpose; profundity of thought and profundity of emotion. His novel engages the mind and the heart, it brings into play the animal and rational sides of the reader. Its content is richer, fuller, and more varied than that of any other novel before it. It is in these attributes—and not in the qualities which do or do not make of it an epic novel or an historical novel or a family chronicle—that we must look for the greatness and originality of Tolstoy's achievement.

# IV: STRUCTURE AND COMPOSITION

IT is customary in England to criticize the lack of shape, architecture and design of many of the great Russian novels of the last century, and especially the novels of Tolstoy and Dostoevsky. Turgenev was the exception, and he was known and read in the West before either of his greater contemporaries. Henry James gave him his blessing, and if in those days one thought about the structure of the Russian novel one probably thought about the harmony, economy and aesthetically satisfying order of Turgenev's works. All the more astonishing therefore was the appearance on the Western scene of translations of the novels of Tolstoy and Dostoevsky. The same Henry James referred to them as 'fluid puddings' and as 'loose, baggy monsters'.[1] The great majority of critics in the West turned their attention exclusively to the exposition or interpretation of the ideas expressed in the novels, or the exploration of the biographies of their authors. One rarely spoke of form in their connexion. In recent years, however, there has been a rising interest in England and America in what is sometimes called the architecture of the novel, and at the same time it has become more widely realized that the standard translations of the Russian novelists badly misrepresent the style of the originals, to say nothing of their literal inaccuracies, omissions and painfully inept dialogue. It is particularly relevant, therefore, to find that a study of the drafts of Tolstoy's novels confirms the suspicion that problems of structure and composition were often in the forefront of his thoughts.

In perusing Tolstoy's vast correspondence one sometimes meets in a literary context such words as *svyazi* ('links', 'ties') and *stsepleniya* ('couplings', 'connexions') which give a clue to the way in which he thought about the composition of his own novels. Writing to Strakhov, for example, in 1876, he said:

In almost everything I have written, I have been guided by the need to gather together thoughts which for the purpose of expression were interconnected [*stseplennykh mezhdu soboyu*]; but every thought

[1] See letter to Hugh Walpole, 19 May, 1912, and preface to revised version of *The Tragic Muse*.

expressed separately in words loses its meaning and is terribly impoverished when taken by itself out of the connexion [*stseplenie*] in which it occurs.[2]

## A little later he continued:

But now that nine-tenths of everything printed is criticism, art criticism needs people who can show the folly of looking for thoughts in a work of art, and can continually guide readers in that endless labyrinth of connexions which is the essence of art, and in the direction of the laws on which these connexions are based. . . .

More explicitly, with reference to *Anna Karenina,* Tolstoy wrote in reply to the criticism that 'there is no architecture' in the novel:

On the contrary, I am proud of the architecture—the arches have been constructed in such a way that it is impossible to see where the keystone is. And that is what I was striving for most of all. The structural link [*svyaz'*] is not the plot or the relationship of the characters (friendship), but an inner link.[3]

Unfortunately it is not explained what this inner link is. We must look ourselves for the *svyazi* and *stsepleniya* in *War and Peace,* to see whether the criticism of its architectural deficiences is justified.

### STRUCTURAL PRINCIPLES

*War and Peace* is too big a novel, and written over too long a period of time, for its author to be expected to be able to carry the whole work in his mind and merely concern himself with putting the different parts together. The book grew with Tolstoy, and its composition must be looked at in terms of growth, dynamically, not in terms of completion, statically. That is to say it is not a finished work. One thing leads on to the next, and there is no real ending. It seems to me that the principle of composition is to think of people and phenomena in terms of their opposites and then to contrive the juxtaposition and interaction of these opposites. The principle operates, in the long view, as a series of sharp contrasts between two dissimilar groups—family and social—which, as groups, each reveal a corporate uniformity. Within these contrasted groups, and in the short view, there is individuality and variety. But

---

[2] Letter to N. N. Strakhov, 23 and 26 April 1876, J.E. LXII. 269.
[3] Letter to S. A. Rachinsky, 27 January 1878, J.E. LXII. 377.

ultimately the individual, however many-sided his personality, remains basically true to his group and does not transfer his allegiance to the other side. The flow of the novel is maintained by this constant juxtaposition of contrasting groups, the individual members of which are in continual contact as they move to and fro and mix with each other. But group solidarity triumphs; the individual is only free within the limits of the group.

The basic contrast in *War and Peace* is the one inherent in the title. This is not simply a contrast between periods when the country is at war and periods when it is not (by this calculation most of the scenes in *War and Peace* take place when the country is at war). War means military actions; peace means non-military actions whether in peace-time or in war. There is a balance held in the composition of the book between military and non-military scenes, even towards the end, when a state of war is permanent. Even then the presence of Pierre, the civilian, the spiritual seeker, towers above that of the soldiers and prisoners among whom he finds himself. Although Pierre and Karataev are both prisoners-of-war one does not think of the episodes in which they appear as belonging to the 'war' side of *War and Peace*.

In the early parts of the novel the principle of juxtaposing and contrasting peace and war scenes is very obvious. Volume I is divided into three parts. The first is exclusively peace; the second war; the third begins with peace and ends with war. Volume II covers the biggest span of years (1806–12), and except for some brief chapters in the second part it is all peace. Volumes III and IV describe a continuous period of war. But the threads of 'war' and 'peace' are no longer separate and parallel. They are very closely interwoven. All the country is involved in war because the struggle is no longer outside Russia, but on her own soil. 'Peace' now means domestic interludes, salons and soirées in war time, civilians in the army, Natasha caring for the wounded. The change in composition from the early juxtaposition of military and non-military scenes to their later integration reflects the change in the nature of the war. When an army fights abroad, war and peace are divisible. When it fights at home they are not.

There is a clearly discernible pattern running through all the

volumes of the novel which invariably begin and end with a
significant scene or happening in peace or war. Taking peace to
mean any non-military activity, we notice that, while Volume I
begins with peace and ends with war, the succeeding volumes
both begin *and* end with the same state—first peace (Vol. II);
then war (Vol. III); then peace again (Vol. IV). Both Volumes
I and IV begin with the same 'peaceful' setting—Anna Scherer's
salon, first in peace-time then in war. Both Volumes II and IV
end with the same 'peaceful' theme—the relations between
Natasha and Pierre, first the beginning of their love, then its
consummation. The two basic states of existence, peace and
war, provided Tolstoy with a useful outer framework for his
novel.

Within this framework the two states are inwardly contrasted.
It is tempting to think that Tolstoy, with his love of contrast,
wanted to draw a dividing line between the 'good' war and the
'bad' war. It might seem at first sight, since the French are the
aggressors while the Russians are their victims, and since the
French leader is made to appear ludicrous while the Russian
commander is the symbol of wisdom, that Tolstoy is opposing
the just to the unjust cause. The antithesis, however, is not as
simple as that. Tolstoy never makes it seem that all right is on
the side of the Russians, all wrong on the side of the French.
In the war scenes of 1812, he places the emphasis on the closing
of the Russian ranks and the spirit of national solidarity
created by the enemy invasion. If there were in fact attempts
on the part of the peasantry to fraternize with the enemy or to
use the invasion in order to rebel against their masters in the
hope of achieving their liberty, they are glossed over by Tolstoy
in the few pages devoted to the Bogucharovo rising. There is
undoubtedly a greater sense of purpose among the Russian
people than there was in 1805. The spirit of the Russian army
is more in evidence than the spirit of the invading troops, just
as its deeds of heroism are more conspicuous than those of its
adversary. But all this does not alter the fact that for Tolstoy
war is an unmitigated evil, and the battle of Borodino as senseless and wicked as that of Austerlitz or any other battle not on
Russian soil. The glorious pages of Russia's military history are
smudged and crumpled in *War and Peace*. Generals and professional soldiers, diplomats, statesmen and emperors—in so far as

they believe that they are planning or directing war in accordance with their own wills—are equally as unsympathetic to
Tolstoy if they are on the Russian side as if they are Frenchmen.
The ordinary man who finds himself a soldier is no worse for
being French than for being Russian. Individual acts of heroism
in battle are as likely to occur at Schöngraben or Austerlitz
when the defence of the motherland is not at stake, as they are
at Borodino, the last ditch before Moscow. Structurally speaking the arrangement of the war material in *War and Peace*
follows the lines not of a just and unjust cause, but of 'good'
and 'bad' men: 'good' in the military context means unpretentious, uninflated, aware of one's own limitations, spontaneous,
non-comformist; 'bad' in the same context means arrogant,
self-opinionated, disingenuous, hidebound, lustful for power. On
both sides in the struggle there is cruelty; on both sides mag-
nanimity; on both sides muddle and confusion. But where
Tolstoy draws the line is between the man who does not pretend
to be in control of the situation, and the man who believes
that he is.

Similarly, at the basis of the construction of the peace scenes
in the novel is the contrast between 'good' families and 'bad'.
The Bolkonskys and the Rostovs are patriotic in the best sense
of the word—not jingoistic or even anti-French necessarily—but
devoted to their country and to its finest national traditions. To
the Kuragins and the Drubetskoys on the other hand, Russia
is not as dear as their own private pleasure or their own personal
ambition. The former are never wholly wrapped up in themselves. They are capable of giving as well as receiving. The latter
are the incarnation of egoism. Here again we have two groups,
fairly homogeneous and totally unlike each other, whose interaction (Vasily's and Anatole's designs on Princess Marya, for
example, or Anatole's attempted abduction of Natasha) weave
another strand into the canvas of the novel.

Within the 'good' families of the Russian aristocracy, there
is a further sharp division between the earnest, intelligent
Bolkonskys and (Vera apart), the gay, impulsive, somewhat
scatter-brained Rostovs, a contrast of thought and feeling. Pierre
moves between the two homes, attached by friendship to Andrei
Bolkonsky and eventually by marriage to Natasha Rostova, and
linked by his first marriage with the 'unnatural', sensual,

Kuragins. He is the keystone of the arch in the building of *War and Peace.*

On another plane one might expect to have found in Tolstoy's novel a contrast between, on the one hand, the Russian aristocracy as a whole—good and bad, pro-Russian and pro-French, the united class of privilege and money—and on the other hand the overwhelming masses of the common people, still for the most part enslaved. But this elementary divorce of the haves and the have-nots, an obvious theme for a novelist who consciously uses the principle of contrast as his main constructional device, is not exploited by Tolstoy. There is little class opposition in *War and Peace,* no unbridgeable gulf between the aristocracy and the common people. None of the *prostoi narod* are treated with the contempt and irony which Tolstoy reserved, for example, for the Kuragin family. Indeed the 'positive heroes' among the aristocracy are at heart far closer to their social inferiors than to their fellow aristocrats in the opposite camp. The most sympathetic sides of Pierre, of Prince Andrei, and of Natasha are revealed particularly in their respective encounters with Karataev, Tushin and 'Uncle'. It is an essential article of Tolstoy's faith that victory over the French was the collective work of the people as a whole, and by the people he meant the best men and women of the nation, serfs and serf owners alike. As distinct from all the other *contrasting* devices employed in the construction of *War and Peace,* we have this time an example of a theme which unites instead of dividing, which compares instead of contrasting.

So far, in speaking of big homogeneous but contrasting groups, we have been talking in terms of virtual absolutes and constants. The Bolkonskys and Rostovs, as families, are good; the Kuragins are bad. Simple soldiers are good; the military caste is bad. Where we have the gradations, the variety, the growth and development (but not *qualitative* change) is in the individual characters within the groups, their vicissitudes, their changes of opinion, their seeking and their finding, their progress towards maturity. Prince Andrei is a very different man in 1812 from what he was in 1805. But even in 1805 he was a Bolkonsky, not a Kuragin. He always belonged to 'us' and not to 'them'. Similarly Natasha, stripped of her vivacity and brought to a somewhat sober motherhood, remains a Rostov—

simple, natural, direct, untroubled by serious thoughts. However great the apparent change in character, it is not big enough to place men and women outside the group to which they belong and always will belong. Contrast between groups; change and development of individuals within those groups: such are the constants and variables in Tolstoy's method of composition.

The constructional device of antithesis, so favoured by Tolstoy, may be seen to operate not only in contrasting groups, but also in contrasting scenes which directly succeed one another. Nikolai in raptures over Natasha's singing gives way to Nikolai in despair as he confronts his father with the news of his gambling debts.[4] The carefree scene of Natasha dancing at 'Uncle's' house is followed in the next chapter by a reminder of all the cares and troubles of the Rostov household.[5] The gaiety in the Rostov ballroom as the sixth *anglaise* is danced gives place to gloom almost at once as the dying Count Bezukhov has his sixth stroke.[6] Pierre goes out to take the life of Napoleon. Instead he saves the life of a child.[7] Or again he loses his faith in humanity as he watches prisoners being executed, only to have it restored by his meeting with Karataev which takes place immediately afterwards.[8] The blow that nearly killed Countess Rostova restored Natasha to life.[9] These and many similar examples in *War and Peace* call to mind the already mentioned juxtapositions such as Nikolai's death and Kitty's pregnancy in *Anna Karenina* or the transitions in the same novel from darkness to light and from light to darkness. They are characteristically Tolstoyan.

These rapid alterations of mood, these sudden *peripeteia*, help to create the illusion of movement which is the very essence of *War and Peace*. Tolstoy's own words in one of the philosophical digressions—'there can be no beginning to an event, for one event always flows uninterruptedly out of another'[10]—can well be applied to his novel. It has no real beginning or ending. The illusion of movement is enhanced by the short chapters and the rapid alterations of scene—Moscow, St. Petersburg, the country, the army. No single episode is dwelt on at any great length, while the longer scenes (the battles) are enacted with considerable

---

[4] *War and Peace*, II. 1. 15 ff.
[6] ibid. I. 1. 20 ff.
[8] ibid. IV. 1. 11 ff.
[10] ibid. III. 3. 1.

[5] ibid. II. 4. 7 ff.
[7] ibid. III. 3. 33.
[9] ibid. IV. 4. 3.

mobility; only historical and philosophical digressions hold things up. There is no obvious climax to the book, but there is a series of culminating points, some in the military action, some in the stories of the lives of the characters, which keep the narrative moving from one low peak to the next. The sense of movement is further intensified by the constant arrivals and departures of the characters. Nobody stays in any one place for long.

From time to time Tolstoy departs from a strict chronological narrative of events. For example, Prince Andrei's story is at one stage carried so far forward that the author has to go back nearly two years in time in order to recover Pierre and bring his story up to date.[11] This is inevitable in such a long novel. There are, however, occasions when Tolstoy abandons strict chronology when he has no need to do so and relates the conclusion of an episode before the events leading up to that conclusion. In the novel the account of Petya's death and the rescue of Pierre from captivity, for example, comes before the description of the prisoners' march and the death of Karataev *en route* which, chronologically speaking, came first. Volume IV, Part 3, Chapter 11 ends with the words: 'Among the Russian prisoners rescued by Denisov and Dolokhov was Pierre Bezukhov.' The next few chapters take us back in time to Karataev, until at the end of Chapter 15 we are told once again that the Russian partisans rescued Pierre from captivity. Something similar, but on a much shorter time scale, happens in the narration of the attempted abduction of Natasha by Anatole Kuragin. Anatole's side of the story is advanced and Natasha's is retarded. All his preparations are gone into in detail. Nothing is overlooked. He arrives at the house. One assumes that Natasha will be waiting for him. Only when he is actually in the courtyard does he realize that he has been betrayed. The events leading up to the betrayal are then briefly recounted in the following chapter.[12] This device which is used sparingly by Tolstoy as a means of varying the narrative sequence also contributes to the sense of movement by taking the reader rapidly on to the next event before the way is wholly prepared.

Another device which Tolstoy commonly uses to sustain the flow and movement of the narrative is the constant repetition

[11] *War and Peace*, II. 3. 7.        [12] ibid. II. 5. 18.

of identical or closely related situations and thoughts which establish links or 'connexions' as Tolstoy would call them. They cast the mind back momentarily, and provide the cohesion vital for a work of this length. We have in mind not the re-curring physical and spiritual characteristics of the main heroes, which we have already mentioned, but the repetition of situa-tions or phenomena, echoes and vibrations of what has gone before, which constitute what has been called in the context of another Russian novel 'situation rhyme'.[13] In spring 1809[14] on his way to his Ryazan estates and shortly before his first meeting with Natasha, Prince Andrei crosses the same ferry he had crossed with Pierre on that momentous occasion the year before when they had spoken of God and a future life. As he lies wounded in a tent after Borodino his thoughts call to mind another scene which takes us back in time:

All he saw about him merged into a general impression of naked bleeding human bodies that seemed to fill the whole of the low tent, as a few weeks previously, on that hot August day, such bodies had filled the dirty pond beside the Smolensk road. Yes, it was the same flesh, the same *chair à canon*, the sight of which had even then filled him with horror as if by a presentiment.[15]

When Nikolai goes to Moscow on leave in 1806[16] he offers his driver a three-rouble tip when the sledge is only three houses away from his own door. When he goes home on leave again[17] (this time to Otradnoe) he again gives his driver a three-rouble tip at the last post-station. On the former occasion he feels that 'all was the same' at home; on the latter occasion the feeling that 'everything is just the same, so why did I hurry?' is upper-most in Nikolai's mind. Precisely half way through the novel, after Natasha's unhappy experience with Anatole Kuragin and the first awakening of Pierre's love for her, Pierre looks up to the skies and sees the brilliant comet of 1812.[18] After the French have entered Moscow, Pierre again looks up at the skies and sees the same comet 'which was connected in Pierre's heart with his love'.[19] The behaviour of Prince Andrei and his kindness in protecting the doctor's wife travelling by cart in a convoy with the retreating Russian army[20] awakens an echo of a similar

[13] J. M. Meijer, *Situation Rhyme in a novel of Dostoevskij*, 'S-Gravenhage, 1958.    [14]*War and Peace*, II. 3. 1.
[15] ibid. III. 2. 37.    [16] ibid. II. 1. 1.    [17] ibid. II. 4. 1.
[18] ibid. II. 5. 22.    [19] ibid. III. 3. 29.    [20] ibid. I. 2. 13.

scene a few chapters earlier where Andrei stops some Russian
soldiers in a retreating convoy of wounded and gives them
money.[21] Prince Andrei again is the subject of the recurring
image of the oak tree before and after his visit to Otradnoe. On
his way there he sees an oak not yet in leaf, unmoved by the
spring, and the oak seems to echo his mood, as nature so often
echoes the mood of Turgenev's heroes and heroines: ' "Spring,
love, happiness!" this oak seemed to say. "Are you not weary
of that same old stupid, meaningless illusion? Always the same
and always an illusion. There is no spring, no sun, no happiness!" '[22] And Prince Andrei thinks: ' "Yes, the oak is right,
a thousand times right. Let others—the young—surrender
afresh to this illusion, but we know life—our life is finished!" '
When Prince Andrei returns from Otradnoe after his first
meeting with Natasha, the same oak has burst into leaf,
and he utters his memorable words: 'No, life is not over at
thirty-one!'[23]

Not only do situations rhyme: thoughts reverberate and echo
in the same way. Prince Andrei's thoughts on the unimportance
of everything he understands and the importance of the incomprehensible something, 'the Great All or Nothing', which
he gives expression to when wounded after Austerlitz,[24] are
recalled during the scene with Pierre on the raft when 'for the
first time since Austerlitz he saw that high everlasting sky he
had seen when lying on the battlefield'.[25] And as he waits in
Yaroslavl for death to come, 'that inexorable, eternal, distant
and unknown thing—the presence of which he had felt continually all his life—was now near to him', and he no longer
feared death, for the hitherto incomprehensible 'something'
became comprehensible as Love and 'Love is God and to die
means that I shall return to the common and eternal source'.[26]

Again Pierre's thoughts on the meaning of life recur throughout the novel in similar forms and sometimes even in identical
images and words. Take, for example, the tormenting question,
what is right and what is wrong. As Pierre ponders over his
action in fighting a duel with Dolokhov and the desirability of
separating from his wife, he thinks: ' "Louis XVI was executed
because they said he was dishonourable and a criminal, and

---

[21] *War and Peace*, I. 2. 9.  [22] ibid. II. 3. 1.          [23] ibid. II. 3. 3.
[24] ibid. I. 3. 19.          [25] ibid. II. 2. 12.          [26] ibid. IV. 1. 16.

from their point of view they were right, as were those too who canonised him and died a martyr's death for him. Then Robespierre was executed for being a despot. Who is right, who is wrong?" . . .'[27] Some time later, as Pierre is resting at Torzhok on his way to St. Petersburg, the same thoughts recur to him: ' "I shot Dolokhov because I considered myself insulted. Louis XVI was executed because he was considered a criminal, and a year later, for some reason or other, they executed those who had executed him. What is bad? What is good?" . . .'[28] In the first case his thoughts are followed by the decision to separate from his wife. In the second case they are followed by his meeting with Bazdeev who reminds him of his decision to separate from his wife.

The fact that clues to the outcome of an eventual situation or relationship are sometimes given at a very early stage—long before that situation or relationship has begun to be determined—may be regarded as another link in the chain which holds the novel together. In the chapter in which Princess Marya is first introduced in the novel,[29] she hears the praises of her future husband Nikolai sung in a letter from her friend Julie. When Nikolai meets Princess Marya for the first time at Bogucharovo 'the meeting immediately struck him as a romantic event'.[30] The first reaction Nikolai has to the news of Natasha's engagement to Prince Andrei (when he sees her for the first time after it became known in the family) is that the marriage will not take place.[31] The ground is prepared very early on for the Natasha-Pierre relationship by emphasizing their mutual attraction and the animation they both feel in each other's company. Pierre's earlier fate had been as good as sealed the moment he received a note from Anna Scherer saying that he would find 'the beautiful Hélène', at her reception, 'whom it is always delightful to see'.[32] These and other similar examples suggest that Tolstoy felt obliged to hint at the likely outcome of a situation well in advance, so that when the expected happens (and there are really very few surprises) the conjectures of the attentive reader may be rewarded. In exactly the same way Anna Karenina's fate is foreshadowed by the words 'an ill omen' which she utters as she witnesses the railway accident on

[27] ibid. II. 1. 6.          [28] ibid. II. 2. 1.          [29] ibid. I. 1. 22.
[30] ibid. III. 2. 13.        [31] ibid. II. 4. 1.          [32] ibid. I. 3. 1.

her very first appearance in the novel. Tolstoy sows the seeds early and they all come to flower.

It was the belief of Tolstoy that the vast majority of ordinary men and women, for all their differences and individual idio-syncrasies, are creatures of habit and routine who react in a recognizable and essentially similar way to the basic situations of life. This belief is reflected in his writings by something of a standard approach to the description of human responses to such universal happenings as love and death. One finds not only in *War and Peace* but also in the early story *Youth* the state of being in love described as an inability on the part of the person in love (Pierre in *War and Peace*) to get up and take his departure.[33] One notices a standard approach to the portrayal of profound emotional disturbance in an almost obsessive con-centration on the movements of the human jaw. Not only does Prince Andrei's jaw quiver at moments of agitation. The same is true in *War and Peace* alone of Natasha, Nikolai, Pierre, Captain Tushin, a doctor, a Frenchman and others too.

There is a similarity between the scene in *War and Peace* where Countess Rostova learns of the death of her son, Petya, and that in *Childhood* where the grandmother learns of her daughter's death.[34] Both scenes have this in common that the two women continue to address their children as though they were still alive. In *Childhood* the little boy enters: 'She [the grandmother] was sitting in her chair . . . "Ah, if only you had known, my dear, how worried I was and how glad I am now that you have come [*chto ty priekhala*]."' In addressing the boy she uses the feminine form as though she were talking to a woman—her daughter. Compare this with the episode in *War and Peace* where Natasha enters her mother's room: 'The countess was sitting on the bed . . . "How glad I am that you have come . . . [*chto ty priekhal*]."' Here the masculine form is used as though she were talking to her son and not her daughter. Finally one must mention Tolstoy's stock description of the fear-courage ambivalence displayed by men in the face of the enemy. Nikolai Rostov, in his baptism of fire at the Enns bridge,[35] shows the same fear of death and love of life, the same awareness of the contrast between the beauty of nature

---

[33] See V. V. Vinogradov, *O Yazyke Tolstogo, Literaturnoe Nasledstvo, 35/36,* Moscow, 1939.      [34] ibid.      [35] *War and Peace*, I. 2. 8.

and the ugliness of suffering, the same momentary fear of being thought a coward as was shown earlier by the obscure heroes of the Sevastopol sketches. His own version of the Schöngraben affair recalls the similar falsification of facts common in Tolstoy's experience among the bravest soldiers in the Crimean campaign, and recorded by him in the same Sevastopol sketches. Prince Andrei's reactions to imminent death in battle as a smoking shell spins near to him[36] remind one very much of the scene of Praskukhin's death in *Sevastopol in May*.

These few examples from among many will perhaps be sufficient to make the point. Certainly Tolstoy's somewhat stereotyped approach to the description of certain states of mind and particularly to the construction of battle scenes in general was not lost on his contemporaries. A satirical article in *The Spark* (No. 17, 1868) says that if an artist wished to paint the battle of Austerlitz as described in *War and Peace* he would paint it as follows:

First of all the sun at Austerlitz, the sun not at all like the ordinary sun, of course. Secondly smoke. There must be smoke at a battle. Thirdly, two soldiers in flight and one wounded officer. The rest of the army can't be seen for smoke. And fourthly and finally Napoleon's 'little white hand', also invisible because of the smoke. That is the whole picture according to L. Tolstoy's plan.[37]

This is not a very accurate parody. What stands out about Tolstoy's description of Austerlitz is the mist and the confusion. What is characteristically Tolstoyan is the confusion. One met it at Schöngraben. One will meet it again at Borodino. Nobody really knows what is happening, least of all the generals. Individuals act of their own accord because they have no orders or because they disobey orders, because they have lost touch or because they have been forgotten. The final result, whether victory or defeat, is quite independent of the preliminary tactics and strategy elaborated by the commanding officers. General confusion coupled with the particular exploits of individual brave men—Tushin, Timokhin, Prince Andrei—the single battery keeping up a lone fire, the single officer charging with standard in hand, isolated acts of daring and initiative unforeseen in the debates at Headquarters—these are standard ingredients in Tolstoy's battle scenes. Generally speaking, the

---

[36] ibid. III. 2. 36.          [37] Quoted by Shklovsky, op. cit. p. 99.

actual description of fighting is kept down to a minimum (in the case of Borodino, only three chapters are strictly concerned with the fighting itself), while scenes of camp life, army head-quarters, and regiments in reserve, or description of attitudes of mind predominate. It would be wrong to imply that the three big battles in *War and Peace* (Schöngraben, Austerlitz and Borodino) all conform to the same general pattern. Schöngraben and Borodino were, if not victories, at least triumphant pages in Russia's military history. Austerlitz on the other hand was a disaster, and is treated with even greater irony and venom. Nevertheless the three battles as described in Tolstoy's novel have much in common, and the very fact of their common denominator is further evidence of that sameness of approach which is characteristic of the structure and composition of significant episodes—and not only military episodes—in Tolstoy's fiction.

Take for example the not infrequent sleep and dream scenes in *War and Peace*. Here the standard compositional device is to direct the sleeper's thoughts to a point where they can sensibly coincide with the words of the man who wakes him. Pierre, on the retreat from Borodino, sleeps the night in a carriage in the yard of an inn at Mozhaisk. Thoughts run through his mind which are channelled into the mouth of a speaker (Pierre's bene-factor) and led up to the point where this voice in his sleep tells him to 'unite the meaning of everything in his soul':

'Unite everything?' said Pierre to himself. 'No, not unite. You cannot unite thoughts, but you can *harness* all these thoughts. Yes, you must *harness them*, you must *harness them*,' Pierre repeated to himself. . . . 'Yes, you must harness them, you must harness them.' 'Time to harness, time to harness, Your Excellency! Your Excellency, you must harness, it's time to harness', repeated someone's voice . . . [38]

Exactly the same device is used when Pierre has another dream a few moments before the Russian partisans rescue him from captivity: 'Again [i.e. in his sleep] real events mingled with dreams, and again someone, he or another, gave expression to his thoughts and even to the same thoughts that had been expressed in his dream at Mozhaisk.'[39] Incidentally, the refer-ence to the earlier dream at Mozhaisk provides yet another 'link' in the story. In both cases there is a voice which speaks

[38] *War and Peace*, III. 3. 9.          [39] ibid. IV. 3. 15.

to Pierre in his dream. This time it is an old schoolteacher of his. Here is the sequel to the dream: ' "Vous avez compris, mon enfant?" said the teacher. "Vous avez compris, sacré nom", shouted a voice, and Pierre woke up.'[40]

Another recognizable feature of Tolstoy's style which may be related to the general subject of composition is his partiality for describing his characters reacting to new situations in terms of old situations with which they are thoroughly familiar. Nikolai Rostov, a keen sportsman, sees battle in terms of a hunt. When he runs away in battle, Tolstoy likens him to a hare fleeing before the hounds. Captain Tushin, a pipe-smoker, sees the enemy's guns as pipes. This is in keeping with the underlying philosophy that gives shape to Tolstoy's novel, that over the larger issues of life there is a basic sameness about the pattern of human behaviour, and that human beings, conditioned as they are by habit, milieu, and social and class prejudices, tend to follow a more or less predictable course. Despite the frequency in the novel of the word *svoistvenny* ('peculiar to'), denoting the distinguishing features of an individual, it is the expressions such as 'the same as ever' or 'as is always the case', denoting habit and conformity, which predominate in *War and Peace*.

### NARRATIVE DESCRIPTION, DIALOGUE AND MONOLOGUE

So far we have spoken about the principles of contrast, movement, repetition, association and uniformity as all playing their part in the structure of Tolstoy's novel. We can now turn to a different question—that of the nature and extent of narrative description, dramatization and author's digression in the presentation of the material.

Not surprisingly, descriptive narrative is the most widely used means of exposition (although it is doubtful whether it is correct to say, as one Soviet critic does, that '*historical* narrative is the basis of the plot development of the novel and forms an almost continuous narrative stream').[41] But the narrative passages in *War and Peace* are constructed along certain general lines which are easily recognizable and which point to the originality (in the sense of distinctive features) of Tolstoy's prose style.

[40] ibid. IV. 3. 15 and see Vinogradov, op. cit.
[41] Saburov, op. cit. p. 53.

First we may mention Tolstoy's general aversion to sustained detailed narrative description of any sort. Attention has recently been drawn to the fact that shortly before beginning *War and Peace* he wrote that the 'accepted method' of logical step by step description had now become impossible in literature, that is to say: 'first a description of the characters, even their biographies, then a description of locality and milieu, and only then the beginning of the action. And it's a strange thing' (he continues) 'that all these descriptions, sometimes dozens of pages long, tell the readers less about the characters than some casually thrown out artistic detail [*cherta*] in the course of an action already in progress between people who have not been described at all'.[42] These words obviously are intended to apply to the beginning of a narrative and seem particularly apt in the context of the opening pages of *War and Peace* over which Tolstoy laboured for so long. Nevertheless they have a wider application also in his novels. In close connexion with this first point, we may add that when Tolstoy *does* narrate at some length, he has a tendency to avoid describing objects, situations and even people in isolation, as it were, and to show instead what sort of impact they make on other people. How did the battle of Borodino appear to Pierre, a civilian who happened to find himself on the battlefield? What impression did freemasonry make on him personally? What did he seem like to Anna Scherer, to Prince Andrei, to Natasha? This is the approach that Tolstoy used, and on the whole he remained consistent to his belief, referred to in our first chapter, that 'description from the author is a bad thing in literature—one should describe how this or that thing is reflected in one's characters'.[43] As a result there is surprisingly little detailed 'objective' author's description in *War and Peace*—of the great battles or the fire of Moscow, for example, or even of the environment in which the characters lived and moved, their estates, houses or furniture.

Just as there is comparatively little 'exhaustive' narrative, of the sort which one associates with Balzac, Flaubert, Goncharov or many nineteenth-century English novelists, so also in my opinion is there little specifically historical or period detail in the novel.

[42] J.E. VIII. 312. Quoted by Zaidenshnur, op. cit. p. 49.
[43] Tolstoy to V. G. Chertkov, 5 September 1909. Quoted in *Literaturnoe Nasledstvo*, 37/38, Moscow, 1939, p. 533.

This last assertion is by no means generally accepted and has been the subject of much controversy in which Tolstoy himself took part. From the very beginning he was criticized for neglecting to define adequately the character of the period—to provide in fact sufficient period *couleur*. He took this criticism to imply the absence of 'the horrors of serfdom, the immuring of wives, the flogging of grown-up sons, Saltykova etc.' (the latter is reputed to have tortured 139 of her serfs to death) and replied in his article *A Few Words about War and Peace* that in his opinion these were not the characteristics of the period at all. 'That period had its own characteristics', he wrote, 'which resulted from the alienation of the upper class from other classes, the religious philosophy of the time, the peculiarities of education, the habit of using French and so on.' This, he said, is the character which he tried to depict. Did he succeed? One critic (without agreeing that the characteristics of the period were the ones singled out by Tolstoy) was so strongly of the opposite opinion that he said very pertinently that as you read and re-read *War and Peace* you cannot help asking yourself—where did Gogol's Russia come from?[44] Another much more influential critic, Merezhkovsky,[45] also ventured to disagree with Tolstoy. He believed that the background of *War and Peace* is essentially Tolstoy's own background, the background too of *Anna Karenina*. He felt that there was no vital difference in historical colouring between the battles of Austerlitz and Borodino on the one hand and the Sevastopol sketches on the other; that Prince Andrei could hardly be thought of as a contemporary of Karamzin's *Poor Liza* ('one feels that he had read Byron, Lermontov, Stendhal, Flaubert and Schopenhauer') and that Pierre as well as Levin might well have been Tolstoy's own contemporary ('Levin had no religious doubt which would have been incomprehensible to Pierre'). As for the domestic life of a Russian nobleman during the Napoleonic wars, the only significant period detail, asserted Merezhkovsky, is the glass entrance-hall with its two rows of statues in niches in the old Count Bezukhov's town house in Moscow.

Merezhkovsky's impressionistic generalizations can easily be attacked on individual points. There have been people ready to

[44] '*Voina i Mir*': *sbornik pamyati L. Tolstogo* (see footnote 6 Ch. II, p. 85).
[45] D. Merezhkovsky, *L. Tolstoy i Dostoevsky, Zhizn' i Tvorchestvo*, St. Petersburg, 1909, pp. 165 ff.

track down in *War and Peace* details of dress characteristic of the times, or more period pieces from the Bezukhov house (the Venetian mirror in the hall, the Persian carpets, the tall mahogany bed with silk curtains, the Voltaire armchair, the reception room with its two Italian windows and the big bust and portrait of Catherine the Great). They have pointed to the songs and dances at the Rostovs' nameday party or the description of the banquet at the English Club in honour of Bagration as lending historical colour and authenticity to the narrative. One might add that Tolstoy not only qualified things in a general way as being 'according to the fashion of the times' (*po togdashnei mode*), but also made specific references which date the work accurately and are at the same time representative of trends and movements—Prince Andrei's emancipation of 300 serfs, for example, which stemmed from the edict of 1803 enabling landowners to sell freedom and land to their peasants; the growth and power of Freemasonry; the foundation of the Bible Society.

Nevertheless the fact remains that Merezhkovsky is right to imply that there is a significant lack of the sort of period detail and historical colouring which one finds, say, in a Balzac novel. It is hard to visualize exactly what the Rostov and the Bolkonsky houses and rooms looked like from what we are told of them. Descriptions of food and dress are meagre. There is little from which to conjure up pictures of towns, shops, churches, streets or vehicles. As for the character of the period which Tolstoy confesses he was at pains to render as accurately as possible—the alienation of the classes resulting from education, religion and the predominance of the French language—it is doubtful whether this was much more true of 1812 than of 1850.

What has been said about the comparatively restrained use of detail in Tolstoy's narrative description of places, houses and domestic paraphernalia may be extended also to his descriptions of nature, which do not figure prominently in the novel and are hardly ever used independently for effect. The pathetic fallacy, the attribution of human characteristics to the world of nature, is not foreign to Tolstoy's art, and it does not come as a complete surprise to find references in *War and Peace* to stars, 'disporting themselves' or 'whispering something joyful and mysterious to one another'. But when Tolstoy observes nature, he generally does so through the effect it has upon a man or woman. Natural description is essentially an element of characterization, not a thing in its own right. Pierre looks at the comet and thinks of his love for Natasha. Prince Andrei gazes at the sky and a series of thoughts are evoked in him. But neither the comet nor the sky are described except in the most general terms. Again, the oak tree which Prince Andrei sees on his way to and from Otradnoe corresponds to a definite mood within him: nature is in harmony with his soul, now dead and now alive. Lukacs[46] singles out this episode and recalls that Flaubert advised Maupassant to observe a tree until he discovered features which distinguished it from all other trees. But to do this, he says, only isolates it from nature and from its relationship to man. In Tolstoy's novel, however, Prince Andrei contemplates the oak before and after visiting the Rostovs, and while it is given no original features, it plays its part in a psychological process.

Just as there is a close connexion between nature and man, so also is there an organic relationship between man and the particulars of his domestic environment. We have said that details of this sort are comparatively few in *War and Peace*. We should add that they are not important as things in themselves, but rather as objects which evoke responses in the characters. Thus when Nikolai Rostov comes home on leave, many objects are mentioned in rapid succession—streets, shops, lanterns, cabs, the broken plaster on the cornice of his house—but they are not details given to fill out the picture. They are objects which give rise to positive or negative responses in the mind of the impatient and agitated Nikolai:

'How much longer? How much longer? Oh these insufferable streets, shops, bread rolls, street lamps and cabs', thought Rostov, when their leave permits had been passed at the town gate and they had entered Moscow. . . . At last the sledge turned right into the entrance; above his head Rostov saw the old familiar cornice with the plaster broken off, the porch, the post on the pavement. He jumped out before the sledge stopped and ran into the hall. The house stood still and uninviting, as though it had no business at all with the person who had entered. There was no one in the hall. 'Oh, God, is everything all right?' thought Rostov, stopping for a moment with a sinking heart and then immediately starting to run along the hall and up the familiar warped steps. The same old door-handle, the dirtiness of which always angered the countess, turned as loosely as ever. A solitary tallow candle burnt in the ante-room.[47]

[46] Lukacs, op. cit. p. 142.          [47] *War and Peace*, II. 1. 1.

'Insufferable' . . . 'familiar' . . . 'still and uninviting' . . . 'familiar' . . . 'the same old'. . . . These adjectives and adverbs tell us little about the streets and the house. There is no accumulation of detail for its own sake. Such detail as there is is there because it evokes a response, and the scene is written, one feels, with the response in the front of the author's mind and the objects in the back. The door-handle is not a wooden one; it is not a glass one; it is just the *same old one*.

If Tolstoy is not particularly interested in *external* detail, he is fascinated by the details of feelings and thoughts. Feelings for him always took precedence in fiction over actual events and he drew the distinction himself long before he became a famous writer:

> I read *The Captain's Daughter* and, alas, I must admit that Pushkin's prose is now already out of date—not in its language, but in its manner of exposition. Now, quite rightly, in the new school of literature, interest in the details of feeling is taking the place of interest in the events themselves. Pushkin's stories are somehow bare.[48]

Tolstoy did not betray his early instincts. In *War and Peace* he strove above all to convey states of mind and processes of thought, no less in his *narrative* passages than in his dialogue, and he remained comparatively indifferent to the recording of events, as he did to the painting of word pictures.

In the draft versions of *War and Peace* narrative is by far the commonest form of exposition. One significant difference between the drafts and the definitive version is the much greater use Tolstoy makes in the latter of the principles of dramatization —the introduction in fact of dialogue, monologue and interior monologue into episodes which had first been written out in continuous narrative. The chapter about the doctor and his German wife, Marya Hendrikhovna,[49] was at first a mere paragraph without dialogue. It had dramatic possibilities and Tolstoy developed it scenically. There are numerous similar examples in *War and Peace*. But what is characteristically Tolstoyan is not the expansion of narrative into dialogue, but the changes rung on narrative, dialogue and monologue in order to express the true and innermost thoughts of the characters. People's thoughts, Tolstoy observed, are far more complex, erratic and unpredictable than people's actions. Men and women are frequently so absorbed in their own private world that they follow

[48] J.E. XLVI. 187.        [49] *War and Peace*, III. 1. 13.

their own train of thoughts to the exclusion of all else. They say words which do not arise naturally out of the conversation in which they are engaged. This somewhat elementary observation is put to good use in *War and Peace*: ' "You are good in every way, André, but you have a kind of intellectual pride", said Princess Marya, following her own trend of thought rather than the trend of the conversation.'[50] Or ' "You talk of Bonaparte and his career", said Prince Andrei (although Pierre had not mentioned Bonaparte)'.[51]

Equally striking is the propensity of men and women to say things quite unrelated to what they are really thinking, their thoughts being revealed very often by their eyes or their smile. When Boris Drubetskoy sees Natasha again after some years have passed, the conversation runs: ' "How handsome you have grown." "I should think so," replied Natasha's laughing eyes. "Is Papa older?" she asked'.[52] Or after dinner on Prince Bolkonsky's nameday: ' "May I stay a little longer?" he [Pierre] asked, letting his stout body sink into an armchair beside her. "Oh yes," she said. "Didn't you notice anything?" her look said'.[53] Or again in the course of the Schöngraben action: ' "Whose company?" asked Prince Bagration of an artilleryman standing by the ammunition wagon. He asked "whose company?", but he really meant "are you frightened here?" '[54]

The disjointed nature of the normal process of articulation is frequently conveyed in *War and Peace* by the casual, apparently fortuitous beginnings and endings of conversations which are struck up at random or break off at random, petering out into three dots. This realistic side of human intercourse is one which Tolstoy reveals commonly in the composition of his dialogue passages. But more common still, as a compositional device for conveying the true nature of thoughts and words and the relationship between them, is the interior monologue. V. V. Stasov once said in a letter to Tolstoy:

Nearly all authors write monologues which are absolutely correct, consistent, streamlined, polished, ultra-logical and consistent. [sic] . . . But is this the way we really think? Of course not. I have only met one exception up to now—Count Lev Tolstoy. He is the only person

[50] ibid. I. 1. 25.
[52] ibid. II. 3. 12.
[54] ibid. I. 2. 17.

[51] ibid. I. 1. 6.
[53] ibid. II. 5. 4.

who in his novels and dramas gives us real monologues with all their irregularity, fortuitousness, incompleteness and jerkiness.[55]

We may take as an example the passage in *War and Peace* where Natasha, aged 16, is wondering whether to marry Boris. She runs into her mother's room, talks to her, runs back to her own room, is unable to sleep and lies on her bed thinking and looking at Sonya.

'Sonya?', she thought, looking at the sleeping, curled-up little kitten with her enormous plait. 'No, how could she! She is virtuous. She is in love with Nikolai and doesn't want to know anything else. And Mamma —even *she* doesn't understand. It's astonishing how clever I am . . . and how nice she is . . . ' she went on, speaking of herself in the third person and imagining that it was some very clever, the cleverest and best man speaking about her. 'She has everything', went on this man, 'She is exceptionally intelligent, charming and pretty, exceptionally pretty, and agile—she swims and rides splendidly. And her voice! It really is a wonderful voice.'[56]

This is an interesting passage, because it shows how the simple interior monologue can be expanded and made more subtle by the introduction of a second voice—a trick which is repeated in very similar words ten chapters later. Tolstoy has said that Natasha was pretty. He could have added in so many words that she was vain. But vanity, unlike good looks, is an inner characteristic and one that is best expressed through the workings of the mind.

Another good example of interior monologue may help to illustrate Tolstoy's technical versatility. This passage is a thought 'dialogue': two people are thinking about each other, but no words are spoken. The occasion is Anatole Kuragin's visit to Princess Marya, as an unwilling suitor to a lady overanxious to be wooed. Externally the emphasis is laid, in Princess Marya's case, on her peculiar hair style, specially arranged for the occasion, and the agitation suggested by her clumsy, heavy tread. Anatole, for his part, 'stood with his right thumb under a button of his uniform, his chest expanded and his back drawn in, swinging one foot and with his head slightly bowed, silently beaming at the princess and obviously not thinking about her at all'. No words are exchanged, but what is at first conveyed

[55] *Lev Tolstoy i V. Stasov, Perepiska 1878–1906*, Leningrad, 1929, p. 265. Quoted by Vinogradov, op. cit.
[56] *War and Peace*, II. 3. 13.

externally by gestures and appearances is later communicated internally by thoughts and feelings:

'But am I not too cold with him?' thought Princess Marya. 'I try to be reserved because in the depths of my soul I feel too near to him already: but then he can't know all I think about him and may imagine that I don't like him.'

And Princess Marya tried, but could not manage to be nice to her new guest.

'La pauvre fille! Elle est diablement laide', thought Anatole [significantly enough in French].[57]

In most of the important episodes in *War and Peace* in which the major characters are involved, there is a subtle blend of author's narrative, outwardly spoken words and inwardly spoken thoughts; and it is in the many different combinations and variations of these three basic ingredients that Tolstoy's originality as a psychological realist lies.

Tolstoy's own intervention in the novel is very much less marked in the definitive version than in the drafts. Nevertheless there are a good many passages which, for want of a better term, are called digressions. They occur for the most part at the beginning of a volume, or part of a volume, and they belong almost entirely to the second half of the novel. None of the eight parts which comprise the first two volumes of *War and Peace* begins with a historical or philosophical disquisition. On the other hand, all three parts of Volume III and two parts of Volume IV open with *ex cathedra* statements on such subjects as rulers and generals, the nature of the course of the events of 1812, the method of history, the cause of historical actions and the nature and character of war. The first epilogue devotes several opening chapters to a discussion of the forces operating in history, to chance and genius, while the second epilogue is given exclusively to an examination of problems of the philosophy of history. In the draft, and even the proof stages of the novel, the epilogues were in the reverse order, the historical reflections preceding the continuation of the story of the main characters. Only in the last proof was the final order arrived at, no doubt to make as independent and detachable as possible the one really long continuous statement of the author's position. The opening chapters of most parts of Volumes III and IV are

57 ibid. I. 3. 4.

preludes to the episodes to be described in those parts and closely related to them. But the second epilogue is virtually a self-contained summing-up of Tolstoy's thought on the subjects ventilated in the novel, whether in narrative statements from time to time, or in the lives and fates of the characters themselves. From an artistic point of view there is little to be said for the digressions. It is, I think, reading too much into them to regard them as genre elements, as indications of an alleged transition from a family novel to an epic. There is to my knowledge no evidence that Tolstoy ever considered them as conscious Homeric elements. He did not connect them one with another in the form of a consecutive thematic digression as sometimes appears to be the case in Pushkin's *Eugene Onegin*. They are all relevant to the main idea of the book, although they are repeated and hammered out with a force and insistence which is offensive to many readers. Their structure is laboured; their syntax cumbersome. They abound in oratorical tricks, heavy irony, questions and answers divisions and sub-divisions, progressions of *firstly, secondly* and *thirdly*. Besides the offence they give to many readers by their tedious style and their uncompromising position, they are structurally unfortunate in that they lay too heavy an emphasis on what should emerge naturally from the course of the fictional narrative. In fact Tolstoy's conclusions, while they can in retrospect be applied to the behaviour of the fictitious characters in his novel and can be made to seem not inconsistent with this behaviour, do not strike the reader spontaneously as he reads the stories of the Rostovs and the Bolkonskys. The consistency between the idea and the fictional illustration of the idea has to be looked for; it is not there on the surface. Structurally speaking, then, there is a serious unbalance in Tolstoy's novel— not a high-handed disregard of 'architecture', but a lapse on the part of a novelist who nevertheless strove after the 'architectural' virtues of order, balance, harmony, contrast, and focus. A major weakness of the digressive passages is that they are concerned so much with the big groups—whether nations, armies, or historians, which as groups make far less impression on the reader than the individual heroes who, forming the stuff of the novel, are, nevertheless, as individuals, given only the scantiest treament in the digressions and have the small area of freedom ascribed to them inadequately defined. In his article on *War and Peace* Tolstoy wrote: 'there are two kinds of actions: some that do and others that do not depend on my will.' This crucial statement ought to be both illustrated in the text of the novel and elaborated in the commentary in order to give that *balance* between reflection and action, between thesis and illustration of thesis, which, for all Tolstoy's preoccupation with compositional problems, seems to me to be inadequately maintained in *War and Peace*.

In drawing attention to the evidence that Tolstoy was far from indifferent to problems of form, a final reservation must be made. Despite all the 'links' and 'connexions', the inadequately explored structural subtleties of Tolstoy, *War and Peace* remains a sprawling work—vast, all-embracing, life-like, unrounded. To many West European writers of the twentieth century—to Proust, Thomas Mann and others—this was the fact which really counted. This was the great lesson which the Russian novel had to offer. It was the shapelessness, variety and richness of life, not the shapes and graces of architecture, which was Tolstoy's literary bequest to posterity.

# V : LANGUAGE

A PERSON who has read only one or two books by Tolstoy will have no difficulty in assigning passages from other books of his to their correct author. He will not confuse the language with that of Dostoevsky or Turgenev, Gogol or Leskov. There is no mistaking, even in English translation, the simplicity and lucidity of Tolstoy's writing. But the English reader may not be so aware of that other distinguishing feature of Tolstoy's style which is everywhere apparent in the Russian text of *War and Peace*—namely, repetition.

Many varieties of repetition are encountered in prose fiction. A novelist who writes at such length as Tolstoy cannot afford to say a thing once only. He is more or less obliged to repeat a piece of information at least once if it has any significance. But Tolstoy is not content with merely saying a thing twice. How often are we told that Julie Karagina became a wealthy heiress on her brother's death? That Kutuzov occupied his leisure time writing to Madame de Stael and reading French novels? That there was straw beneath the windows of the dying Bezukhov's house? That the French envoy Michaud knew no Russian? These facts are repeated two, three and four times even. Their repetition aids the memory. It facilitates reading. It is the novelist's concession to his reader. But there is no doubt that in this respect Tolstoy was much more considerate than he need have been.

Another variety of repetition, and one which is characteristically Tolstoyan, is the constant reiteration of some external detail designed to characterize an individual: a repetition which has nothing to do with the fact that the novel is long and the reader's memory is short. No one can fail to notice how the essence of a Tolstoyan character is distilled into a mannerism, a gesture, a physical feature, an outward and visible sign which recurs continually and is the permanent property of that character. Such attributes are not repeated to remind us of something we may have forgotten. Nor are they generalizations like the epithets *pius* or πολύμητις which qualify Aeneas and

Odysseus, whether or not their behaviour happens to be dutiful or resourceful. They resemble rather musical *leit-motivs*. They identify the person by something more meaningful than a name, and something less ossified than a stock epithet. The repeated reference to Napoleon's small white hands, Hélène's bare white shoulders, Princess Marya's radiant eyes is not a conscious epic device. It is a combination of the assertion of a permanent, individualizing feature with the expression of a moral judgement. As well as suggesting what is most significant about his heroes, Tolstoy tries to evoke in the reader at the same time a positive or negative response to them. Napoleon's small hands suggest effeminacy and the absence of work; Hélène's inadequate clothing is a sign of her brazenness; the light in Princess Marya's eyes reflects the inner light within her soul. We are intended to disapprove of Hélène and Napoleon, and to approve of Princess Marya. This type of repetition of external detail, involving as it does the frequent recurrence of identical words, is an example of how closely related a novelist's language and characterization are. Words are repeated because aspects of character have to be repeated, and once the words chosen to convey those aspects are altered, the characterization itself is altered, however slightly.

Another type of repetition to which Tolstoy was prone also demonstrates how difficult it is to divorce words from the ideas they express. Nobody who has read *War and Peace* carefully could fail to notice the frequency of such words or phrases as, for example, 'peculiar to' (*svoistvenny*), 'simple' (*prostoy*), 'natural' (*estestvenny*), 'as is always the case' (*kak vsegda byvaet*), or 'all this must be so' (*eto dolzhno byt' tak*). Sometimes one can regard a frequently-recurring expression as nothing more than a linguistic mannerism, characteristic of one author and not another. Such phrases as 'to experience a feeling similar to that experienced by . . . ' (*ispytyvat' chuvstvo podobnoe tomu, kotoroe ispytyvaet . . .*) or 'as a sign of' something or other (*v znak chego . . .*)—are good examples of obtrusive verbal idiosyncrasies characteristic of Tolstoy's style of writing, but having no real significance in themselves. But the phrases quoted earlier in this paragraph belong to a different category. The crux of Tolstoy's thought is that every human being has features which mark him off from every other human being—

hence the frequency of the word 'peculiar to'—while at the same time human beings in the mass exhibit a sameness, a uniformity, a predictability, an inevitability which is conveyed in Tolstoy's language by the repetition of 'as is always the case', 'as all people do', or 'all this must be so'. The insoluble problem of the individual personality and mass uniformity, of free will and determinism, is reflected on the linguistic plane by the insistent use of identical words to express identical content.

What has been said so far concerns the tenuous distinction between form and content. Tolstoy repeats the same words because he wants to repeat the same ideas, which can only be repeated exactly by using again the form in which they originally occurred. This is a justification for some repetition, but not for all. There are certain limits within which a writer can express his meaning in more ways than one, and within these limits, meaning is not affected by style. Tolstoy, in his old age, remarked that 'the basic content of a work of art in all its fullness can be expressed only by itself'[1]—that is to say that you cannot describe it without reproducing it word for word, and that the change of a single word means a change, however minute, in the content of the whole. But this is only true if we understand content as the sum total of everything in the work of art. It is possible to make stylistic alterations, without affecting the meaning to the slightest extent. And this brings us to another aspect of Tolstoy's repetition, which is not inevitable. Let us examine the following typically Tolstoyan sequences. The subject of the first one is Pierre, and he is scrutinizing his feelings for his first wife Hélène (the italics here and in the passages which follow are mine):

'But how often have I *felt proud of* her, *felt proud of* her majestic beauty, her social tact', he thought, '*felt proud of* my house in which she received all Petersburg, *felt proud of* her unapproachability and beauty. So this is what I *felt proud of*! I thought that I did not *understand* her. How often when considering her character have I told myself that I was to blame for not *understanding* her, for not *understanding* that constant composure. . . .'[2]

In Russian the single word *gordilsya* ('I felt proud') occurs five times and the word *ponimayu* ('I understand') three times.

The next passage is self-explanatory:

[1] Goldenweiser, op. cit. p. 68.                    [2] *War and Peace*, II. 1. 6.

. . . thought Prince Andrei, as he waited among a number of important and unimportant people in Count Arakcheev's *reception-room.*

During his service, chiefly as an adjutant, Prince Andrei had seen
the *reception-rooms* of many important men, and the different types of
these *reception-rooms* were well known to him. Count Arakcheev's
*reception-room* had quite a special character. The faces of the unimportant people waiting their turn for an audience in Count Arakcheev's
*reception room* . . .[3]

Here the Russian *priemnaya* recurs five times in as many lines—
a fact which is glossed over in the Maudes' English translation
by omitting it once, calling it a 'waiting room' once, an 'ante-
room' twice and simply a 'room' once.

When Prince Andrei died

. . . everyone came to take leave of him and everyone *wept.*

Little Nikolai *wept* because of the painful perplexity which rent his
heart. The Countess and Sonya *wept* from pity for Natasha, and because
he was no more. The old count *wept* because he felt that he would
soon have to take the same terrible step.

Natasha and Princess Marya also *wept* now, but they *wept* because of
their own personal grief; they *wept* because . . .[4]

To translate these seven past tenses of *plakat'* ('to weep') the
Maudes say 'wept' three times, 'cried' three times, and omit one
altogether. Finally one might add the second half of a sentence
which occurs when the Russian prisoners, Pierre included, are
waiting their turn to be shot by their French captors, who are
the subject of the sentence: '. . . and it was noticeable that
they were all *hurrying,* and were *hurrying* not as people *hurry*
in order to perform a comprehensible task, but as people *hurry*
to complete a necessary, but unpleasant and incomprehensible
task.'[5] These few examples out of many hundreds (one is
tempted to add that in describing Platon Karataev, Tolstoy
uses the word *krugly* ('round') five times in a single sentence!)
are more than enough to make the point. It will be noticed,
incidentally, that very commonly a basic verb is met at the
beginning of a sentence and is then repeated at the beginning
of several successive sentences or clauses. One example will
suffice, in literal and abbreviated form, from the opening scene
in *War and Peace*: '*There arrived* the highest Petersburg
society . . . ; *there arrived* the daughter of Prince Vasily . . .
*There arrived* too the youthful little Princess Bolkonskaya . . .

[3] ibid. II. 3. 4.          [4] ibid. IV. 1. 16.          [5] ibid. IV. 1. 11.

*There arrived* Prince Hippolyte . . . ; *there arrived* too the Abbé Morio and many others.'[6] The monotony of the reiterated past tense of the verb is quite unjustifiably disguised by the Maudes, who translate it in five different ways: 'was assembled', 'came', 'was also there', 'had come', 'had also come'. Consequently English readers do not notice as readily as Russians these sledgehammer blows: 'She could not understand . . . She did not understand . . . She did not understand . . . Still less could she understand . . .' Or: 'Pierre did not know that . . . He did not know that . . . Pierre did not know that . . . He did not know that . . . And therefore Pierre . . .'.

This recurring pattern for introducing sentences and clauses, a variant of the pattern of single word repetition which we meet so commonly in Tolstoy, is a characteristic device for achieving balance and rhythm. In this matter of balance, furthermore, Tolstoy was particularly addicted to a classical, rhetorical arrangement of his material in groups of three—three adjectives, three nouns, three verbs, three prepositions. Take for example the following sentence, in which I have inserted letters and numbers:

On his return to Moscow from the army, Nikolai Rostov was welcomed (A) by his home circle as (1) the best of sons, (2) a hero and (3) their darling Nikolenka; (B) by his relations as (1) a charming, (2) agreeable and (3) polite young man; (C) by his acquaintances as (1) a handsome lieutenant of hussars, (2) a good dancer and (3) one of the best matches in Moscow.[7]

Or the description of the preparations for the Olmütz review:

Now thousands of feet and bayonets, with colours flying and at the officers' command, (1) halted, (2) turned and (3) formed up at intervals, wheeling round *other* similar masses of infantry in *other* uniforms; *now* could be heard the rhythmic hoof-beats and jingling of the smart cavalry in (1) blue, (2) red and (3) green braided uniforms with smartly dressed bandsmen in front on (1) black, (2) roan or (3) grey horses; *now,* deploying itself *with its* brazen clatter of cannons, (1) polished, (2) shining and (3) swaying on their gun-carriages and *with its* smell of linstocks, the artillery crawled up between the infantry and the cavalry and took up its appointed positions. *Not only* the generals *wearing* full parade uniforms with their thin and thick waists drawn in to the utmost, their red necks propped up by their collars and *wearing* scarves and all decorations; *not only* the elegant, pomaded officers, *but every* soldier with his (1) fresh, (2) washed and (3) shaven face, and

[6] *War and Peace*, I. 1. 2.          [7] ibid. II. 1. 2.

his weapons polished and shining to the last degree, every horse, groomed till its coat shone like satin and every hair of its wetted mane lay smooth—all felt that something (1) serious, (2) important and (3) solemn was happening.[8]

Running through the syntax of Tolstoy's narrative passages is every device of arrangement and balance known to Cicero and Demosthenes (excluding the rhetorical question). There are the 'threes', the 'not only . . . but also', the 'either . . . or, neither . . . nor'; there is the fondness for 'in the first place', 'in the second place', 'in the third place'; there is the frequency of 'some said', 'others said', 'yet others said' (in one passage the pronominal sequence 'some' . . . 'others' . . . 'others' . . . (*kto* . . . *kto* . . . *kto* . . .) is carried to the length of ten successive repetitions); there is the love of 'now' . . . 'now' . . . 'now' . . . (*to* . . . *to* . . . *to* . . .); and there are the divisions of people and opinions into parties, groups and categories. We saw in the first chapter, in examining the draft versions of *War and Peace*, how some of Tolstoy's alterations were conditioned by the need to achieve greater balance and symmetry. It is this same objective which Tolstoy is continually pursuing through his use and abuse of the repeated word. There is no subtlety here, no attempt to disguise his method. But there is a blunt, simple, overwhelmingly direct attack which is characteristically and unmistakably Tolstoyan. Perhaps the following few sentences contain the quintessence of his unashamed repetitiveness:

It *seemed* to Pierre so *natural* that everyone should *like* him, and it would have *seemed* so *unnatural* if anyone had not *liked* him, that he could not help believing in the *sincerity* of the *people* around him. Besides he had no *time* to ask himself about the *sincerity* or *lack of sincerity* of these *people*. He was *constantly* short of *time*, he *constantly felt himself* in a state of mild and cheerful intoxication. He *felt himself* the centre of some important and general movement; he *felt* that something was *constantly* expected of him . . .[9]

The principle, broadly speaking, is to introduce a word and then repeat it in the next sentence; introduce a new word in that sentence and repeat this new word in the following one. It is not a consistent principle, of course, but the pattern is clear, and there is often an easily discernible system of links between consecutive sentences, and even, on occasions, between consecutive paragraphs.

[8] ibid. I. 3. 8.   [9] ibid. I. 3. 1.

Before we leave the subject of repetition we may mention those sequences, common in Tolstoy's writings generally and not merely in *War and Peace,* in which a person's thoughts which have been expressed in narrative are repeated in direct or indirect speech. When Prince Bolkonsky is reflecting on the possible betrothal of his daughter to Anatole Kuragin the thoughts attributed to him by Tolstoy are immediately repeated in his own words:

'Well, I've nothing against it,' the prince said to himself, 'but he must be worthy of her. And that is what we shall see.'

'That is what we shall see,' he added aloud. 'That is what we shall see.' [10]

One recalls the passage in *Anna Karenina* where Anna and Vronsky meet on the train in the snowstorm on Anna's return from Moscow to Petersburg. 'She had no need to ask', writes Tolstoy, 'why he was there. She knew as surely as if he had told her that he was there in order to be where she was.' At once Anna asks why he is there and Vronsky replies that he is there in order to be where she is. When Princess Marya imagines herself setting off from home as a pilgrim, her thoughts are described initially in narrative form and then voiced in the first person:

She pictured herself walking by Theodosia's side, dressed in coarse rags, walking with a staff . . . and reaching at last the place where there is neither sorrow nor sighing, but eternal joy and bliss.

'I shall come to a place and pray there. I will go on until my legs fail . . . and I shall at last reach that eternal quiet haven where there is neither sorrow nor sighing,' thought Princess Marya. [11]

Repetition, then, of one type or another, is the most characteristic single feature of Tolstoy's style. Perhaps next to it one might place a certain unorthodox 'incorrectness' of grammar and syntax. For all his preoccupation with balance and symmetry, Tolstoy was very far removed from academic fastidiousness or pedantry. Rules irked him and the student will not find his prose a model of grammatical conformity. One is surprised at times by his inability to distinguish the gerund from the participle, a confusion which is, of course, concealed in English translations. Again, one meets such examples of syntactical clumsiness as 'Today, having caught a glimpse of her, she

[10] *War and Peace* I. 3. 4.                    [11] ibid. II. 3. 26.

seemed to him still more lovely'.[12] On several occasions, too, one notices the redundant pronoun 'he', acting as the subject in a sentence in which the same subject has already been denoted by a noun: 'Trembling and panting, the old man, flying into a state of fury . . . *he* fell upon Eykhen . . .[13]

These un-Russian turns of speech can in some cases be ascribed to the influence of French syntax on the Russian language—as also can the peculiar use of prepositions which astonish one from time to time in reading *War and Peace,* or lexical combinations such as *delat' vpechatlenie* for the normal Russian *proizvodit' vpechatlenie (faire impression).* There are at least three ways of looking at these 'mistakes'. It can be argued that Tolstoy was deliberately using an archaic, gallicized syntax as a period detail in order to recapture the flavour of the language spoken in the days of his characters. But this is far too clever to be true; and in any case the gallicisms are mostly confined to the author's narrative and are comparatively rare in the speech of the characters themselves. Secondly, one can say that Tolstoy's gallicized syntax is not untypical of the Russian language as spoken in his own day, when the influence of French constructions was still strong and when the French language was known at least as well as Russian by most educated men. This fact undoubtedly explains some 'mistakes' in *War and Peace,* but does not explain their absence in other contemporary novels. Thirdly, one can give credence to Tolstoy's own statement on the subject of language: 'I like what is called incorrectness, that is to say what is characteristic.'[14] His words could be taken to strengthen the suggestion that he deliberately tried to capture the inaccuracies of the living spoken word, the looseness of syntax, the unfinished sentences of the average speaker. And there is certainly some truth in this, at least in so far as it concerns the dialogue of *War and Peace* or the author's reproduction of the thoughts of his characters. But the fact still remains that Tolstoy neither knew nor cared much about formal grammar and was a good deal more careless than, say, his sophisticated contemporary Turgenev. He thought aloud, transferred his thoughts to paper and sometimes forgot that he was writing, not talking.

[12] ibid. II. 1. 1.                    [13] ibid. IV. 2. 5.
[14] Letter to Tishchenko, 1886, quoted by Vinogradov, op. cit. p. 141.

If we continue to look for distinguishing features of Tolstoy's language, we will not find, as we do with many other Russian authors, that he has a marked preference for any one particular part of speech. Vinogradov has observed the frequency of the verb in Pushkin's prose, Turgenev's love of adjectives and adverbs; Goncharov's fondness for the noun. We find no obvious partiality in Tolstoy. But one cannot help observing a particular type of *sentence* structure which, while not confined to Tolstoy, is a stylistic feature which is certainly associated with him. This can only be conveyed in English by a translation which exactly follows the word order of the original: 'And a joyful, and at the same time pathetic, asking forgiveness for her joy, expression, settled on Natasha's face.'[15] This is a fairly typical example of his marked tendency to insert between adjective and noun a complex adjectival or participial expression in parenthesis as it were. Although economical of words it creates an impression of overcrowding. It has been remarked that not only individual sentences, but whole periods in Tolstoy's narrative are weighted down and unwieldy. Chekhov noticed this fact and saw in it a virtue: 'Have you noticed Tolstoy's language? Enormous periods, sentences piled one on top of another. Don't think that it happens by chance or that it's a shortcoming. It's art, and it only comes after hard work. These periods create an impression of power.'[16] Now and again sentences reach monumental proportions. The final sentence of Volume III, Part 3, Chapter 5 contains more than 230 words, and follows a not uncommon pattern: 'Count Rostopchin now removed . . . , now distributed . . . , now forbade . . . , now seized . . . (the word *to* "now" is repeated seventeen times)—this man did not understand . . . but merely wanted to . . .'. The sentence ends characteristically enough with the type of insertion just referred to: 'he tried with his puny hand now to speed on, now to hold back the course of the enormous, carrying him away together with it, popular tide.'

Such enormities are comparatively rare in Tolstoy. But what has been noticed—and it deserves further examination—is a tendency for Tolstoy's paragraphs (especially in the historical

15 *War and Peace*, IV. 4. 20.
16 S. Shchukin, *Iz vospominanii o Chekhove, Russkaya Mysl'*, No. 10, 1911, p. 45. Quoted by Bychkov, op. cit. p. 220.

and philosophical sections of the book) to begin and end with a simple sentence and to grow in the middle into a series of long, complex sentences: to start simply, become increasingly involved, and then relax again.[17] Personally I would say that it is more common for the complex sequence to continue throughout a paragraph, and for the *next* paragraph to revert to the simple statement. It seems to me that the example I now quote is more typical of Tolstoy's method of paragraph construction:

Prince Andrei arrived in Petersburg in August 1809.‖ It was the time when the reputation of the young Speransky and the energy with which his reforms were being carried out reached their highest point.‖ That same August the Emperor was thrown from his carriage, injured his leg and remained three weeks at Peterhof, receiving Speransky every day and no one else.‖ It was the time of the preparation not only of the two famous decrees which so agitated society on the abolition of court ranks and on the institution of examinations for the ranks of collegiate assessor and state councillor, but also of an entire state constitution intended to change the existing legal, administrative and financial system of Russian government from the state council to the district tribunal.‖ Now the vague liberal dreams with which the Emperor Alexander had ascended the throne and which he had tried to put into effect with the aid of his associates Czartorysky, Novosiltsev, Kochubei and Stroganov, whom he himself jokingly called his *comité de salut public*, were taking shape and being realised.‖

  Now all these men were replaced by Speransky on the civil side and Arakcheev on the military.‖[18]

The last statement is not easy to substantiate, but one can safely say that there are many examples of the above type of sentence sequence in the author's narrative in *War and Peace*. Chekhov admired the weight and power of Tolstoy's periods. To some of Tolstoy's contemporaries, however, his style of writing appeared cumbersome and archaic. One reviewer, writing in 1870, said:

What sort of language is this in Tolstoy's latest novel? When the author himself is recounting the story, the language is often woven together from sentences piled one on top of another in such ugly periods and with such frequent repetition of one and the same word that one is involuntarily reminded of mediaeval Latin or the writing of our old chancelleries. Is it possible after the graceful and refined speech of Pushkin and Lermontov to go back again to the language of the pre-Karamzin period?[19]

[17] See Saburov, op. cit. pp. 541 ff.    [18] *War and Peace*, II. 3. 4.
[19] *Syn Otechestva*, No. 3, 1870, quoted by Vinogradov, op. cit. p. 136.

The reviewer, incidentally, might have mentioned in confirmation of his point the extraordinary proliferation of 'that' and 'what' and 'which' in Tolstoy's longer sentences: 'She only repeated *that* she asked him to forget *that which* she had said, *that* she did not remember *what* she had said, and *that* she had no sorrow except *that which* he knew—sorrow *that* Prince Andrei's marriage . . . etc.'[20] Both he and Chekhov have some right on their side. There is nothing graceful or refined about Tolstoy's periods. They are not short, or economical of words. They are not varied or subtle. But they do have the weight, the power and the balance of Roman declamation—and something of the archaic, artificial flavour too. One feels when reading the historical and philosophical passages of the novel that Tolstoy believed that weighty subjects needed weighty treatment. As Chekhov said—it did not happen by accident.

Equally contrived and equally important in an examination of the style of *War and Peace* is the use of the French language. This is a subject which must be clearly separated from the one touched on earlier, namely the French elements or gallicisms in Tolstoy's language (a feature not confined in his writings to *War and Peace,* and which in any case is rather an unconscious reflection of the language of educated Russian society in his day than a conscious linguistic device). By the use of French in *War and Peace,* I mean the presence of French words in the text of the novel. Academician Vinogradov, the most diligent student of Tolstoy's style, was so carried away by the apparent quantity of French in *War and Peace* that he called the novel bilingual. This is an exaggeration, particularly since the percentage of French words can hardly be as much as 2 per cent of the total (although it strikes the Russian reader more than the English, since in the Maudes' translation the French is sometimes translated into English, sometimes not). As the writing of the novel progressed, there is evidence that Tolstoy began to doubt the wisdom of his use of foreign words in a Russian novel. In December 1867 he wrote to Bartenev, who was doing his proofreading for him, and said: 'there are a good many French and German phrases in Book IV. They need to be translated, especially the German.'[21] In his article 'A Few Words about

[20] *War and Peace,* II. 5. 4.
[21] Letter to P. I. Bartenev, 6 December 1867, J.E. LXI. 188.

*War and Peace'* he refers specifically to the criticisms levelled against his use of French; and one might add at this point that he was criticized not only for *using* French, but for using *bad* French! One reader wrote in 1865: 'I don't much like Tolstoy's *1805*—there is more bad French than Russian in it.'[22] while a reviewer in the April 1868 number of the journal *The Spark* said in a bantering tone: 'The new novel *War and Peace* is nothing but the story of two battles—Austerlitz and Borodino. In the intervals between these battles, some nice young officers fall in love with some no less nice young ladies, while the old people speak French very badly and Count Tolstoy translates their words into Russian in footnotes.'[23] Tolstoy, as far as I know, did not take up this rather flippant challenge but while in general defending his point of view in his article on *War and Peace* he did go so far as to say that in depicting the Russians of a certain class and also Napoleon and other Frenchmen: 'I was involuntarily carried away to an unnecessary extent by the form in which they expressed their French way of thought.' Eventually in 1873, when Tolstoy drastically revised the published novel, all the French words were cut out. Writing later in the same year to Strakhov he confessed: 'I was sometimes sorry about doing away with the French, but on the whole I think it is better without it.'[24]

Although Tolstoy veered round to this conclusion in the 1870's, the fact remains that the French words were later restored in the definitive edition, and had presumably been introduced originally for some definite reason. It is not enough to say that they were intended as authentic period details, for Tolstoy need only have said that most of the Russian educated classes in the early nineteenth century spoke French more easily than Russian to have made his point: and as for the French, it can safely be assumed that the reader knows they spoke French without Tolstoy having continually to remind him. It is quite clear that the French language was used largely as an element of characterization. At an elementary level, Tolstoy makes many pronouncements *in Russian* about the fluency in French of a score of major and minor characters, referring to

[22] Letter of A. D. Bludova to P. Annenkov, March 1865, quoted by Vinogradov, op. cit. p. 147.
[23] Quoted by Shklovsky. op. cit. p. 208.
[24] Letter to N. N. Strakhov, 22 June 1873, J.E. LXII. 34.

their accent, their intonation, or the occasions on which they
resort to French; and often he has some ironical comment to
make: that French was used by Prince Andrei when he wished
to express disdain; that a word was pronounced in a specially
'refined' manner by Anna Scherer when speaking French; that
Akhrosimova, who always spoke Russian, used a French expression to Sonya to imply mild contempt; that Pierre 'expressed
himself so artificially because he was speaking in French' (this
despite his French upbringing); that Hélène did the same to
defend herself against the charge of wanting to marry again
when her husband was still alive, the implication being that
she could deceive herself more easily in French than in Russian.
There are numerous references of this sort—some seemingly
quite pointless, as for example the mention of the orderly officer
in Bagration's detachment who spoke French fluently but badly
—but they are not relevant to the present question because no
French words are used. When French words are actually spoken
by or with reference to a character in the novel, they are either
spoken by or about Frenchmen, because they are Frenchmen,
or Russians because they are un-Russian (or else find themselves
in an 'un-Russian' environment where they are obliged to conform). French in fact commonly means sophisticated, artificial,
mendacious even; Russian means native, simple, natural and
true. The principle is not followed with absolute consistency
throughout the novel (Prince Andrei, for example, occasionally
speaks to Pierre in French), but it is followed sufficiently often
to make it easily recognizable and effective. Sometimes Tolstoy
uses a French word and gives its Russian equivalent in brackets
immediately after it. 'Boris Drubetskoy, *en garçon* (a bachelor)
as he put it, having left his wife behind in Moscow, was also
at the ball . . .'[25] This affectation of a French phrase when a
Russian equivalent exists goes down as a black mark against
Boris. Equally ironical is the use made of individual French
words in the scene between Pierre and Captain Ramballe in
Moscow in 1812, when the two are discussing love: 'It was
obvious that *l'amour* which the Frenchman so loved was not
that low, simple sort of love which Pierre had once felt for his
wife, nor that romantic love which he felt for Natasha. . . .'[26]
Pierre's feelings, whether for Hélène or Natasha, were sincere

[25] *War and Peace*, III. 1. 3.       [26] ibid. III. 3. 29.

and natural even if in the first case they were misguided; they were therefore Russian. Ramballe's concept of *l'amour,* on the other hand, is something unnatural and affected and so the French word is retained. When the conceited Anatole Kuragin visits the unpretentious Princess Marya as a prospective suitor, he is made to think in French—'La pauvre fille. Elle est diablement laide.'

Another ironical use to which French phrases are put is the expression of some conventional sentiment. Tolstoy describes how the words 'ma pauvre mère' figure in the thoughts and speech of three of his French characters whose vanity or artificiality are especially distasteful to him—Napoleon, Ramballe and Mlle Bourienne. When the Emperor Alexander utters the truism 'what a terrible thing war is' Tolstoy follows the Russian words by their French translation: 'Quelle terrible chose que la guerre.'[27] When he wishes to ridicule the idea of Napoleon's greatness he writes: ' "Du sublime" (he sees something "sublime" in himself) "au ridicule il n'y a qu' un pas", he says. And the whole world has been repeating for fifty years: "Sublime! Grand! Napoleon le grand! Du sublime au ridicule il n'y a qu'un pas." '[28]

Irony and ridicule of the theatrical and the self-important underly most of the French phrases used in *War and Peace.* As such they serve a legitimate purpose as long as French is readily understood by the reader. But when that language ceases to be understood and there is a need for footnotes to explain the meaning, their purpose is no longer useful. This is not to say that they ought to be deleted. It is only to emphasize that a knowledge of both French and Russian is essential for a full appreciation of the language of Tolstoy's novel.

There is a further side to the study of the language of *War and Peace,* namely, the exploration of words and phrases which do not belong to a neutral, literary language and which, taken collectively, constitute the distinguishing features of an author's style. There are a good many examples in Tolstoy's vocabulary and syntax of archaic linguistic mannerisms derived from an official 'civil service' style of writing known to philologists as the 'language of the chancelleries'. Such examples occur at random in the author's narrative, in certain documents such

[27] ibid. I. 3. 10.        [28] ibid. IV. 3. 18.

as Kutuzov's letter to old Prince Bolkonsky, and in the mouths
of statesmen such as Kochubei or Arakcheev. Tolstoy knew how
to impart to his characters and situations the appropriate,
stylized linguistic flavour. The language of the freemason who
introduces Pierre to his masonic lodge has a strong Church
Slavonic tang. A sentimental Karamzinian aura pervades Julie's
correspondence with Princess Marya. There is a popular gnomic
element in Karataev's speech, salted as it is with expressions of
folk wisdom. The language of the soldiers and peasants in *War
and Peace* is rich in colloquial words and idioms. The passages
devoted to hunting, bee-keeping or horse-breeding are sprinkled
with local dialect words which will not be found in dictionaries
of the standard Russian literary language. In short, Tolstoy
consciously, but *with restraint,* employs a wide variety of linguistic idioms, the effect of which is of course lost in translation;
but at the same time he avoids an excess of obscure jargon or
recondite professional terminology, the over-naturalistic reproduction of peasant speech, the proliferation of dialectisms or the
flirtation with neologisms, one or other of which extravagances
mar some of the works of Gogol, Leskov, the writers of the
'natural school' of Russian fiction and many early Soviet
novelists. The hallmark of Tolstoy's style is lucidity, and such
lucidity demanded moderation and caution in departing from
the best standards of Russian spoken by the educated people of
his own class and day—the basis of the language of *War and
Peace.*

The spoken language of the principal characters in the novel
is not generally marked by any special idiosyncrasies or even by
any individual colouring. Prince Andrei and Pierre, Nikolai and
Natasha are immediately recognizable by the sort of things
they say and the opinions they express, but the actual words
they use might well have been taken, one imagines, from the
day to day language of Tolstoy and his family in the 1860's. An
exception might be made for Prince Andrei, whose gallicisms
obtrude from time to time. But he, like the others—and this
is the surprising thing—is a person of few words. The main
characters in the novel in fact are given relatively little direct
speech. When they speak they do so briefly; they do not declaim
at length or figure in long conversation pieces. One has the impression that more is said about them than they say themselves,

and still more is expressed through interior monologue or through the author describing their thoughts, feelings and re-actions. Idiosyncrasies of language, favourite words, witticisms, stylized mannerisms such as brusqueness or directness—all these things are found in the minor characters. Karataev has his popular saws and his frequently repeated *sokolik* ('my little falcon', 'my dear'). Akhrosimova is fond of slang and salty terms of abuse, and is moreover blunt and abrupt in her de-livery. 'Uncle' has his favourite Dickensian untranslatable tag *chistoe delo marsh* (which the Maudes render as 'that's it, come on'). Bilibin is always ready with a *mot*. Count Rostov is dis-tinguished by his gastronomic vocabulary, simple, colloquial Russian, bad French and the abuse of *ma chère*. The speech of Prince Bolkonsky, a survivor of an older generation, is studded with archaisms, gallicisms and colloquialisms which, when Prince Vasily visits him at Bald Hills, are so obvious that Vasily him-self tries to imitate them. These subtleties of language which are lost on the English reader are a real, if minor part of Tolstoy's art, and perhaps only a Russian can fully appreciate them. The English reader, however, while having to accept on trust that there is more to Tolstoy than the best English versions can convey (though at least he suffers much less than, say, Gogol, the standard 'Everyman' translation of whose *Dead Souls* is so inaccurate as to be quite ludicrous) will more readily notice another idiosyncrasy of his language—the attribution of words to inanimate objects. The oak tree 'speaks' to Prince Andrei. After Borodino the rain 'seemed to say: "Enough, men, enough. Desist. Think what you are doing."' Gestures, faces, eyes are all made articulate, and often seem to say things which con-tradict the spoken word—all of which emphasizes Tolstoy's belief in the inner truth of involuntary facial and bodily move-ments and the dictum of the poet Tyutchev that a thought, once uttered, is a lie.

The student of Tolstoy's language is bound to admit that there is comparatively little richness of imagery in *War and Peace*. Metaphor and metonymy are quite rare, and even similes, which are Tolstoy's commonest literary image, are not especially prominent when viewed against the novel as a whole. The objects of his similes are drawn for the most part either from the animal world, the processes of nature and the daily round of country life, or from the physical world with its mathematical laws. In the former case they reflect the author's profound knowledge and observation of rural life, and stem directly from his own experience; in the latter they savour more of textbooks of elementary physics or mechanics and suggest the influence of Tolstoy's learned, scientific friends of the 60's, an influence which is geared up and put to the service of a providential, determinist philosophy. The one group of similes has to do with ants, bees, flies, hares and hounds, herds of cattle, rams, wounded animals, the action of water, and household objects such as spinning wheels and looms. The subject matter of the other group is mass and momentum, velocities, parallelograms of forces, attraction, gravity, heat, engines, clocks, watches and mathematical equations. Seldom is a startling image produced or a *recherché* simile concocted, but now and again one is arrested by the thought behind a simile such as that of the old man sitting in the deserted grounds of the abandoned Bald Hills estate 'as impassively as a fly on the face of a loved one who has died',[29] or that of the smile which came to Natasha's face 'with difficulty and with an effort just like the opening of a door which has long been rusty'.[30] The comparisons are thoughtful and unstereotyped. They do not pass over the reader like hackneyed phrases which have long ceased to evoke any response. At times they run into many lines—in one case two whole pages!—and inevitably bring to mind the epic similes of Homer and Virgil. It is quite possible that a complex extended simile such as the one comparing deserted Moscow to a queenless hive is a conscious imitation of an epic device, a prose counterpart of the bees similes in the *Georgics* or in *Paradise Lost*. Less obviously inspired are the frequent comparisons of battle scenes, acts of war and troop movements with fishing, hunting and agriculture, or the actions of society men and women at soirées and dinners with simple domestic or rural activities. They are both comparisons and contrasts: comparisons of two superficial likes, but with ironical allusions to the distance separating abnormal and unnatural things like war or high society and the natural, simple activities of normal country life. It has been well pointed out[31] that the simile of

---

[29] *War and Peace* III. 2. 5.     [30] ibid. IV. 4. 15.
[31] Steiner, op. cit. pp. 85 ff.

the guests 'shaken together like rye in a shovel'[32] at the English Club dinner to honour Bagration or the comparison of Pierre, confronted by his deceitful wife, to a hare crouching motionless before the surrounding hounds[33] have the effect, among other things, of contrasting the false social world with that of the land and the rural life. And there is no doubt that irony, which lies concealed in these images, is a sharp weapon in Tolstoy's hands. One may recall his scathing remarks about the Frenchman sent to announce to the Emperor Alexander the news of the abandonment of Moscow: 'This envoy was the Frenchman Michaud who knew no Russian, but was *quoique étranger, russe de coeur et d'âme,* as he used to say about himself.'[34] One remembers Bilibin's sallies against the Prussians; 'Les Prussiens sont nos fidèles alliés, que ne nous ont trompés que trois fois depuis trois ans.'[35] Tolstoy's irony may also be seen in his many forthright statements levelled against classes of men and women whom he disliked. Doctors were one such group: 'But despite the fact that the doctors treated him, bled him and gave him medicines to drink, Pierre recovered.'[36] Diplomats were another, and it is said in favour of Bilibin that 'He was not one of the great number of diplomats who are bound to have only negative qualities, to avoid doing certain things and to speak French in order to be very good diplomats.'[37] Historians were yet another, and in writing about the causes of the French Revolution, as advanced by modern history books, Tolstoy says: 'Louis XIV was a very proud and self-confident man; he had such and such mistresses and such and such ministers, and he ruled France badly. His descendants were weak men and they too ruled France badly. And they had such and such favourites, and such and such mistresses. Moreover certain men wrote some books at that time.'[38] This last passage is a good example of a naïve oversimplification whereby Tolstoy refuses to view a thing in the conventional light and contrives to 'make it appear strange', in the expression of the Formalist writer and critic Shklovsky. Shklovsky regarded Tolstoy as an exponent of 'the device of making it strange' (a cumbersome coinage of his own), which meant, simply speaking, removing

[32] *War and Peace*, II 1. 4.        [33] ibid. II. 1. 6.        [34] ibid. IV. 1. 3.
[35] ibid. II. 2. 9.        [36] ibid. IV. 4. 12.        [37] ibid. I. 2. 10.
[38] ibid. Epilogue, Part 2, 1.

a word or object from its conventional context, calling it by a different name, refusing to recognize it, pretending it is something else, doing anything with it, in fact, to rescue it from being a verbal cliché with no power to evoke a response. Perhaps the classic example of this 'device'—this ironical oversimplification as I would prefer to call it—is the description of the opera in Moscow as seen through Natasha's eyes, which begins:

The floor of the stage consisted of smooth boards, at the sides was some painted cardboard representing trees, and at the back was a cloth stretched over boards. In the centre of the stage sat some girls in red bodices and white skirts. One very fat girl in a white silk dress sat apart on a low bench, to the back of which a piece of green cardboard was glued. They all sang something . . .[39]

To Natasha, newly arrived from the country, the artificiality of operatic convention seemed ludicrous and grotesque, and these deflationary sentences with their ironical naiveté, well convey her mood. In a similar deflationary spirit Tolstoy alludes to military standards, the highly prized symbols of valour and glory, as 'scraps of material on sticks'.[40]

There is little subtlety in Tolstoy's irony, but much publicist force. Yet again one is made aware how closely linked are an author's language and linguistic devices and the basic idea or purpose of his novel. As language is controlled by the thought it is designed to express, so it is bent to the service of characterization as we saw with reference to Tolstoy's use of the French language, and as we shall see again in the next chapter. The conventional compartments into which we separate our material break down under pressure and spill their contents one into another.

[39] *War and Peace*, II. 5. 9.          [40] ibid. III. 2. 39.

# VI: CHARACTERIZATION

In this chapter we shall try and consider how Tolstoy's characters are introduced and developed, and what are his particular methods of characterization. The subject is complicated by the sheer number and variety of the dramatis personae, but we can narrow it down from the very start by drawing a general distinction between the treatment of historical and non-historical characters in the novel. It is a fact that the generals and statesmen, the great historical names of the period of the Napoleonic wars, are almost without exception flat and static figures. Little or nothing is revealed of their private lives. We do not see them in intimate relationships with other people. Their loves, their hobbies, their personal dramas are a closed book to us. This is not accidental. As Prince Andrei reflects at Drissa in 1812:

> Not only does a good commander not need genius or any special qualities; on the contrary, he needs the absence of the highest and best human qualities—love, poetry, tenderness and philosophic, inquiring doubt. He must be limited . . . God forbid that he should be humane, love anyone, pity anyone, or think about what is right and what is not.[1]

Their thoughts are rarely scrutinized either through interior monologue or by extended description from the author. Some characters, such as Arakcheev, for example, use only direct speech. Nothing is conveyed of their thought processes or the motives behind the words they utter. Nor do they develop with the action of the story. The statesmen and the generals in *War and Peace* are either bearers of a message or bureaucratic Aunt-Sallies for Tolstoy to knock down. This fact illustrates the unity which exists between Tolstoy's ideas and their expression through his characters. Static characters generally speaking deserve static treatment. Theme and style are at one.

An exception to the rule that generals are flat characters might be made in the case of Kutuzov. Although he is a general, he is not, as Tolstoy understands him, arrogant or self-satisfied. The Kutuzov of *War and Peace* has some claim to be

[1] *War and Peace*. III. 1. 1.

three-dimensional. It is not that he is shown by Tolstoy to have grown sufficiently in stature with the course of events to justify the remark—true though it may well have been in real life—that 'In 1805 Kutuzov is still only a general of the Suvorov school; in 1812 he is the father of the Russian people'.[2] But his little acts of kindness, his friendly words to the soldiers who fought with him in his earlier campaigns, his unaffected behaviour in the company of his inferiors, his present of some sugar lumps to the little girl at Fili, his request to have some poems read to him—all these small things reveal positive and humane qualities which more than balance his lethargy and lechery. Again it is in keeping with Tolstoy's purpose that a general who is not a *poseur* or an egoist or a careerist should emerge as a more rounded personality than any of his professional colleagues.

In this chapter our remarks will be confined to the fictitious or, rather, non-historical characters. Here again the range is enormous, and in order to restrict it as much as possible we shall concentrate mainly on the men and women who figure most prominently in *War and Peace*. We have already seen that Tolstoy's first step as a novelist was to draw thumbnail sketches of his future heroes and group their main characteristics together under such headings as wealth, social attributes, mental faculties, artistic sensibilities and attitudes to love. In this respect, incidentally, his rough notes and plans are very different from those left by Dostoevsky, and illustrate an important difference of approach. Dostoevsky in the preliminary stages of his work is concerned with how to formulate his ideas (a generation earlier, Pushkin had tended to jot down first of all the details of his plots). But Tolstoy was interested primarily in the personalities of his characters—in the fact, for example, that Nikolai 'is very good at saying the obvious'; that Natasha is 'suddenly sad, suddenly terribly happy'; or that Berg has no poetical qualities 'except the poetry of accuracy and order'.[3]

The problem of actually bringing his major characters on to the stage was one to which Tolstoy attached the greatest importance, and one which, as we have seen, gave him a great deal of difficulty. Broadly speaking, the problem was tackled in a

² Saburov, op. cit. p. 372.          ³ J.E. XIII. 16–18.

fairly uniform manner, and the technique employed is clearly recognizable, though not of course invariable. All the main characters are introduced very early on. They are introduced with a minimum of biography and with a minimum of external detail (but such as there is is typical and important, and likely to recur). Attention is drawn to their features, the expression on their faces, the expression in their eyes and in their smile, their way of looking or not looking at a person. This is a fact which has attracted the notice of most critics of Tolstoy's novels, and inspired Merezhkovsky to make his much-quoted *mot* 'with Tolstoy we hear because *we see*' (and its corollary 'with Dostoevsky we see because *we hear*').[4] From the very beginning, the fundamental characteristics of the men and women as they then are are enunciated. There is little or no narration to elaborate these characteristics. Almost at once the men and women say something or make an impression on somebody, so that the need for any further direct description from the author disappears. Pierre, for example, is introduced with one sentence about his appearance (stout, heavily built, close cropped hair, spectacles); one sentence about his social status, and one sentence about his life to date. He is then portrayed through the impression he makes on other people present. He is summed up by four epithets which all refer to his *expression* (*vzglyad*)—clever, shy, observant, natural—and which at the same time distinguish him from the rest of the company and reveal the essence of his character as it then is. Similarly Prince Andrei is given a sentence or two of 'author's description'—handsome, clear-cut, dry features, measured step, bored expression (*vzglyad*)—while the impression he makes on the company and his reaction to them is at once sharply contrasted with the mutual response of Prince Andrei and Pierre to one another. Virtually nothing is said about the earlier lives of these two men. What did Pierre do in Paris? Why did Prince Andrei marry Lisa? We are not told. Both men immediately catch the eye, for both are bored and ill at ease. They are introduced in fact into an environment which is essentially foreign to their real natures, although their way of life requires that they should move in this environment. Despite the fact that the manner of their first appearances attracts attention, there is nothing to suggest that they will be

---

[4] Merezhkovsky, op. cit. p. 235.

the main heroes of the novel, in the sense that no extra length or detail goes into their description.

By contrast, Natasha and Nikolai are both introduced in their own domestic environment—home-loving creatures on their home ground—integrated in the family and, as it were, part of the furniture. But again they are presented with a minimum of external description (in which facial expressions are conspicuous); again their salient characteristics—Natasha's charm and vivacity, Nikolai's frankness, enthusiasm and impetuosity—are conveyed from the very start; and again we are told nothing about their earlier lives (for example, Nikolai's student days). This lack of biographical information is important in the sense that it enables us to be introduced to the characters as we usually meet people in real life—that is to say, as they now are, and without any knowledge of the forces which shaped them before we met them and made them what they are. It could even be argued that a novelist who introduces his heroes by reconstructing their past when that past plays no direct part in the novel, actually risks sacrificing, by the accumulation of historical detail such as we do not have about people whom we are meeting for the first time, that immediate lifelikeness which, in the case of Tolstoy's greatest characters, is so strikingly impressive.

Once the men and women have made their entrances the author has to face another problem. Are they to remain substantially as they are, with the reader's interest diverted towards the details of the plot? Or are they to grow and change as the plot progresses? If they are to develop, must they do so because the passage of time and the inner logic of their own personalities dictate it? Or because of the pressure of the events which form the plot? Or because the author wishes to express an idea of his own through their medium? In *War and Peace* the main characters do grow and change, and they do so for all these reasons. In the course of the time span of the novel the adolescents grow to maturity and the mature men reach early middle age. War and marriage make their impact on men and women alike, and experience teaches them what they failed to understand before. The Pierre of the opening chapter of the novel, with his self-indulgence, his agnosticism and his admiration for Napoleon, is very different from the spiritually rejuvenated

middle-aged man who has discovered a focus for his restless
and dissipated energies, and who no longer has any illusions
about the grandeur of power. The course of events brings Prince
Andrei round from a cynical disillusionment in life, through
a feeling of personal embitterment, to a belief in the reality of
happiness and love; in the face of death his vanity and ambition
are humbled by the realization of the insignificance of this
world, and he acquires a hitherto unknown peace of mind.
Natasha acquires an unsuspected strength of character after her
younger brother's death, and an unaccustomed staidness as the
wife of Pierre—to some readers an astonishing violation of her
nature, but to others a change which is fully comprehensible in
the transition from adolescence to motherhood. Even Nikolai's
impetuosity is curbed and experience gives him greater solidity
and stability. These changes do not result from the fact that
our knowledge of the main heroes gradually increases throughout the novel, as it inevitably does, and the picture of them
grows fuller and fuller with each successive episode. They are
changes of substance, qualitative rather than quantitative
changes. Tolstoy's achievement in contriving the development
of his main characters lies in the fact that all the reasons mentioned above for their development are so carefully interwoven
that the reader is not conscious of many strands but only one.
The characters change because they grow older and wiser. But
the events which form the plot, and in particular the Napoleonic
invasion, give them greater wisdom and experience, for characters and events are organically connected. And the state to which
the main heroes come at the end of the novel—marriage, and
the simple round of family life—the state which is the ultimate
expression of Tolstoy's basic idea—is the natural outcome of the
impact on them of the events they have experienced as they
have grown older and their realization of the shallowness of
society and the vainglory of war. The profoundly subjective
basis of Tolstoy's art may be seen in the fact that Pierre and
Natasha, Nikolai and Princess Marya all achieve the state
which he himself had achieved, however imperfectly, and which
he sincerely believed to be the most desirable of all states. But
this does not mean that their characters are distorted in order
to force them into the channels which for him were the right
ones. Pierre has so much of Tolstoy in him that he needs no

forcing. Natasha, we may remember, was from the very earliest draft of *War and Peace* 'crying out for a husband', and needing 'children, love, bed'. Nikolai and Princess Marya, for all the difference between their personalities, interests and intellectual attainments, never seem likely to stray far from the family nest or to be seduced from the family estate by the allurements of *le monde*.

Change and development are at the centre of Tolstoy's characterization, and the process is a consistent and logical one. But however great the changes in his main heroes may seem to be, it must not be forgotten that they occur within certain well-defined bounds, and that the characters themselves remain in the camp to which they have always belonged and continue to be what they have always been—some of the finest and most sympathetic representatives of the Russian land-owning aristocracy.

There is no need to labour the point that Tolstoy's principal heroes change and develop. We can turn instead to the question how he achieved the effects he desired by the devices of characterization at his disposal. It seems to me that the essence of Tolstoy's technique is to show that at every stage in the life of his heroes the likelihood of change is always present, so that at no time are they static, apathetic or inert, but constantly liable to respond to some new external or internal stimulus. Very often the stimulus is provided by a person from the opposite camp—a 'negative' character, a selfish, complacent or *static* man or woman. These people act as temptations to the heroes; they are obstacles in their path which have to be overcome. Pierre, for example, is momentarily blinded by the apparent greatness of Napoleon. He is trapped into marriage with Hélène, with whom he has nothing in common, and is in danger of being drawn into the Kuragin net. After their separation he is reconciled with her again, only to bemoan his fate once more as a retired gentleman-in-waiting, a member of the Moscow English Club and a universal favourite in Moscow society. Prince Andrei, like Pierre, is deceived by the symbol of Napoleon, and like Pierre he finds himself married to a woman who is as much his intellectual inferior as Hélène is morally beneath Pierre. Natasha for her part is attracted at first by the social climber Boris Drubetskoy and later infatuated by the same Anatole Kuragin who had actually begun to turn Princess Marya's head. Julie Karagina looms for a while on Nikolai's horizon. From all these temptations and involvements the heroes and heroines are saved, not by their own efforts but by the timely workings of Providence. Prince Andrei's wife dies. Pierre is provoked by Dolokhov into separating from his wife, and after their reconciliation he is eventually released by Hélène's death. Natasha is saved from herself by the solicitude of her friends. By chance Princess Marya catches Anatole unawares as he flirts with Mlle Bourienne. (Nikolai, to his credit, is never likely to obey his mother's wishes and marry Julie.) It seems as if fate is working to rescue them from the clutches of egocentricity. But it is not only external circumstances such as personal associations with people of the opposite camp which are a challenge to Tolstoy's heroes and heroines. There are internal obstacles against which they have to contend, without any help from Providence. Tolstoy made it a main object of his characterization to show his positive heroes at all important moments 'becoming' and not just 'being', beset with doubts, tormented by decisions, the victims of ambivalent thoughts and emotions, eternally restless. As a result, their mobility, fluidity and receptivity to change are constantly in evidence, as they face their inner problems. Princess Marya has to overcome her instinctive aversion to Natasha. Nikolai has to wage a struggle between love and duty until he finds in the end that they can both be reconciled in one and the same person. Pierre's inner disquiet and spiritual striving express his determination, now weak, now strong, to overcome in himself the very qualities of selfishness and laziness which he despises in other people. Outward and inward pressures are continually being exerted on Pierre, Prince Andrei, Princess Marya, Natasha and Nikolai, and their lives are lived in a state of flux.

And yet Tolstoy felt himself bound to try and resolve their conflicts and bring them to a state which, if not final and irreversible, is a new and higher stage in their life's development. It is not a solution to all their problems, a guarantee that they will not be troubled in future. The peace of mind which Prince Andrei attains before his death might not have lasted long if he had lived. Pierre's uneasy religious equilibrium may not be of long duration. The very fact that we can easily foresee new threats to their security, new stimuli and new responses, is a proof of the depth, integrity and lifelikeness of the two finest heroes of Tolstoy's novel. But although there is not and cannot be any absolute finality about the state to which Tolstoy's men and women are brought, there is nevertheless an ultimate harmony, charity, and sense of purpose in their lives which represent the highest ideals of which they are capable, given the personalities with which they have been endowed and the beliefs of the author who created them.

The novelist who wishes to create a vivid illusion of immediacy and mobility in his heroes must avoid exhaustive character studies and biographical reconstructions concentrated in a chapter or series of chapters in his novel, whether at the beginning, in the middle or at the end. Many novelists begin with lengthy narrative descriptions of their main heroes. Gogol in *Dead Souls* leaves Chichikov's life story to the very end of the novel. Turgenev in the *Nest of Gentlefolk* asks the reader's permission to break off the thread of his story in Chapter 8 in order to spend the next few chapters filling in Lavretsky's background. In Chapter 33 he does the same thing for his heroine, Lisa. But Tolstoy by dispensing largely with 'pre-history' and allowing his men and women to reveal themselves little by little as the novel progresses, avoids the necessity for set characterization pieces, static and self-contained as they often are in other writers.

Another factor which aids the illusion of reality—and movement—is the continued interaction of all the elements which make up Tolstoy's novel—men and women, nature, and the world of inanimate objects. Very seldom is a person seen or described in isolation—just as in real life, human beings cannot be divorced from the infinite number of animate and inanimate phenomena which make them what they are and determine what they do. Tolstoy is at pains, therefore, in striving after truthfulness to life in his characterization, to show the interdependence and interpenetration of man and nature. The stars, the sky, the trees, and the fields, the moonlight, the thrill of the chase, the familiar objects of the home all affect the mood and the actions of the characters no less than the rational processes of the mind or the persuasions of other human beings. That this is so in life is a commonplace; but there have been few authors with Tolstoy's power to show the multiplicity of interacting phenomena in the lives of fictitious men and women.

Movement is the essence of Pierre, Prince Andrei and Natasha and this is shown both externally and internally. Externally their eyes, their lips, their smile are mobile and infectious; their expressions continually alter. Internally their thoughts are in a state of turbulence and their mood is liable to swing violently from one extreme to another—from joy to grief, despair to elation, enthusiasm to boredom. There are times indeed when two incompatible emotions coexist uneasily and the character does not know whether he or she is sad or happy.

Princess Marya is not such a forceful or impulsive character as her brother or sister-in-law. Her qualities of gentleness, deep faith, long-suffering, humility and addiction to good works are not combined with a searching mind or a vivacious personality. But she is, nevertheless, a restless person, and as such is clearly a favourite of Tolstoy (she even quotes his beloved Sterne!). The anxieties and disturbances in her relations with Anatole Kuragin, Mlle Bourienne and Natasha are evidence that she is a rounded and dynamic figure, and not, as it were, conceived in one piece. In the presence of Nikolai she is brought to life with all the magic of Tolstoy's art. Nikolai too, for all his apparent complacency and limited horizons, does not stand still. He has his moments of doubt, uncertainty and fear just as he has his outbursts of uninhibited enthusiasm and emperor worship. He is given his own inner crisis to surmount when at Tilsit 'a painful process was at work in his mind'[5] as he tried to reconcile the horrors of the hospital he had recently visited, the amputated arms and legs and the stench of dead flesh, with his hero the Emperor Alexander's evident liking and respect for the self-satisfied Napoleon. The crisis, it is true, soon passes after a couple of bottles of wine. But it could never have been allowed to come to a head at all by his friend Boris Drubetskoy.

By contrast, the less prominent figures in *War and Peace* are not shown in the critical stages of their change and·development. Even Sonya's conflict (she is described in an early portrait sketch in typically Tolstoy fashion as 'generous and mean')[6]— the conflict between her loyalty to the family and her love for Nikolai—emerges rather through Tolstoy's description of it

---

[5] *War and Peace*, II. 2. 21.          [6] J.E. XIII. 19.

than through the inner workings and sudden vacillations of her mind. Vera and Berg, Akhrosimova, Bolkonsky and many other minor figures, however vital and many-sided they might be as individuals, are fundamentally static characters who are fully-grown from the beginning. The ability to respond to change, the qualities of restlessness, curiosity, flexibility and dynamism are essentially the perquisites of the main heroes of the novel, and in particular Pierre, Prince Andrei and Natasha. And one may add that it is the growth and development of precisely these three people which reflects above all the changes in Tolstoy himself and those closest to him at Yasnaya Polyana, and is a convincing proof of the personal basis of Tolstoy's art.

In examining the characters of a novel with an historical setting, three questions immediately spring to mind. In the first place, do they emerge as individuals? Secondly, do they un-mistakably belong to the historical environment in which they are made to move? And thirdly, do they embody universal characteristics which make them readily comprehensible to people of a different country and a different age? If we apply these questions to Pierre, Prince Andrei and Natasha, the answer to the first is indisputably yes. There is nothing bookish, contrived or externally manipulated about their actions. They can never be confused with any other characters. They have an outward presence and an inner life which mark them off as highly individualized personalities. To the second question the answer is less obvious and critical opinion is divided. For my own part I am inclined to think that there is nothing about them specifically representative of their own age, which is not also representative of Tolstoy's own generation. They are the products of a class and a way of life which had not materially altered when Tolstoy began to write. That they experienced the impact in their homes of a great patriotic war is a fact which distinguishes their lives from the lives of Tolstoy's own con-temporaries, but the development of their characters cannot be explained solely in terms of that particular war. Pierre might ask different questions from Levin or put the same questions in a different way, but his spiritual journey is fundamentally the same. Prince Andrei's reactions to war could have been those of one of the many obscure defenders of Sevastopol. Natasha's progress to motherhood, while it is not identical with Kitty's, is not peculiar to the first half rather than to the second half of the nineteenth century. The third question, however, like the first, is easily answered. In Tolstoy's heroes in *War and Peace* there is a basic denominator of human experience which is common to all men and women regardless of class, country, age and intellectual attainment. Their mental, spiritual and emotional problems, their pleasures and pursuits, their enthusiasms and their aversions are as relevant to England today as they ever were to Tolstoy's Russia. And it is ultimately this fact which ensures that *War and Peace* and especially the main heroes of *War and Peace* will always be a part of the literary heritage of the reading public throughout the world.

Characterization cannot be considered in isolation from the many other sides of a novelist's art. In previous chapters different aspects of the subject have been touched upon in different contexts, and all of them are really relevant to this chapter too. First there are the changes which occur in Tolstoy's characters themselves as the successive draft versions are written and discarded. Then there are the features which they inherit from their various historical and living prototypes. There are the ideas of the novelist himself which are transmitted to his heroes and heroines, so that they in turn express his own prejudices and beliefs and in Pierre's case, the gulf between what Tolstoy was and what he wanted himself to be. There is the question of the composition of the novel which is so designed that the character development should proceed *pari passu* with the development of the plot, and not fortuitously or independently of the main action. Finally there are the different linguistic devices at Tolstoy's disposal which play their part in characterization—interior monologue, the contrasting use of the French and Russian languages, speech mannerisms, irony. The specific chapter headings of the evolution of the novel, the use of sources, idea and genre, structure, composition and language all relate directly or indirectly to the broad general subject of Tolsoy's methods of creating character, and although it has been necessary for the sake of convenience to write several chapters and not one, it must not be thought that they are self-sufficient entities unconnected with each other.

In the final analysis it is the characters which a novelist creates

which are the greatest and most memorable part of his achievement. In *War and Peace* they range over the scale of good and
evil and they are treated by the author with varying degrees of
sympathy and dislike. In later life Tolstoy wrote to the artist
N. N. Gay that in order to compose a work of art: 'It is necessary for a man to know clearly and without doubt what is good
and evil, to see plainly the dividing line between them and consequently to paint not what is, but what should be. And he
should paint what should be as though it already was, so that
for him what should be might already be.'[7]

   This opinion was expressed some twenty years after *War and
Peace* was written, but the first part of it at least is applicable
to that novel. Tolstoy knew, as well as any man can, the dividing
line between good and evil, although in *War and Peace* he
devoted much more time to painting things as they are than
as they should be. For a novelist, however, to know what is right
and what is wrong is not the same thing as to concentrate
virtue in one character and vice in another, or to pass an unqualified moral judgement on any of the people he creates. 'The
Gospel words "judge not" ', Tolstoy wrote in 1857, 'are profoundly true in art: relate, portray, but do not judge.'[8] Tolstoy's
purpose in his first novel, as a creator of living characters, was
to entertain and not to judge. One of the most interesting pronouncements he made about the function of an artist occurs in
a letter which he wrote in 1865 while actively engaged on his
novel, but which he never sent, and a quotation from it will
make a fitting conclusion to this study of *War and Peace*. The
letter was addressed to the minor novelist Boborykin and contains some mild strictures on the latter's two latest novels.
Tolstoy wrote:

   Problems of the Zemstvo, literature and the emancipation of women
obtrude with you in a polemical manner, but these problems are not
only not interesting in the world of art; they have no place there at all.
Problems of the emancipation of women and of literary parties inevitably appear to you important in your literary Petersburg milieu, but
all these problems splash about in a little puddle of dirty water which
only seems like an ocean to those whom fate has set down in the middle
of the puddle. The aims of an artist are incommensurate (as the mathe-
maticians say) with social aims. The aim of an artist is not to solve a

---

[7] Letter to N. N. Gay, 21 February 1887, J.E. LXIV. 15.
[8] J.E. XLVII, diary entry for 29 March/10 April, 1857.

problem irrefutably but to make people love life in all its countless inexhaustible manifestations. If I were to be told that I could write a novel whereby I might irrefutably establish what seemed to me the correct point of view on all social problems, I would not even devote two hours work to such a novel; but if I were to be told that what I should write would be read in about twenty years time by those who are now children, and that they would laugh and cry over it and love life, I would devote all my own life and all my energies to it.[9]

To make people laugh and cry and love life is a sufficient justification for even the greatest of novels.

[9] Letter to P. D. Boborykin, July . . . August 1865, J.E. LXI. 100.

# INDEX